THE LOTTERY

Survival takes on a new meaning in The Lottery

AM JOY

Book Cover by Miblart

First edition 2024

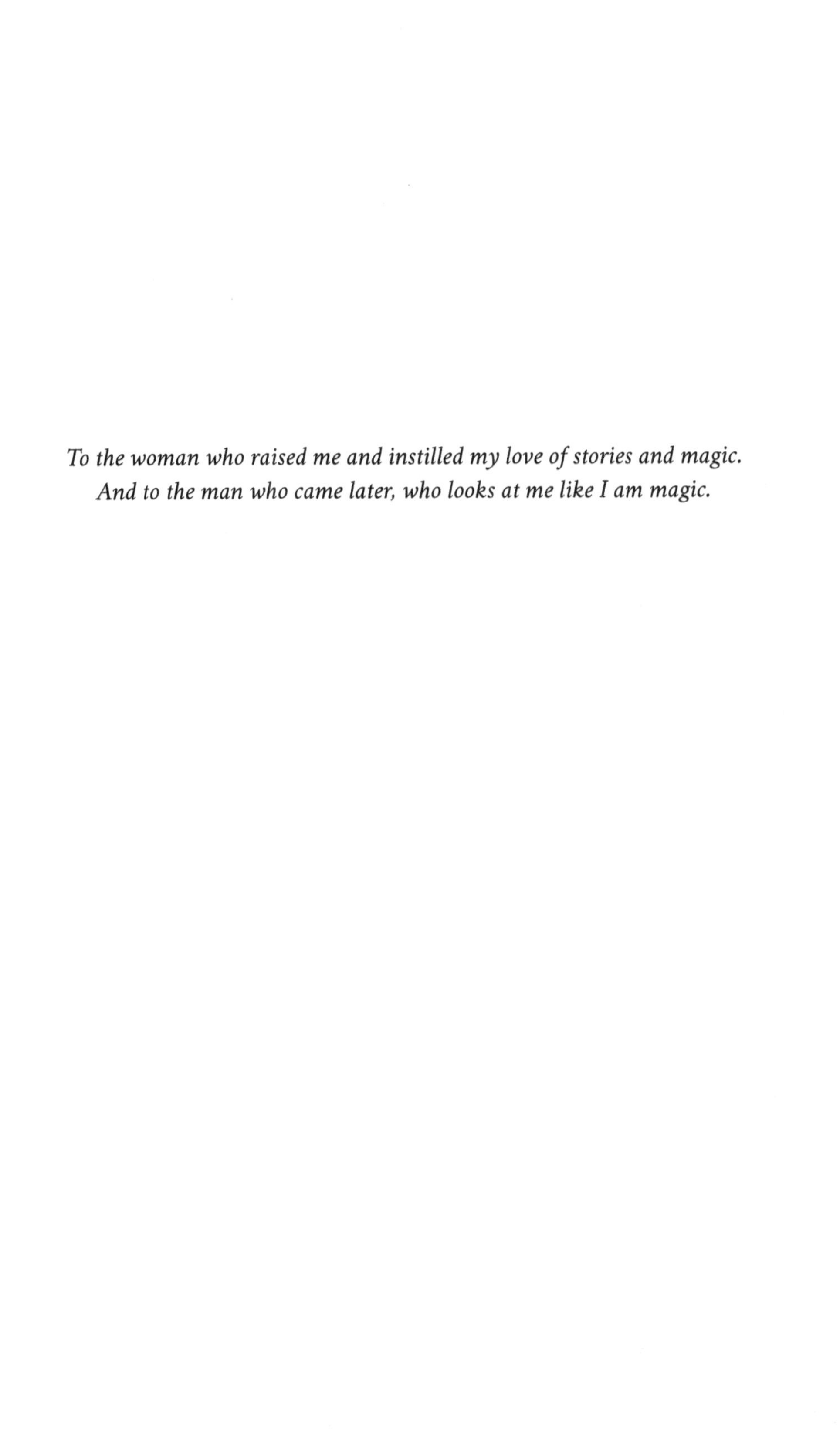

To the woman who raised me and instilled my love of stories and magic.
And to the man who came later, who looks at me like I am magic.

PROLOGUE

THE BEGINNING

The day *The Lottery* was announced, the women held their tongues.

When the Speaker took the stage, a hush fell over the crowd. The women looked on, too numb from years of mandates to speak up, too broken from being silenced to keep fighting.

The mandates had institutionalised the women of Australia. When the changes first started, it had been to legalise abortion and provide free birth control. It felt like the golden age; a time when women were taken seriously as equals.

Avery remembered when the government added incentives to stop growing their families. Cash for women to remain childless, financial motives to entrap them in a new system .

The government called on women to help the country address the exploding population. Australia was suffering under the crushing weight of its people – rising poverty, food shortages, a housing crisis, and crippling inflation.

They called on women to put the greater good above their own desires.

But the women didn't hear the undertones of the plea, didn't heed the warning. They didn't take the slow changes to law seriously.

Slowly, mandates and sponsored Bill's chipped away at their fundamental freedoms, deliberate and calculating, each incremental change a step into a new Australian normal.

Five years after the first rumblings, the women woke up in a country where having a baby had been banned. It was only then that some women marched, but it was too late; the law was ratified. Abortion became a way of life, both for accidental and wanted pregnancies. Life changed slowly and then all at once. Overnight, Australia became a different place.

And now, women stood silent again, as they listened with bated breath to the government's new initiative.

The Speaker shattered the world by announcing a *chance*.

The government had heard the women. They *understood* the sacrifices made the last few years.

After years of heartache, trials, famine, and war, Australia was showing a few signs of recovery, and the government wanted to reward them.

There was a new solution. They claimed they were showing a hint of mercy, a touch of kindness, a shred of hope, as they announced *The Lottery.*

The Lottery was a new-age competition.

The first chance women had after years of oppression.

The Lottery was a chance to battle against one another, pitted against other women for a chance to continue a pregnancy.

A chance for women to prove the worth of their genes through stringent testing.

A chance for anyone, regardless of money or status, to compete for the privilege of keeping their baby.

One baby per quarter was all the government could offer.

They sold it as a tiny step in the right direction.

The first tenuous steps as Australia recovered.

For twenty-five long years, the government would control the population like this.

Every quarter a new chance to compete.

Every pregnancy now scrutinised to see if it met all the markers for future success.

When Avery heard the broadcast, she sighed.

Another empty promise, another backhanded chance. More rules and regulations, more updates to the mandate.

Avery knew what *The Lottery* really was.

Another chance for rigorous control on women's bodies, hidden under the guise of hope.

She wasn't fooled. But she was unaffected. So she stayed silent.

At seventeen, she knew nothing of the adult world, nothing of her future.

Avery was a girl with no desire for children.

A girl born without the mothering gene.

A girl with no need to speak up,

Until she grew into a woman and the rules came back to haunt her.

Survival takes on a new meaning in *The Lottery,*

Pregnancy is just the beginning.

CHAPTER ONE

ALICE AVERY

I SQUEEZED MY EYES SHUT AGAINST THE SHINING SUN FILTERING through the window. The slow, ragged breathing, and hot skin against my back was the perfect reminder that I wasn't in my own bed.

I cursed my choices as I crushed my eyebrows together. Through heavy-lidded eyes, I inched my naked body up off the mattress to sneak a peek at the body that lay beside me. Mason's pale skin looked almost tan in the sunlight that streamed in through the open, top-floor window.

I fumbled to grab my phone and tapped *SOS* into my group chat. as I eyeballed my scattered clothes.

Mason rolled onto his stomach, his blonde hair falling over the side of his face as he let out a loud, sighing snore.

Where did you disappear to last night? came the reply from Kit, as I methodically stuck one leg out of the blanket, and slowly shimmied and rolled my body out of the bed, glancing back at Mason more than once to make sure he was still asleep.

You bring deets, we'll buy coffee? shot Darcy, as I silently snapped my bra on, and dressed in yesterday's wrinkled and smoke-infused t-shirt and jeans.

I've got to escape first, I quickly typed back. *Coffee at Grind, half an hour?*

I didn't wait for a response. Instead I shoved my phone into my rumpled pocket and scanned the room for my wallet and keys. The only two things I couldn't leave behind.

Mason's large bedroom was oddly clean, the walls sporting smiling pictures and multiple framed records in thick glass cases. The corner desk held a framed copy of his doctorate, side-by-side with a goofy picture of him in a cap-and-gown, showing off his trademark toothy grin.

Scientists can be so smart and *so dumb*—I would know.

I groaned internally as I stared at him, skulking to his side of the bed and sinking to my knees to commando-crawl forward; all while wondering what the hell was wrong with me.

As I inched my body past Mason's sleeping frame, I pressed my lips together, slowly easing my wallet out from between the headboard and bed frame. My eyes kept darting to Mason's tranquil face, cursing myself for sleeping with him, only to hatch an escape plan the next morning. It was my typical pattern—never get too close, never get hurt; my parents and their perfect marriage had set me up for failure.

Wallet in hand, I picked my way back across the room; Mason's clothes from last night were the only mess strewn across the floor now.

I froze as the floorboard at the end of his bed creaked loudly under my bare feet and Mason turned over. With bated breath, I backed toward the door, arms outstretched; as if my tightrope walk would keep me quiet and him asleep.

His arm sleepily reached toward my now-empty side of the bed, his fingers fumbling and gripping the sheets for a few seconds before a soft snore echoed through the room again.

I crept silently towards the door on my tiptoes, grabbing my boots and leaving my socks as a dirty memento. The second the bedroom door was shut, I hightailed it through the tidy living room. Two red-ringed glasses of wine were placed neatly on coasters on the coffee table. A memory flashed of me mounting Mason on the couch—and my cheeks burned red-hot.

Mason was too much of an adult for a girl who snuck out of people's apartments without saying goodbye. Frazzled, I fumbled with the front door, my head flicking back every few seconds to his still-shut bedroom door.

"Let me out, let me out," I mouthed as I desperately pulled at the lock. Finally, the door opened, only for it to slam to a stop a few inches in, struck by the silver chain lock running across.

I cursed drunk, responsible Mason as my stomach knotted and I fumbled with the last obstacle, shooting one final look back at Mason's closed bedroom door.

With a rushed breath, I squeezed my body out and broke into an almost-run towards the elevator.

My stomach lurched and I slowed to a walk, leaning on the wall for support. How had I ended up here, *again*? My brain circled on loop, the fuzziness of last night's alcohol consumption making it difficult to string together a coherent chain of events.

"Come on, come on," I whispered, as I jammed my finger against the elevator button, my head swivelling back and forth to apartment number 247 again and again.

The apartment building was eerily silent for a Sunday morning. I looked down at my watch. *7:55a.m.* Thankfully both Kit and Darcy couldn't sleep in after a night out; we all needed a hearty breakfast.

The early hour explained the quiet as the elevator doors clunked to a stop. As I stepped in, I knew everyone who made good choices on a Saturday night was still asleep.

Guilt crackled in my stomach as the elevator doors clamped shut, and I let out a loud sigh of relief. Sadly for Mason, the old saying, *it's-not-you-it's-me,* was more than true in this situation.

I jiggled and tapped my feet as I waited impatiently for the doors to creep open. As soon as they did I sprang out, run-walking across the polished, marble-floored lobby. I couldn't wait to reach the rotating door and the outside world. As if in a movie, the doorman tipped his head to me, a gleam in his eye. I smiled weakly as my phone buzzed in my pocket.

Back corner table, read the message from Kit. I broke into a jog, turning the corner at the end of Mason's street and walking into the Sunday morning market crowd.

The fruit and vegetable stalls were already brimming with bright colours and proper adults milling about. All of Melbourne must have decided to head to the Market this Sunday morning, forcing me to weave my way through the bustling crowd. My head pounded, an ache settling behind my eyes as I reached the hidden coffee shop; my favourite place tucked away down a back alley on Flinders Street.

I squeezed my way in, waving shakily at Kit and Darcy, whose beaming faces stared up at me expectantly. Their wide grins told me everything I needed to know. I was busted, and I was going to have to pay for both the girls' breakfast and provide last night's details.

Kit pushed a large, black coffee in a pink mug towards me as I collapsed into my chair.

"And how are *you*?" Darcy asked, her voice sickly sweet as I took my first sip of coffee, my body rejoicing. My shoulders jiggled as I did a happy dance.

"You look *amazing*," Kit said, both her and Darcy looking me up-and-down with sympathetic head-shakes.

"Oh, thank you," I said, grinning and giving them a fancy head nod with pursed lips. "It must be the orgasms." I laughed as they broke into a fit of giggles.

A smiling waitress trotted over carrying three giant plates of pancake stacks, and a few bakery treats crammed on the side. "You guys are the *best*," I said, wrapping my arms around Kit's pale, bony shoulders. Her curly, red hair spilled across my arm as I pulled her in.

I moved to the other side as Darcy put her hand up, fork already gripped tightly towards me. Her dark eyes and deep frown warned me not to get between her and the first bite of her syrup-laden pancakes.

"The food is forward payment," Darcy said with a wink, holding my knife and fork hostage. "Details will be needed." I groaned as I snatched a fork from her hands and stabbed my first pancake. The soft dough was soaked in a thick layer of syrup and melting ice cream, and my stomach immediately gave a groan that screamed *eat*.

Darcy and Kit broke into fits of giggles as they both shovelled food into their mouths.

"Worked up an appetite?" Darcy snort-laughed as she jokingly blocked my fork to mouth movement for a few seconds before moving her hand away, graciously allowing me to shovel the enormous bite into my mouth.

"Looks like it," I said, the gooey fluff of the second bite already rocketing towards my watering mouth. "His name is Mason," I added through my chewing as they both eyed me.

"Mason…Mason…" Kit wondered aloud, clearly trying to picture him from her own vague memories of the night before.

"The *other* nerd-scientist?" Darcy's dark eyes shot upwards as she thought. I cringed every time my friends made fun of *nerd-scientists*, they always seemed to forget I was a biologist and fit right in with that crowd.

"He's an astronomer," I said. "If you call that a scientist," I whispered with an eye roll, the words shooting out under my breath, making the girls giggle. "In my defence, he suckered me in by promising to show me his lab." I groaned again, taking a long sip of coffee as we all collected ourselves.

"Is that how he *tempted* you?" Darcy teased, both her and Kit knowing I didn't take sex too seriously.

"You can see the entire night sky through his telescopes." I shook my head, only a very fuzzy memory of glittering black remaining after last night. "Though I barely remember the view." I shot a lopsided grin at them.

"My boyfriend shows me the *world*," Kit said, throwing her arms around herself and swooning. Her bouncy red hair fell over her face and covered her eyes.

"My boyfriend is a poet of the *stars*," Darcy took over, wrapping her arms sensually around her upper body. Her biceps bulged as she hugged herself and made horribly loud smooching sounds.

I snorted, choking on my sip of coffee and cringing. As a defence, I shovelled another two mouthfuls of pancake in, trying my best to chew and swallow as my cheeks grew redder and hotter.

"My boyfriend dreams in *planets*," Kit said, jumping up onto her knees and flinging her fingers through her thick red hair, frizzing it out.

"My boyfriend holds the *galaxy* in his hands," Darcy giggled, swooning and batting her thick fake eyelashes at me.

"Stop, stop," I said, pleading and giggling. The coffee shop had filled up around us; the other tables full of young couples on sweet breakfast dates shooting us side-ways glances.

"You seeing him again?" Darcy asked, lowering her voice a little, all of us acting quiet and normal until the stares disappeared.

I shrugged and said, "Probably not," as Kit and Darcy shook their heads. Truthfully, I couldn't imagine calling him after I commando crawled out of his apartment at 7a.m. the morning after.

"But *how* will you find a *husband*?" Kit asked in fake outrage, putting her hand to her heart and sighing deeply.

"How will you succeed in life without a *husband*?" Darcy gasped, clapping her hand over her mouth, grinning at me as she copied Kit's fake outrage.

I laughed. "The sex was *great*." A mental image of Mason's naked body against mine flashed in my mind for a few seconds. "But I want to *be* the husband, not marry one."

"The big promotion?" Darcy and Kit asked in unison, their voices creepily similar when they spoke at the exact same moment.

"I was shortlisted," I said, casually twirling my fork in my hand and keeping my face blank as the girls squealed. "There are checks and references and hurdles," I added "But, ten weeks from today, the final candidate will be announced."

The girls cooed and hyped me up as I complained, "It's the same day as my bloody pregnancy screening." I realised that meant my next mandated screening was just two-weeks from now, and I gave a long, drawn-out sigh.

"Every eight weeks is ridiculous," Kit piped up while Darcy silently nodded along, giving me a sad, sympathetic smile. Every Australian woman knew the pain of the screenings and the pride of competing in the elusive *lottery.* Instead, I wished I could rip out my ovaries so I could avoid being poked, prodded, and tested as a vessel for the next generation, only to be told I wasn't good enough.

I sighed and bit my tongue; I would only be preaching to two women who understood. We had spent many nights debating and devolving into drunkenness and ranting over the current state of our country and our fight for bodily autonomy.

I made a mental note to look up women's marches for this year and see if any protests were happening close by; maybe it was time to do something other than complain.

"Whatever. Nothing can dampen my spirits." I smiled, scratching absent-mindedly at my wrist. The tiny chip tingling beneath my skin. "Great sex last night and a promotion soon." I giggled as the girls clapped alongside me; my own personal cheer squad. "And you two are always here," I wrapped my arms around them both and squeezed them tight. Kit leaned in while Darcy clearly fought the urge to pull away.

"We got your back," Darcy whispered, finally giving in.

"Always," Kit chimed in as they both hugged me tighter, squeezing a burp out of me, and sending the three of us into another fit of laughter.

CHAPTER TWO

STIRRUPS

My stomach rolled over itself, collapsing and crumpling inward as I awkwardly grappled with the stirrup's hooks. My fingers grasped the silver buckles, the metal clanging together as I struggled, my fingers a few inches too short.

I let out a loud sigh, rolling my eyes as I flopped backwards onto the firm, black leather chair, leaving my legs to swing in the air untethered. It was always the same at these appointments. Too much time spent waiting, too much time with my legs in the air, my body too cold and sterile—and a dash of anxiety thrown in.

To pass the time, my eyes drifted to the right and landed on the wall where in-depth pictures of female anatomy danced across my vision. The giant uterus and reproductive systems sent a strange shiver down my spine. Seeing my insides pictured and framed on the wall was a tangible reminder of why I was here, why we all had to submit to these tests and screenings. All you needed was a uterus and the rest was history. The reminder sent a gurgling, nauseating swirl through my stomach.

"Miss Avery?" a muted voice called from the hallway.

"Come in," I hollered, my legs trembling as I lifted my body up onto my elbows and tried to smile at the young nurse who ripped the curtain back. She barely looked at me, all business as her dark black curls bounced behind the clipboard glued to her face.

"Miss Avery?" The nurse confirmed again, her blue eyes peeking out from the side of the clipboard, only meeting mine for a split second.

"Otherwise known as Alice Avery." I put on my most serious superhero voice, cracking a smile that wasn't returned.

The nurse placed the clipboard to the side. Her face was round and sweet, but her tight-lipped mouth and furrowed eyebrows were harsh. Her hands clasped the buckles that looped from the bottom of my feet to my ankles, strapping me in with a tight tug and *click*. She managed to do this in seconds, when I had struggled for minutes.

"Not your first day?" I asked, trying to make conversation as I shoved the blue sheet down, my hands automatically fighting against the taut fabric as I lay naked from the waist down, awaiting my fate.

The nurse said nothing in return, instead pushing a red button affixed to the wall and busying herself with her back to me. She pulled out swabs, needles, and a large, clear speculum, which she held up. The clear plastic shone under the fluorescent lights. I gulped and laid back as the door creaked, followed by the forced cough of a man announcing his presence. I heard the tug of curtain against wire before a middle-aged doctor strode in.

His forehead was full of deep lines, and he wore a pained look on his face. I watched him and craned my neck as he made a beeline for the nurse. Twisting away, he turned his back to me, scrunching his shoulders inwards. *This can't be good,* I thought, my stomach shaking as I pulled myself up to stare at them. Their hushed, whispered tones were manic, the doctor repeatedly flailing his hand and pointing to a chart gripped in his left hand.

A groan escaped my lips as the stirrups creaked and wobbled, my legs flailing open.

The nurse returned to my side, unbuckling my feet in two swift movements.

"Sit up," she whispered, retreating to the furthest corner of the room and turning her back to me again, but not leaving me alone.

I swung my legs closed slowly, buying a few extra seconds to put on my best blank and confused face. My body betrayed me as a slight ache shot into my pelvis and hips, leaving me to grimace and sigh. As I arranged myself, I looked up, startled that the doctor was now seated in front of me, rolling toward me in his chair at a rapid pace.

"Alice Avery," the doctor said, his voice smooth. His eyes were glued to the clipboard and chart in front of him as if the answer to every question was written there. "What kind of scientist are you?"

"I'm a biologist," I said, my eyebrows knitting together. Why was he reading the life-and-times-of-Alice-Avery? My file was one of the most boring out there – minus a few additional STD screenings from a little drunken sex.

"Clever, clever," he muttered, and I knew he was being condescending. I opened my mouth to say something back when he enunciated the worst sentence I have ever heard. "You are pregnant, Miss Avery."

His words hung in the air as he finally looked me in the eye. His dark brown eyes shone almost black under the harsh lighting; the lines carved into his forehead creating deep shadows. It was all I could focus on as his words seeped into reality.

I shook my head slowly and then sped up to shake it vigorously.

"Impossible." Counting back dates on my fingers, visions of Mason's sweaty body and heaving chest flood my vision—entirely unhelpful as I tried to concentrate.

"Blood tests don't lie," the doctor interrupted, cutting off my rambling of numbers and random syllables with a clap of his hands.

I cleared my throat and took a deep breath, looking the doctor in the eye. I knew what happened next, every woman did. "When will my abortion be scheduled?" My voice was meek but it didn't shake.

"*Ten weeks pregnant*, Miss Avery," the doctor replied, his voice curt, as if this explained everything.

"T-ten?" I stammered almost before he had finished his sentence. "How was this not picked up at my last mandated check eight weeks ago? You just said *the tests don't lie,*" I snapped, hurling his words back at him as my heart hammered. No wonder I was feeling more agitated than usual. Had it really been ten weeks since Mason?

"Alice, tests, doctors, and women often don't pick up a two-week pregnancy. Your body barely knows you're pregnant at that stage." He paused as if this explanation made everything okay. He shook his head. "You know your circumstances are rare." He raised an eyebrow at me as if to remind me, mid freak-out, that *I know this.* This has been explained countless times and caused countless arguments. "Good genes, high-IQ, familial success," he cooed at me, repeating things doctors had said to me time-and-time again over the years. Words that sounded like compliments but were not. "Due to your personal circumstances—*and* the timing—the Government mandate deems you are ineligible for an abortion." The doctor dropped his eyes, his chest deflating and head shaking as he looked away. He looked disappointed *in* me as he shook his head.

"There must be a mistake." I was almost pleading now, staring at him with my mouth hanging open. My eyes looked down at my stomach; my round, curvy stomach, normally only full of bakery treats, tacos, and margaritas. I *couldn't* be pregnant, even drunk, I was *always* careful—I never wanted to be threatened with *the lottery* again.

"I-I…" the words tumbled out, jagged and jumbled. "Australia…" I stuttered, forcing myself to suck in a deep, slow breath. "Abortion is our way of life now." The words burned like acid as they left my mouth, my mind spinning as I tried to recite the words that had been splashed across the news, calmly spoken by politicians, rioted against in the streets every day in dwindling numbers for years. "The mandate," was all I could manage haphazardly, the reasons spruiked by the Australian Government for the last thirteen years in my mind but stuck in my throat.

"The lottery," I finally cried as I looked the doctor in the eye and tried to steady my quivering nerves. The two words I loathed but might save me now - might remind the Doctor that only *certain women* get the chance to carry children.

The doctor forced a smile, reaching out and patting his stiff hand against my knee.

"The mandate is complicated, Miss Avery." He leaned backwards in his chair, the clipboard flipping up and resting against his deep blue button down shirt. "For certain women," he eyed me, his eyes flicking between my chart and my face, "protocol is to wait until twelve weeks and test the foetus for intelligence markers." A small smile danced on his lips as he spoke, as if this would be the revelation I was waiting for, not my own personal nightmare. "It's important you remember the goal, Miss Avery. High markers lead to productive members of society."

"But I want an abortion," I hadn't been clear before, but I would be now as I swallowed down the burning acid. The doctor's cool demeanour unnerved me, so I kept talking. "I know many women would kill to be in my position—A chance," I said, my voice getting louder and squeakier. I stood up, hopping up on my leather chair with both knees, and pushing myself up to my feet. "*To win the lottery,*" I said, my voice sickly sweet, as I kissed my hands and threw them into the air, waving at a non-existent crowd of onlookers. "I am *not* interested." I fell back onto the chair and crossed my arms, hopeful my face showed both the disgust and determination I felt.

The doctor looked amused as I stepped down, tumbling back to catch my breath.

"Alas, Miss Avery," he shook his head, "with the gestation, and your circumstances..." He trailed off and paused, eyes scanning across the pages in my file again, widening as he took in the words. "That baby —" He jabbed at my stomach without his fingers touching my skin. "—*must* continue to develop." I could have sworn his eyes lit up as he looked back at me, tearing himself away from the paperwork.

I snorted, a giggle tumbling out of my lips, turning into a loud, choked laugh. "This *foetus,*" I corrected the doctor, already irritated by the use of the word *baby* for a clump of cells. "This *foetus* is the product of a one-night stand." I shook my head, pressing my hands hard into my eyes. He must have sensed my disbelief as a curt smile tugged at the corners of his lips.

His face was blank and expressionless as he pushed on, undeterred by my opinions or assertions. As always, my words didn't matter.

"Be that as it may..." He fidgeted, smoothing down his hair multiple times. "The Government *requires* you to submit for further testing." His words hung in the air as my frown deepened. He kept his eyes cast down, and his hand scrawled across the clipboard as I sat there in silence. My heart thumped; the skin on the back of my neck prickled as I desperately tried to formulate a single sentence, a single argument he might listen to.

"And how are *you* qualified to make this decision?"

The doctor eyed me as the silence returned and stretched on. I shifted uncomfortably in my seat, my thighs sweating and sticking to the leather.

"I *am* the Government, Miss Avery, whether you like it or not."

My eyes narrowed as the doctor stood and started tearing out pieces of paper and handing them to me in rapid succession.

"Supplements," he said, shoving the papers into my lap. "Ultrasound booking." He balanced another piece of paper on top of the first. The doctor's rigid frame stood in front of me, his feet tapping from side-to-side as he stood and placed the last piece of paper on the stack. "Referral to a psychiatrist." He stepped away as the bold heading caught my eye. I stared at it as the paper balanced precariously on my fist.

"Dealing with a miracle pregnancy?" I read aloud before grabbing the three layers of paper and crumpling them as I shoved them towards his face.

"The feelings you are experiencing about your pregnancy should be discussed," he said dryly, "*with a professional.*" He snapped my file shut. Clearly, in his mind, this conversation was over.

"Do you not understand?" My voice was incredulous as I stared at the doctor who clearly didn't understand. "*There is nothing to discuss.* As a grown, educated woman of sound mind, *I do not want to have a baby,*" I said, enunciating each word. I stared at the doctor's forehead as he fidgeted and picked at non-existent lint on his shirt.

His head gave a slight nod at the nurse as he looked over my right shoulder and a second later, a loud *click* reverberated through the room. A chill ran down my spine, prickling my skin as I geared up to have the same argument I had had a hundred times. It felt almost like a practiced speech now, and suddenly my flicker of fear turned to anger.

"First, they told us not to have children." I snorted, my heart racing as I ripped the paper dress down enough to stand. "Too many children, rampant overpopulation, homelessness, scarce resources," I listed off the reasons the Australian Government had presented in the years leading up to the abortion mandate and *the lottery* thirteen years ago.

Furiously, I tugged my plain black knickers and blue jeans on under the paper dress. "Then, they began subjecting us to pregnancy screenings every ninety days. Then every sixty days." I fidgeted with my newly created wedgie and uncooperative button without taking my eyes off the doctor. "And when I wanted to be sterilised, they said *no*," I said through gritted teeth, pulling up the zipper of my jeans, my fingers fumbling and shaking. "*Twelve* doctors said no." I was panting now. "This isn't about population control. This is *just* about control." I looked the doctor square in the face. His head was tilted to the side, his eyes glazed—the same look I had seen a hundred times when half the population tuned out because the mandate and its testing didn't directly affect their autonomy. The sound of footsteps echoed behind the door. "*You* play a part in this," I said, my voice quiet as I picked up my bag to leave, his papers now littering the floor. As the silence grew I decided to try my luck and step forward to leave.

As if they read my movements, the door burst open. Three mask-clad male nurses in scrubs and blue gloves towered in the doorway, blocking my exit.

"What now?" I snapped, my voice steady as my veins turned to ice and I faced the nurses. My elbows pressed into my sides as a shiver snaked through my body. I took an involuntary step back, and my legs wobbled slightly as the air turned cold.

A nod from the doctor, and four warm hands gripped my arms. Their fingernails jabbed into my skin, shoving my head down.

All I could manage was a muffled squeak as I struggled, my voice disappearing as I pulled my arms backwards, my skin pinching and ripping.

"It seems apparent..." the doctor started, hunching his body forward. He leaned in close to me, his hot breath hitting my face. "...that you cannot be trusted to report for the next phase of testing."

Another hand gripped my hair, jabbing hard fingers into the nape of my neck and shoving my head down.

"A shame," the doctor said as I struggled to lift my head.

A sharp stinging pain sliced across my neck. The sound of ripping skin and the warm gush of blood turned my stomach. I gritted my teeth so hard they ached as the knife sliced deeper into my muscle. It felt like the back of my neck was ripping apart, the searing pain shooting down my spine as I let out a blood curdling scream.

"It'll hurt more," the doctor whispered in my ear, "if you struggle."

His words echoed through me, and I fought harder, ripping my head to the side. The knife dragged diagonally across my skin. The four hands tightened, gripping my hair in fistfuls to hold me still as they sliced again and again.

The doctor cooed. "*Only* a little tracking device, Miss Avery." His voice slithered across my skin. "We wouldn't want to *lose track* of you."

I let out a tiny whimper as the knife pierced deeper into my skin, the point poking sharply into the middle of my neck.

The curly-haired female nurse stepped forward, her bright purple shoes shuffling to the doctor's side.

With a piercing prick, the doctor shoved something with sharp edges into my neck. The knife chased it and pushed it deeper, every muscle in my neck tensed and fought, the searing pain slipping deeper and deeper into my sinew. Blossoming pinpricks of pain on each side of my neck rippled and the feeling of tugging told me I was being stitched back together. My skin screamed with each stitch, the pain simmering under the surface.

"I'll just pull them out." I forced the words out past the pain as they held my body at an awkward, splayed angle.

"I don't think you will, Miss Avery." The doctor tugged the last stitch hard, the sound of snapping and sizzling metal pinging into the air. "Titanium self-sealing stitches; an invention of the Aortic Lab." He pushed on the back of my neck, a final few zapping sounds ringing in my ears.

With a *snap,* the nurses let me go. Their thick, brawny bodies backing out of the room as quickly as they had appeared to do the doctor's dirty work.

With an effort, I pulled my body upright. My head spun and my legs wobbled.

The black-haired nurse steadied me on her way past, squeezing my arm once. It was the only kind gesture.

My fingers ran across the uniform line of stitches. The bubbled metal clung to my skin, its thin tendrils spun deep into my neck muscles.

"This," I said weakly, my head still down as I tried to steady myself, my fingers dancing across the cool, flat surface of the stitches buried deep into my skin.

"Yes, Miss Avery: a new technology."

I nodded, my fingers unable to stop running up-and-down against the stitches. I would have been full of questions and curiosity under different circumstances.

I wanted to ask *why* I needed another chip, *why* they couldn't use the one implanted in my wrist – but I knew I would have to keep guessing as this man would never tell me.

"That will be all," the doctor said, walking forward. His bony fingers pushed against my shoulder and led me out of the room. I looked up at him as his lips moved and tried to focus on what he was saying. "You will be summoned for your twelve week tests shortly. *Best of luck, Miss Avery.*" He said with a wry smile as he pushed me out of his office and snapped the door shut in my face.

CHAPTER THREE

HUMAN BIOLOGY

My hands shook as they hovered above my phone screen, and I debated what to type into our group chat. I could barely explain what had happened in the last hour to myself, let alone to my two best friends. I opted for a little terror and humour combined; it was essentially my trademark, and the girls would immediately understand.

FUCKING PREGNANT!!!!!! My first message read as the train began to slow. My heart raced and my fingers automatically went to my new stitches as if to confirm I *wasn't* going crazy. I would have been distracted by the metal if the little dots had popped up any slower from my two confidants.

Drinks??? was the first message from Darcy. Her use of question marks made me laugh, knowing that it wasn't a question—and then immediately pondering if I *could* drink.

WHAT, WHEN, HOW? the next message from Kit shot over a second later. She had matched my energy, screaming at me in capital letters and full of questions and curiosity.

These two were my perfect balance, and I breathed a little easier knowing I could lean on them.

Who? pinged the next two messages simultaneously, one in all caps, the other with ten exclamation marks. I sighed as the train shuddered to a groaning halt in unison with my own groan. The door opened again and more people bustled in; their sweaty bodies slid past me and pressed up against me from all angles as my legs wobbled on the packed early morning commuter train.

You couldn't tell I was pregnant yet, but should that still get me a seat?

Assembly, 8pm. I tapped back, my hand instinctively going to the back of my neck to fiddle with the stitches again. They half-itched, half-burned under my fingers.

You two shout, I'll bring details. I punched out left-handed as I weaved my way through the train. Their replies buzzed, but I didn't read or answer, too busy with the chorus of "excuse me," and "pardon me" echoing as I jumped down onto the concrete platform. The trains might be faster now, but commuting was still commuting.

As my feet hit the ground, the smell of cotton-candy, freshly baked bread, and strong, black coffee intermingled, and I breathed in the familiar scent.

I pushed my body against the dirty, tiled wall, slinking past the two teams of volunteer workers trying to sell new solar and phone plan deals. I was surprised they still had jobs with the way of the world.

I glanced at my watch and groaned as I weaved through the crowd. I had to twist, turn, and shimmy through the wall of people until I reached the escalator and clambered on. I wrinkled my nose, now standing shoulder-to-shoulder with a man with terrible body odour.

Turning and breathing through my mouth, I watched the black-and-white flecked stairs as we slowly ascended to street-level. Suit-clad people ran up-and-down them two at a time; everyone was in a hurry, glancing at their wrist-screens or phones. Half of them shoved whole bakery treats into their mouths and chewed haphazardly as they rushed past. I wasn't jealous at all—Friday was the only day I didn't have to rush.

My legs jiggled as I reached the top and spun a full three-hundred-and-sixty degrees on the spot before snaking left and making a beeline for the exit. Shimmying my wrist out, I swiped it across the pod entrance and the door flung open, the token *low balance* I had come to expect flashed across the screen.

"*I'll show you* low balance," I grumbled as the pod closed around me and scanned over my body. I shivered, the cold air always surprising me. The pod beeped and the doors popped open. For the first time I wondered if the pod only scanned for metal and guns, or if maybe the technology also picked up *other* private information.

Shoving the thought away, I rubbed my hands together in the cool morning breeze as I approached the large, red-brick archway.

Outside, I took a quick left. My feet led by my howling stomach, I almost ran to the little coffee shop on the corner.

"Happy Friday!" the barista called as I threw open the door, panting. A huge grin crept across my lips as the smell of baked treats and sweet coffee smacked me in the face.

There was nowhere else I would rather be on a Friday morning as I took my place in line behind a loved-up couple who couldn't stop caressing each other's hands, their fingers intertwining and grabbing at each other.

I rolled my eyes as they stepped away.

"O—" I opened my mouth, and was immediately cut off by the barista.

"One large, flat, white, three sugars," Rory said mocking me with a grin, as he punched in my daily coffee order.

"Wait." I threw my hand up, and he spun to grab the card machine. He raised an eyebrow as I lowered my head to stare into their glass pastry pantry. Homemade treats packed the enormous glass dome. I stared at the croissants, large slabs of banana cake, chocolate dipped éclairs filled-to-the-brim with fresh cream, piles of biscotti, and cookies and cupcakes in every flavour. I may as well have pressed my tongue up against the glass.

"Could I also get..." I trailed off, chewing my lip. "A pumpkin scone and a chocolate—no, caramel—no, chocolate slice?" I paused briefly. "Yes." I smiled and I nodded my head at Rory, his hand perched a few centimetres away from the chocolate slices. It was harder to pick a Friday treat than a Saturday screw.

"And a double chocolate chip cookie," I blurted as he finished packing up the first two bags. He looked at me, his eyebrows dancing as he threw in two cookies without a word. I smiled sheepishly, scanning my wrist to pay and hoping that *low balance* wouldn't flash up for the second time this morning

"It's busy out there today," Rory called, and I replied with an audible groan.

Without hesitating, I ripped open the scone and threw Rory a wave over my head. I would need a delicious sweet treat if the protestors were outside the lab again today. They always made me feel guilty, and today would be worse given this morning's news.

I grinned as I sipped my sweet coffee and tried to chew slowly, ambling towards work. I had been in a hurry for coffee, but work could wait.

"Women's rights are human rights," chanted a chorus as I licked my buttery fingers.

Rosalind Institute loomed in the distance. The paved street was lined with trees, and the changing leaves fluttered towards the ground in thick, red-and-yellow clumps.

"Game face, Avery," I whispered as I rounded the corner, taking another gulp of coffee.

"Do you believe in women's rights?" A thick pack of pamphlets were shoved in my face, gripped by a hand with red taloned nails.

I sighed. "I certainly do," I said, rummaging through my messy handbag. The two treat bags were now oil-stained and in the way as I fished my heels from the bottom—underneath everything I owned. "Alas, I have to get to work." I waved my shoes towards the woman who stepped back, crossed her arms, and huffed. A deep scowl was painted across her forehead. I admired the protestors, continuing to show up after being ignored, spat at, or arrested every day for years. But today, I didn't have the strength to debate or discuss. Today of all days, I couldn't fathom how they kept going.

"Those who do not fight cannot complain," she said before spinning on her heel and leading another loud chorus of *women's rights are human rights*. The huge placard she waved had the same slogan plastered across it in thick, block letters. The small, all-woman crowd joined her as they shouted and thrust their signs in the air.

I hovered on the front step of the large skyscraper building where I worked. The mismatched glass windows that made up Rosalind Institute towered over me as I stared up.

My foot hovered at the bottom step. As I took the first step, I turned around, peering back at the small crowd of women chanting and waving their hand-written signs. Their feet trudged against the cement, the thick layers of wet autumn leaves sticking to their sneakers, boots, and sandals.

There were women of all ages, sizes, and colours, and each held a clearly homemade placard that shone brightly in the morning sun.

"MY BODY, THE GOVERNMENT'S CHOICE!"

"STOP THE WAR ON WOMEN'S RIGHTS!"

"GOVERNMENT MANDATES NEVER AFFECT MEN!"

"THE AUSTRALIAN GOVERNMENT: WAGING WAR AGAINST WOMEN."

The chanting women yelled out-of-sync, their voices strangely vibrant. Each yelled their own slogan, the words jumbling and mashing together.

The signs made me swallow hard. The reality of my situation was written on those cards. They may be mostly for women who were forced to have abortions they didn't want, but I liked to think they were also protesting for women like *me*.

I sighed, aching for a moment to join them, to yell my own obscenities at the Government who wasn't listening, to let myself *feel* the rage, sadness and confusion that bubbled within. Instead, I spun on my heel and marched up the stairs. I caved and shot a quick look back as I reached the top, shakily changing my shoes under the soft glow of the inner office foyer.

"8:58a.m., record time for a Friday." I nodded to security who grunted as I drained the last few drops of my coffee.

Throwing my shoulders back, I strode inside. I had my entrance and exit down to a fine art. With a twirl, I placed my handbag down on the conveyor belt, wrist poised to scan my embedded ID. The machine beeped and I strode through the full body scanner. Overhead a green light flashed, and on cue, the tiny chip flashed green underneath my skin.

I shuffled forward as the other side opened with a loud *beep*.

I forced myself to keep my mind on the mundane task as I stepped off the platform and onto the mottled marble floor. The word *pregnant* seemed to flash into my mind every other moment. I gripped the handle of my bag and made a beeline for the elevator, swiping my wrist again; my skin glowing green again as I summoned the elevator.

Pregnant. My fingers shook as I pressed the illuminated *seven*.

Pregnant. The letters flashed before my eyes as my stomach lurched in time with the elevator. The floors sped by, the scientists switching from Friday casual, to lab-coats, to pencil skirts and crisp suits depending on the level.

The doors lurched open at level seven, the red carpet shrouding everything in a red glow. I practically ran to the coffee machine, flicking it on with an audible sigh as if I hadn't already had a coffee today.

Coffee gripped tightly, I darted into my office, dumping my coat, handbag, and rubbish onto my overcrowded desk and stared down at the towering, haphazard piles. The papers spilled over onto each other as I plonked myself down into my chair, head resting on my palms. My eyes glazed over just by looking at the messy mounds. Today's priorities pinged into a shared tablet.

"Avery?" A sweet, singsong voice interrupted my paper-work wallowing. An enormous mug of strong, black coffee now waved in my face.

"My saviour," I cooed, smiling and stifling a yawn. "Daily report?" I took a huge swig of the dark brew and rested the coffee on my thigh. The cup left a small, blotchy ring on my black stockings—you'd think after a hundred pairs of ruined stockings I would learn.

"Dealing with this…" Chase said, half-grimacing, half-smiling as I groaned, the paperwork taunting me.

"Unimportant appointment at two with Mr. Venter," Chase said, her smile now faltering as her eyes flicked down to the tablet in her hands. The click of the tablet signified the end of today's scheduled events.

I looked up at her with a pathetic half-smile. I had *almost* forgotten about my meeting after such a disastrous morning.

"Out of here by four?" I said, gliding past the awkwardness that hummed between us. "Three-thirty?" I raised my eyebrows as I tried to tempt her to remain my friend and paperwork-assistant.

"The scientist in me knows this is a great opportunity," Chase retorted, circling back to the meeting. "The human in me is selfish, and wants you to stay." She followed her words with a large shrug that moved her black-buttoned jacket up to her ears.

"The human in us wants many things." I wiggled my eyebrows at her. "Yet sometimes, we are destined for other pathways," I continued, my voice going all low and sarcastic as I spoke, dropping my head into a bow.

Chase snorted, and a small dribble of coffee snaked down her chin. Her dark brown eyes lit up for a few seconds as she giggled.

I smirked, placed my coffee down, and sighed.

"See..." Chase whined, "who will do things like that to make me smile?" She whinged as I grabbed the thickest stack of paper and rifled through it.

"The next Scientist might be a hottie," I countered, already skipping ahead and visualising the spicy hot wings, cheesy fries, and beers I would scarf down in a few short hours. The mere thought of food and my stomach gurgled.

Pregnant. My mind raced as my hands moved from habit, ripping the staples out of the first three pages and re-stacking them in the correct order.

I wondered if the twinge of guilt I had felt was from knowing I was pregnant, or knowing I was supposed to be on another already unsuccessful diet. I argued with myself that this was the *perfect* excuse to break my promises.

Sunlight shone in from the window, the glare making me squint as I held up the next stack of pages, half of them coffee-stained.

"How do I stain *everything*?" I dramatically waved the pages from the report on *DNA: Decoding the Origins of our Humanity*.

"Re-print and refill?" Chase offered, holding out both hands for my mug and the thick wad of paper before dashing out the door.

I flopped back into my chair, sinking down a little and hunching my back as a loud siren blared outside my window. "Right on time." My body automatically swivelled to look out the window as four policemen in riot gear hopped out of a doorless jeep. The front man held up a large white speaker.

"Time to move along." His gruff voice echoed through the closed window, cracking and blasting at the small crowd of women. His free hand shooed them, waving them off dismissively.

Chase jabbed my elbow and handed me my coffee.

"Fresh pot. Fresh printing." She waved the new report across my vision. I barely saw her as my eyes locked down on the police and protestors.

"Did I miss anything?" Chase sipped her coffee and closed the gap between us, staring out the window with me.

Pregnant. The word returned with more force inside my brain.

"No. Maybe? No–Not really." I stumbled on my words, unable to pull my gaze away. "Why do we just accept this as our fate? Why have so many of us stopped fighting?" I was asking Chase, but really, *I was asking myself*.

"We know our place," Chase said with a shrug, her voice low and sad and ringing in my ears as the police gave their second barking direction for the women to move on. "Why do you care all of a sudden?"

Chase turned away from the window. The rustling and flicking of papers filled the room until the loud siren blared and the police split up. They circled the women, ripping the signage from their hands, and broke them into pieces across the pavement.

As the women scampered off in different directions, a thick, green hose drenched them, the water gushing from a nearby fire hydrant—the hose held by a smirking policeman.

I shuddered as they separated the women, and a loud direction was given for them to put their hands behind their heads.

"They're being arrested," I murmured, shaking my head.

"They always are," Chase said. "Every Friday...what's gotten into you today?"

My stomach curdled as the woman with red-taloned nails was roughly shoved into the back of a police car. Her head smacked hard against the metal door as the police officer shoved her in, her wailing yells for equality muffled as they shut the door in her face.

"Chase," I said, swivelling on my heel. I turned to face her, her deep eyes narrowed and looking me up-and-down as I whispered, "can you keep a secret?"

CHAPTER FOUR

THE ELUSIVE LOTTERY

"Pizza or baby?" I whispered as I swivelled side-on and stared at my stomach in Rosalind Institute's luxurious bathroom mirror.

I stared at my reflection. My sweaty fingers grappling with my stockings and shirt, trying to contort them to sit flat. I sighed as I reminded myself that the curves and bulges were part of my body—and that my body hadn't changed overnight *or* from finding out there was an unwelcome clump of cells growing within. That little extra pudge came from a love of all things sweet and deep-fried.

I pushed my stomach out with force. The tops of my tights protested as I held my breath. My cheeks turned puffy and rosy, blue eyes wide before flicking into a deep scowl.

I let it go, turning to face the mirror, not bothering to attempt to smooth my unruly brown hair.

I nodded at my reflection, trying to psych myself up and prove *I was ready*. My stomach had other plans; it twisted and back flipped hard as I pulled open the bathroom door. My heels echoed down the long hallway.

As I stood with my back against the cold, glass elevator wall, mumbled lines of acceptance and loss tumbled out of my mouth.

"Thank you for this opportunity, Mr. Venter. It was an honour just to be considered, Mr. Venter. I appreciate the nomination, Mr. Venter."

As I walked past the six glass-enclosed labs on the top floor corridor, I forced my mind to go blank. I plastered on my scientist smile, usually reserved for grant nights and rich donors, and locked my eyes on the only solid door.

I ran my fingers across the cool, gold lettered plaque that hung in the centre of the door. The letters read *Chief Scientist* and nothing else.

Without hesitating, I knocked twice. My knuckles echoed against the wood. I took a step back, my breath sticking in my throat as I forced myself to stand still.

Fifteen seconds had passed when the door finally swung open. Mr. Venter was standing back with a warm, friendly smile as he ushered me in.

"Sit, Alice," he said, waving his hand at the large blue velvet chairs to the left.

He stalked across the room, taking residence in the other identical chair and pouring two glasses of water.

I closed the gap, sinking down into the soft chair, trying to perch my body on the tip and not slump backwards.

"T-Thank you, Mr. Venter." His gaze was fixed on me as he sipped his water, his lean, suit-clad body relaxed; the exact opposite of the sweaty, nervous mess I was.

He waved his hand at me, a smile cracking across his weathered face. "Don't thank me yet."

I nodded once as he suddenly stood back up.

"This is an incredible opportunity." He paced forward, his hands clasping behind his back, salt-and-pepper hair neatly combed into place.

"It was an honour to be considered." I pressed my lips shut. *Shut up, shut up,* I thought, as I smacked myself internally.

"You graduated with a bachelor's degree in biology?" Mr. Venter asked, turning to face me with a thick manila file in his hands, *Alice Avery* scrawled across the front. I had seen enough files marked *Alice Avery* for one day.

"Yes." I nodded. "With honours…Sir," I added as he leafed through the pages in front of him, as if to confirm I was telling the truth. I wondered for the first time what other information was shared between Government and Employer.

"Top of your class, master's degree, spotless work record," he listed, his eyes fixated on the paper, the top of his thinning hair pointing at me as he looked down. "A star in the academic world. The perfect candidate." He snapped the Manila file shut. "Almost…"

My heart raced. An electric shock shot down my back, tingles spreading into my arms and legs. I fought to keep my face blank, hoping I could portray a face of slight confusion and interest at the same time.

"Pregnancy is a gift, Miss Avery." He dragged the blue velvet chair forward, the wooden floor beneath its legs groaning as it bumped along.

"Pregnancy?" I repeated, unable to get out any other words.

"You are pregnant, are you not, Miss Avery?" His eyes were fixed on my face.

I could feel myself turning a shade of pink, and then deep red as he stared at me expectantly, as if only I knew the answer to his question. It had been half-a-day and I barely knew how I felt; and now Mr. Venter had been advised.

"It will be *taken care of*," I said after a drawn-out pause, my voice a little harsher than intended.

"Possibly, yes…but maybe not."

I swallowed hard. "Sir." I looked him in the eye now and pleaded. "With all due respect. This was a momentary, *personal* lapse in judgment." A deep frown was creeping onto my forehead. "I ask for your professional understanding, and that I still be considered for this opportunity—should I be the top candidate choice?" I quickly added, the words coming out like a question instead of a statement. I didn't want to sound arrogant on top of everything else.

I could feel the pull of my shoulders up around my ears, the muscles contorting.

"Miss Avery, you have a chance at *the lottery*. The odds," he swooned. I opened my mouth to speak but he pressed on. "*Scientifically*," he said, enunciating this word, his eyes flitting between my face and my stomach. "This could be huge. Both for you and your career—*and* for the institute. Most women don't even get to cross the starting line." His eyes flared. "Most women aren't *extraordinary*."

I stared at my boss; a man of science with a sudden gleam in his eye. He looked giddy with excitement, but I couldn't be sure exactly where that excitement stemmed from.

"Sir," I said, scratching the back of my head hard. "Respectfully, I don't want to have a baby. Why was it that I had to keep explaining this to the *men* I was surrounded by? Women seemed to grasp this concept with ease.

"I know the arguments," I went on, holding up my hands as Mr. Venter opened his mouth, the Government's pretty words on the tip of his tongue. "I have a proposition... two weeks." My voice echoed in my ears. "My confirmation test is in two weeks. If by some miracle I am carrying the next Darwin or Einstein, I will concede, and throw my hat into the lottery to compete...not that I have a choice," I mumbled the last part under my breath. The notion of *the lottery* sickened me. Fighting against other women for the *chance* to carry a pregnancy to term always felt archaic; and here I was, pleading with my boss, *a man of science*, for his approval.

"And if—" Mr. Venter interrupted, "—that happens, you'll mention the Rosalind Institute? Tell the world what we are, what we do, how we can bring change?" His voice shook, his pitch uneven.

"Yes." I nodded, internally rolling my eyes and outwardly forcing a smile. "But, if this situation is taken care of," I interjected before he could continue to speak, "and the opportunity we were just discussing is still available..." I trailed off. "If I am the best candidate..." I didn't want this to sound like a bribe; a foetus traded for a promotion.

"Miss Avery," Mr. Venter said, putting his hand up to stop my awkward rambling. "You were the most qualified candidate." His eyes darted to my stomach again, and for a split second, I wondered if he would ever truly see me as an equal while I had a uterus. "You were to be my recommendation—of course this is now dependent..." He trailed off, eyes darting again to my stomach. I understood that everything hinged on my entry to *the lottery*. I sighed as his face broke into a smile, the edges of which tugged at the corner of his mouth, shooting tiny cracked wrinkles across his cheeks. "You would be a superstar behind the scenes, but also in court." A nod accompanied his words as if that added to their weight.

"Thank you, sir." I smiled and let myself imagine for a moment standing up to give expert testimony, backing up my words with science, helping the system put away the bad guy.

"Justice," Mr. Venter said, "should always be the focus. We need people who understand that on our side." His eyes darted to my stomach once more. It was like an in-built twitch now and my heart skipped a beat every time.

"Can I ask you a question?" I interjected. "If you were in charge, and the decisions surrounding the Australian population were yours to make—" I swallowed hard, knowing I should have simply thanked Mr. Venter and not let the door hit me on the ass on the way out; but my curiosity and wonder got the better of me, like it always did.

"Miss Avery." Mr. Venter stood up, pacing back-and-forth, his hands clasped behind his back. With each step he took, my heart thumped harder in my chest. *The lottery* was a touchy subject for men and women alike, and even more so for scientists.

"You—" He cut me off with a hand and I withered and clamped my mouth shut.

"The ideals and decision-making surrounding *the lottery* came from a good place." He paused for a moment. "But, *I believe,* the process is flawed." He was choosing his words carefully.

The breath I was holding deflated like a balloon. My knees knocked together in the same rhythm as my nodding head. He was right, of course, but his admission didn't feel like the victory I was hoping for.

"I don't envy your position. Society has always dealt women the short straw in matters of reproductive freedom and bodily autonomy."

"Freedom?" I scoffed, only allowing a tiny smirk to appear on my lips and swallowed the seething anger at society and the men who made the rules. I bit my cheek hard and forced myself to stay quiet. This wasn't Mr. Venter's fault and my anger shouldn't be directed at him.

Mr. Venter's forehead was deeply indented as he waited for the words that never came. I stared at his concerned face, realising this might be the first time he had considered the impact this competition had on real women in his life. It was amusing, in an irritating way. I wanted to hold onto the anger, but if I was being honest, I was just as guilty. The mandates had never been more than an inconvenience to me, and so I never bothered to speak up or fight it, and now here I was. *Fucked,* I thought—in more than one way.

Twenty-five years hadn't felt so long when they announced *the lottery,* but thirteen years in and the women of Australia were suffering.

"Thank you," I said, giving Mr. Venter a smile and standing up to leave, my own guilt at what was happening gnawing at my insides. "No matter how this turns out..." My hands gripped the side of my tight pencil skirt, the sweat seeping into the bunched up fabric. "I'll have something worth fighting for."

CHAPTER FIVE

THE SOLIDARITY OF WOMEN

Sinking down into the squishy leather couch, I cradled my drink. Darcy and Kit slid in beside me, cramming into what would normally be a two-person booth.

Our sweaty shoulders knocked together. My tanned skin vibrant against Kit's pale, freckled arms, and more natural against Darcy's almost-orange fake tan.

"What is going on with that colour?" I asked, giggling as the first rush of alcohol reached my brain and I poked Darcy's bicep.

She chugged down three-quarters of her mojito, staring at me with forlorn eyes.

"Disaster," she finally said, sucking in a breath and letting out a commanding burp. "It's the story of my life written on my skin." This time she winked at me.

My laughter sent a small sip of beer dribbling down my chin.

"*So*, what's new with you?" Kit interjected and both my friends rounded on me. Kit stared at me, batting her eyelids, while Darcy crossed her arms and leaned back in her chair.

These two simple gestures told me my fake nonchalance was about to be forced to an end.

I sighed, putting my hand to my forehead in a damsel-in-distress motion. "In all honesty," I said, almost immediately dropping the act and swigging another sip of beer. "I think I'm still in shock." I cast my eyes towards the small dance floor and stared at the three awkward strangers jiving to the music together, out of sync and rhythm. "Mr. Venter told me I was the best candidate and *would have been* his recommendation to the board."

Kit and Darcy squealed beside me. Their arms clambered over me and their squeaky voices squawked my praises. Two hands squeezed and grabbed at my shoulders as fingers jabbed into my rib cage. Until Kit reeled back and said, "Wait, *would have*?" in an incredulous tone.

"Alas, I have a uterus." I sighed. I wanted to say so much more, but couldn't bring myself to rehash the same point with the two women in my life I *knew* would understand.

"What does that have to do with *anything*?" Darcy asked, pulling back and looking at me.

"When your boss finds out you're pregnant," I said coldly, closing my eyes and leaning my head back, "they become crazed at the possibility of a Rosalind employee competing in *the lottery.*" I made sure my sarcasm was over-the-top.

"Is he kidding?" Kit asked, her jaw dropping open. Her pale, overgrown eyebrows pinched together over her bright green eyes, a furious glint radiating from them. The expression on Kit's face summed up how I felt without words.

"He basically said to me to *imagine the publicity*," I said, putting on my best deep voice to impersonate him. He didn't say that—but he implied it, and that was enough.

Darcy sculled the rest of her drink, her eyes flashing between anger and joy as the waitress sauntered our way with a tray stocked to the brim.

"Loaded potato skins?" the waitress cooed sweetly.

"Yes!" we said in unison as she dumped the metal tray down in front of us, followed by our second round of drinks.

We eyed each other before digging in. The silver cutlery the waitress had placed to the side all but forgotten and replaced by ravenous hands.

"So," Darcy said, half a potato skin hanging out of her mouth as she licked her lips. Her fingers were covered in sour cream and sauce, and she tried unsuccessfully to brush her long, dark hair out of her face. "Who's the father?" Her smile turned almost shy as she looked at me, still chewing her last enormous bite.

"Who *is* the father?" Kit echoed, staring at me incredulously, like I was hiding the secret to eating whatever you wanted and staying a perfect size six from her.

I groaned, shovelling another huge potato skin in and then pointing to my full mouth and shrugging my shoulders.

"Is it Blake?" Darcy asked, her deep brown eyes staring into my soul as she spoke.

"Is it Spencer?" Kit interjected, immediately waving away Darcy's possibility.

"No way!" Darcy said, shaking her head vigorously. The two of them shared a long glance, talking without audible words.

"It has to be Mason!" Kit and Darcy said in unison, high-fiving across the table as they both looked at me for official confirmation.

"We fucked *once*," I said, feeling the groan in my words. Visions of Mason's sweaty body against mine flashed in my mind and sent a burn to my cheeks.

"Isn't he a scientist, too?" Darcy asked, her dark eyes shooting upwards.

"He's an astronomer," I said. "If you call that a scientist," I added with an eye roll, the words shot out under my breath and made the girls giggle. I had said the same thing about Mason to them last time—and a tiny pang of guilt wiggled through me.

"Have you seen him since?" Darcy eyed me and crossed her arms. We all knew the answer to this question, but I shook my head, not saying another word as I shovelled more potato skins into my mouth.

"I thought you liked this one?" Kit said.

A shrug hit my ears. "I-I did…I do? He's been calling." I could feel the pink creeping up my neck and burning its way onto my cheeks and neck. I hated that my skin gave away my discomfort with dazzling displays of red and pink.

Kit and Darcy both raised an eyebrow in unison before Kit pressed on. "You've kept in touch?"

"I want him all up in my personal *space*." I winked and swooned with an over-exaggerated giggle. "But things have gotten more than a *little* complicated now..."

"What are you going to do?" Darcy whispered, her eyes darting around the club. Mine followed hers, running over the bottle laden bar and half-filled stools.

"Two things." I sighed. "I'm going to call Mason back." I rolled my eyes as the girls exchanged looks. "And I'm going to procure a remedy for this situation."

"Alice," Kit whispered, first-naming me as her nostrils flared under her green eyes. "You know you *can't*."

Kit placed her warm hand on my back, followed by Darcy's icy hand pulling my hair out of my face and laying her head on my shoulder.

"It's brutal," Kit whispered. "Unless you can get the pill." Kit's fingers dug into my skin, her chest heaving against my shoulder.

"I-I'm sor—" I tried to speak, but was silenced by Kit's tightening grip. I was half-sad and half-grateful as my apologies weren't what Kit or I needed at that moment.

Kit's fingernails dug in deeper, cutting off my words. *"Don't you dare."*

I shot a glance at Kit. Her eyes were narrowed, her lips pressed into a thin, white line.

"Nineteen-year-old-Kit couldn't have handled a baby. Hell, thirty-year-old-Kit *still* couldn't handle one," she said, a flush of colour rushing across her pale cheeks. "Don't compare what I went through to your situation..."

"Where do you—" Darcy whispered, not finishing her sentence as Mason's name lit up on my phone—almost the perfect saviour. Three sets of eyes were immediately glued to it.

"I don't know," I swallowed. "The tracker is likely to pick it up anyway." I rubbed the nape of my neck and the prickly stitches under my fingers.

"The *tracker?*" Darcy said through gritted teeth.

"Bathroom," Kit said, shooting me a stern look.

I groaned internally as I scooted out of our booth and weaved my way through the crowd to the bathroom. My stomach was in my throat as we moved, and I knew I was about to be grilled about leaving out that crucial, disastrous detail.

I pulled open the door, and the stench of urine and burnt hair smacked me in the face. I scurried towards the only empty stall in the back left corner. Heaving the door open, I scooted in, closing and locking the door behind me.

"Avery?" Kit and Darcy called, their voices ringing against the muted music of the club.

I stuck my foot out of the stall and wiggled it, making no move to unlock the door.

"What do you mean, *THE TRACKER?*" Darcy's fist pounded on the door. The hinges rattled under the weight of her battering.

"*What tracker?*" Kit said, her voice low and ominous; she was calmer and more deadly when she was mad.

"Apparently, I'm unpredictable." I shrugged behind the closed door. The stench from the toilet wafted up my pinched nose. The smell made me gag. "I can't do this," I said, sinking down onto the floor and curling myself into a ball.

"Come on," Kit insisted, shimmying the lock of the toilet door and pushing her weight against it. With a snap, the door swung open.

Kit started mothering, slamming the toilet lid shut, perching herself on top and flushing it twice. The loud gurgling sound rang in my ears, but it didn't help the searing smell.

Darcy ungracefully clambered in too, her black boots scuffing against the floor as she squeezed herself into the corner and pushed the door shut.

"Right," Darcy said. "No more of this nonsense."

"Tell us what the hell is going on?" Kit prompted.

They both squatted, contorting themselves into the small spaces on either side of me. I owed them an explanation, but my mind was so jumbled it was hard to get the words out.

"They implanted a tracker in my neck." I bent forward so they could see the silver stitches. "And they've denied me an abortion due to my past intelligence testing." Kit and Darcy shared a glance. They had both heard about my arguments with doctors before and immediately knew what I meant. "I *refuse* to let the government continue to decide my choices. I won't go back," I finally whispered, pulling out my phone.

I opened my texts and sent Mason a message to meet tomorrow morning. I hoped he still pictured the cool science girl he met at the bar, rather than this reality where I was stuck in a crammed, reeking bathroom stall, crying about my mistakes.

"He's already replied." Darcy smirked, staring down at my phone.

"*How* is that possible?" Kit grumbled, followed by our loud laughter. I appreciated them more than ever as they wiped my tears and pulled me out of my spiral.

"*Maybe it's because your ass is from outer space*," Darcy said, pushing herself to her feet and reaching down to drag me up as I burst into a fit of half-sobs, half-giggles.

"*Your legs are out of this world*," Kit chimed in, standing up, too.

We burst out of the small stall, and I felt like I could breathe a little easier.

"Thank you," I said with a wonky smile as they laid their heads on my shoulders, two chins poking into my skin.

Our reflection stared back at us as we stood side-by-side at the small, mirrored sinks. Smiles were painted on each of our faces. I wasn't sure if they were all real or all fake, but it didn't matter. At least I felt less alone.

"*I can do this*." I said as I stared at Kit's out-of-control red curls and blue velvet blazer, and Darcy's bare arms, the thin straps from her patterned midriff top lining her skin.

I looked at my girl gang, sandwiched between my two best friends.

Pulling them closer, I dropped my head down, the tears that had formed in my eyes falling onto their skin.

"Will you b-both come with m-me?" I pleaded as my body heaved with choked sobs.

Tighter grasps and nodding heads was the only reply as I felt their tears run down my back. The solidarity of women was unparalleled.

We stood quiet for a long while, breathing in the comfort from each other until I pulled back and wiped my tears.

"Thank you." I smiled at both of them. Their outstretched hands were enough to keep me fighting for one more day.

CHAPTER SIX

THE REAPPEARANCE OF THE FATHER

SIPPING ON MY CHAI LATTE, I STARED OUT THE WINDOW OF THE TINY coffee shop, my view distorted by my own stark reflection.

I glanced down at my half-empty cup, its blue rim covered in a dusting of cinnamon and blush-pink lipstick. I didn't want to admit it, but the make-up on my face was proof of my nerves.

"Alice?" a deep, croaky voice said, followed by a swift cough and clearing of the throat.

I stared up at Mason as he hovered next to the empty chair at my table; always the gentleman, he waited patiently to be invited to sit.

"H-hi," I stuttered, not sure how to greet someone you had a one-night stand with eleven weeks ago and haven't spoken to since outside of texts.

His face burst into a huge grin as he sat down, pulling the chair sideways and leaning up against the solid frame with his shoulder. His smile turned goofy as it widened. "The elusive Alice Avery. Here she sits."

I smiled, remembering how dorky and charming Mason was as his cheeks flushed a hot shade of pink under his light brown eyes.

Heart thumping and knee bouncing, I sipped my latte in silence.

The words I needed to say were stuck in my throat like a boulder that was too big to move on my own.

"How did your grant proposal go?" I asked, suddenly remembering that we had a great conversation about all things science before we jumped into bed together—it was one of the things that attracted me to him.

"You remembered?" he asked, raising his unruly eyebrows and beaming at me as he sipped his black coffee. "Well…" He leaned back and smirked at me, as if he was about to give me a full run down.

"I'm pregnant," I blurted, unable to stop the words from tumbling out of my mouth and smacking him in the face. The rosy pink that had flushed his cheeks vanished. His face turned violent shades of green and grey.

He stared at me, his coffee cup frozen in mid-air.

"You're—" he cut off as if his brain had short-circuited.

"I am ten weeks and two days pregnant." I tried to keep my voice quiet inside the small, crowded café. "With your baby," I added, just in case there was any confusion.

His face was frozen, his eyes wide and unblinking.

"Pregnant," he repeated. The pause between his words stretched to the brink of a sentence.

He placed his cup down, his eyes rising to meet mine.

"How are you still *allowed* to be pregnant?" His eyes darted around the room as if a secret government spy might be lurking nearby.

"I'm a medical marvel," I said with a sigh, running my finger up and down against my cup as its contents turned from warm to cold. "A genius," I added with a wink. I could feel myself cringing internally with each word I spoke.

Mason nodded, the hint of a smile dancing on his lips. His fingers interlaced with each other as he stared at me with intense, unbroken eye contact. It unnerved me, as if he was *really* looking at me, *really* seeing me.

"I thought you didn't want kids?" Mason mused, scratching the back of his head. He looked suddenly concerned and confused, and I switched from a little flirty to enraged in a split second.

"I don't," I snapped. "Alas, our brilliant healthcare system is impossible." I rolled my eyes as Mason stared at me with raised eyebrows. I could feel bile rising in my throat and swallowed it down, forcing myself to breathe.

"Do you know how many doctors I *begged* to have my tubes tied?" I said, as the silence stretched out between us and Mason twitched uncomfortably in his chair. "Twelve," I continued, my anger slowly replaced by an ache in my stomach. "Twelve doctors who all said no. Who all asked me *what would my future husband think*? Who prioritised a non-existent man and future baby above my own desires." I felt the tears welling behind my eyes and dropped my voice even lower. "I could *win the lottery*. The line I heard from doctors so many times. Never mind that I don't *want* children." Mason looked at me with sympathy, and I felt a tiny pang of guilt as I chewed on my lip.

Mason scooted his chair closer to mine with a loud, dragging noise. He winced, almost-embarrassed, but undeterred.

"It's okay." His light brown eyes were full of worry as he wrapped his arm around my shoulders and patted me awkwardly on the arm. His warm skin radiated through the sheer fabric of my long-sleeved shirt. "It's okay to be upset," Mason said, giving my arm a little squeeze as he spoke.

I shrugged away, rolling my eyes. I tried and failed to swallow the words that came next.

"I'm not upset." I held his gaze. "I'm *angry*," I said, my voice harsh but calm. "Angry that I am stuck in a situation I tried desperately to avoid."

Mason nodded in startled agreement as he dragged his chair back, scooting away from me. I struggled to calm myself.

"Can I help?" Mason asked, fidgeting with his hands under the table. He was clearly on edge, and my enjoyment of his squirminess waned almost immediately.

I tried for a genuine smile as I shook my head and sipped my cold latte, before pulling a face of disgust. "I hope you're not as smart as the intelligence tests think you are," I said half-jokingly, biting the inside of my lip. "Otherwise I might be in real trouble."

Mason laughed, and his shoulders relaxed from their tensed spot near his ears.

"Like my genes are the ones to worry about." He cracked a wide grin and pushed an out-of-place strand of blonde hair out of his face. Mason opened his mouth a few times before smiling at me. He clearly had something he wanted to say.

"I'll text you in a week to let you know the result," I said, pulling my bag up off the table and draining the rest of my cold latte, wincing a little at the wrongness of the taste.

I turned on my heel, leaving Mason's confused face and awkward waving arm behind.

I took a few deep breaths, my heart racing, as I looked right and left before crossing the road. Ambling along the cracked bitumen, my feet and ankles knocked together as I stumbled past the post office. It was packed with Saturday morning shoppers who wanted to retrieve their parcels. Life seemingly went on as normal—for me, it was as far from normal as it had ever been.

With a tug, I pulled my jacket closed, shakily buttoning the thick, gold buttons. The fabric pulled against my skin as my fingers dug into the pockets.

Within my left pocket was a sharp-edged card. My fingers poked at the flimsy paper, folded into thirds and scrunched up as if it was nothing.

I picked up the pace at the reminder of the card's contents. My feet pulled me past my regular bookshop, its doors closed to keep out the dancing gusts of wind. The beautiful displays in the window were lit up by fairy lights and brilliant signage.

A woman's face stared back at me from the display. Her perfect white, toothy smile was plastered along every banner, book jacket, and sign in the front window.

Every quarter, a new woman splashed her smile for the cameras and interviews for a few months before disappearing into hiding with her precious bundle. With so many women desperate for children, it wasn't safe to remain in the public eye for long.

Around the corner I fumbled and pulled out the scrunched card. I could have kissed Kit's friend-of-a-friend when she handed this to me in silence with a knowing look.

An address a few streets away was scrawled in red pen, the ink smudged from my sweaty fingers. I scrambled to straighten the card out.

I checked my watch. I had thirty minutes to convince myself this was a good idea.

"Alice," came a husky voice.

I spun around, and Mason and his dorky smile was closer than I expected. The lump in my throat swelled as I shoved my hands in my pocket. The edges of the paper sliced at my skin as I stared into Mason's eyes.

"What are you—" Before I could get another word out, Mason stepped forward and his mouth met mine. All the pent up fear melted away at the feel of Mason's lips against mine.

He stepped away, pushing his hair back and flashing a grin.

"I couldn't let you go without something to remember me by." His lips twitched. He clearly thought he was clever speaking the *most cliché* line in history aloud.

The smile that blossomed on my lips was involuntary. I could feel my cheeks burning with heat and yet somehow, the only thing I wanted was for him to step forward and kiss me again.

"Go, go," Mason said. He was the least nonchalant person I had ever met, and here he was, trying to act casual.

A smile on my face and holding my chin and shoulders back in an uncomfortable position, I walked past my Mason and my favourite bookshop to go onto the main street. The paper was burning a hole in my pocket. I walked the route I had traced on my maps without ever plugging in the address. I didn't look back, and forced the thought of Mason out of my mind. I couldn't think about him now.

I could feel my jaw clench and unclench, my fists ball and let go, my brow pull and furrow as I picked up my pace. The red ink of the card was burned into my eyes as I rounded the last corner.

Gasping and fighting to control my hurried steps, I inched my way forward, counting the house numbers on the plain suburban street. I knew I looked out of place as I stood outside a house with a white picket fence.

The gate squeaked as I pushed it open, a little bell attached to the top ringing in my ears. My slow footsteps inched forward, creeping towards the looming blue-painted door.

I ascended the stairs, knees shaking, and I said a silent prayer before pounding on the door three times.

The door swung open, and a squat, balding man stood in the entrance. His bug-like eyes narrowed on me and darted back-and-forth down the deserted street before pulling me inside roughly.

He snapped and twisted five bolted locks shut.

"Avery?" His voice was questioning, but the file he held in his stumpy fingers had my name scrawled across it in thin, cursive letters. It was a bit late to ask my name, but I nodded, adding my own question.

"Doctor?" I hovered near the door. He looked me up and down, his bugging eyes wide as he tucked the folder under his arm and nodded once before ushering me down a small hallway.

The house was grimy and dusty, as if it had sat boarded up for years.

I wrinkled my nose as we turned a corner, almost bumping into the doctor as he bent down to pull up a trap-door.

"What is that?" My voice trembled when I spoke, all the nerves ricocheting around inside my body.

"The lab is downstairs," the doctor said, flashing me a forced smile with discoloured teeth.

I chewed on the inside of my lip as he hovered, dithering from foot-to-foot, his eyes still darting around. A sense of dread had settled deep within my bones.

"Come, come," he said finally, descending the inner stairs first, his loud footsteps echoing in my ears.

With a nod, I followed. My shoulders curled in and my arms clenched around my body.

Halfway down, the doctor hit a large red button, and a stream of weak light flickered on. The plastic casings were covered in a thick layer of dirt, like everything else in the house. The doctor waved his hand to one of the grubby armchairs in the back as he bustled around the room, not facing me.

I sunk into the chair, tiny puffs of dirty air escaping as I tried to sit still.

The room was small: two tables, two chairs, and a small bench attached to the back wall. I stared at the walls, the cracks filled with a thick layer of dust, the photographs that hung there discoloured.

"How far along are you?" The doctor's gruff voice echoed in the small room, bouncing off every wall.

"Ten weeks, and a few days," I said, trying to sound matter-of-fact as my insides squirmed. I wasn't scared of the procedure itself, but this place sent a creepy, deathly chill through my body.

"A clever girl like you," the doctor sneered as he bustled around, pulling things down from the shelves above the back counter and lining them up. "It's always the smart ones," he added, shaking his head, his back still to me. He fidgeted with glass cups and beakers, holding them up to examine them before placing them on the bench. I hoped the instruments he planned to use were cleaner than the room we were currently sitting in. "They *never* see it coming." He held up three fingers as he turned to face me, a wide smile splitting his face. "Three…" I shot up from the chair, eyes wild. "Two…" I took one step forward as he smirked. "One."

My body trembled as an alarm sounded. The blaring beeping rang in my ears as I shoved my way past the doctor and bolted up the stairs. The thick, wooden trap door was clamped shut. The sound of thundering footsteps were already hammering above.

With a giant creak, the trapdoor was yanked open, my face only a few centimetres away from a pair of shiny black boots. I reeled back as the man forcefully pushed his way into the room.

"Subject has been located." The man with black boots stood face-to-face with me, talking into a small device on his wrist.

I let out a muffled scream as calloused hands grabbed at me, and a gaggle of men with slicked-back hair suddenly tumbled into the small room.

A loud *click* echoed in my ears as a pair of thick handcuffs were clamped shut against my wrists, their grip cutting into my flesh.

"What—" I choked out as a hand was flung into my face.

"No more questions, Miss Avery." A white-lab coat clad chest pushed through. "The fight is over." His hot breath hit my face as his rough hands pressed into my cheeks, squeezing them together.

"The fight has just begun," I said through clenched teeth. "The fight has just begun!" I yelled as I was shoved forward, my head forced down, my body caving in on itself as I was lifted and pushed up the stairs.

"This fight has just begun." I screamed as my mouth was clamped and taped shut, a sting on my neck sending a shiver down my spine, and my vision slowly faded to black.

CHAPTER SEVEN

THE TESTING

For the third time in as many days I perched myself over the shiny porcelain toilet in the doctor's corridor bathroom. The cup had my name printed in big block letters, but the label was smudged from my sweaty grip. My stomach roiled at the combination of smells in the bathroom, and I wasn't sure if it was pregnancy related or pure disgust.

Three loud reverberating bangs echoed on the other side of the door as I awkwardly perched the half-full cup onto the back of the toilet. The knee-length hospital gown bunched up, and I wrinkled my nose.

I rolled my eyes and twisted the lid tighter. I wouldn't be rushed, not today. Pinching my lips tight and holding the cup less than gracefully, I pulled open the door. Three hulking suit-clad men were waiting outside the cubicle, their arms folded against their chests, no smiles to be seen.

I wasn't sure if I felt more angry or mortified in that moment; my face glowed bright red as I placed the cup on the silver tray. The first suit-clad man swivelled away, almost running out the door whilst somehow ensuring my cup stayed still.

"Miss Avery," the man at the front spoke, both men lurching forward to grip my wrists.

"This is unnecessary," I said through gritted teeth as my arms thrashed against their grip.

"Is it, sweetheart?" the man cooed. My blood boiled. "As we hear it, you've tried to *slither away* before." His hot breath sent a shiver down my spine.

"Let's go," the other one spoke, his tone softer. The men marched me out of the small bathroom and back into the corridor. The grip on my wrists tightened as we walked past three closed doors, a faint echo of sobbing behind each one.

With a tug, we came to stand in front of the last door in the corridor. A loud echoing knock rang out three times. The name *Dr. Anna Aslan GP, MD, OB/GYN* was plastered across it. The sticker was crooked, and made my eye twitch the longer I stared at it.

The door cracked open and a middle-aged doctor stood in the doorway.

"Miss Avery," she beamed, her cheery voice high and grating. She grabbed my full pee cup with her bare hands and waved the men away. "Leave us." Her eyes narrowed, and she shifted to block the doorway and the view into her office. Her eyes flared as she looked at where they held my wrists, and she crossed her arms across her chest.

"Ma'am." The two suited men unwrapped their fingers from my wrist one-by-one and dipped their heads—their stomping footsteps retreating slowly.

The doctor stared down the hallway until the men disappeared around the corner.

With a nod and a smile she spoke to me now. "Come in, come in." Then she waved me into a new office.

As she cracked the door a little wider, I did a double take. Kit and Darcy sat holding hands, beaming at me, their eyes spilling over with tears.

"What are y—" I ran to sit down between them, the large lounge letting us all squish in together. They both immediately interlaced their fingers with mine, one hand hot, the other icy against my clammy palms.

They each squeezed my hand three times in unison, sharing our unspoken love code.

"Please wait here," Dr. Aslan said, her voice squeaky and her cheeks flushed red. She rushed out of the room, a huge stack of paper clutched against her chest as she locked the door behind her.

"How? Who?" My eyes widened. I hadn't expected anyone to know I was here, let alone be allowed to visit after being trapped in isolation here for the last few days or weeks; I shivered – *I was no longer sure*.

Time had melded together in a blurry clump in my brain, littered with moments of sickness, testing, cravings, and utter loneliness. I swallowed down the tears. It was a relief to see them both.

"She called," Darcy shrugged.

"We came," Kit said as the two of them wrapped their arms around me.

"What happened to you?" they both said in creepy unison, and I wondered if they had been practicing their line of questioning.

"The abortion doctor was a set-up," I said in a hushed whisper.

They grimaced and then nodded. We had all heard the rumours of spies and crooked doctors utilised by the government to rat women out, but I had been too confident it wouldn't happen to me.

"Are you safe here?" Darcy asked, her voice trembling.

"You know...you're not in danger, right?" Kit pried. Her eyebrows knitted together.

I shrugged as loud footsteps echoed in the hallway, clearly announcing their approach. "Minus the whole kidnapping and holding-me-against-my-will issue, it's been okay," I said, throwing in a pathetic wink and wincing.

Dr. Aslan unlocked the door, stepped in, and halted, leaving the two additional doctors outside the door. Her once pink cheeks now splotchy, the colour running down her pale neck and up into her hairline.

"Miss Avery," she said, raspy and breathless. "It is time for phase two." She pushed her glasses up from the bottom of her nose to the bridge, the smile she was sporting taking over her entire face.

"Can I—"

"You *alone,* Miss Avery," Dr. Aslan cut me off. She shot me a warning glance before she stalked out the door. I could hear the silence in the hallway as she gave me a fleeting moment to say my goodbyes; it was more than I thought I'd get and I was grateful.

"We'll wait," said Darcy, her narrow eyes focused and her voice quiet enough to hide her presence.

"Right here." Kit squeezed me a little tighter before latching herself onto Darcy as I stood up.

"You got this," Darcy whispered, as she gave Kit's shoulder a tight squeeze. At least they had each other.

I nodded at them both as a goodbye, a weird, forced smile plastered on my face as I slipped out the door without a backwards glance. I wouldn't give Dr. Aslan away after her kindness.

"This way, Miss Avery," Dr. Aslan said, her chirpy voice masked by the click-clack of her high heels. I watched her back as we exited the room. She had been kind enough to hide Kit and Darcy here for me, but it didn't quite bolster me enough to trust her.

The other two doctors flanked me, their footsteps in perfect unison with each other, their shiny black shoes shimmering against the stark white tiles.

Dr. Aslan hurried, tapping her pristine white swipe card as we passed through a multitude of glass doors. The building twisted and turned more times than I could count before we stopped. With a swipe and a tap of her manicured nails, Dr. Aslan summoned the elevator.

"After you," Dr. Aslan said, her smile so wide it must have been hurting the edges of her mouth and her cheeks by now.

The door slid open, and I stepped forward, scooting to the back, right corner and taking three deep breaths with my eyes closed. I could feel the downward clang of the elevator and my stomach lurched—even the simple downward *whoosh* made its contents curdle, and I wondered if it was the foetus's revenge or my nerves.

The door clanked open and Dr. Aslan placed her hand on my shoulder, steering me into a large, black leather chair inside a new office. I let my body sink into the soft cushions, the cool leather prickling against my sweaty skin.

The two silent doctors stood on either side of me, their hands clasped together in front of them as if they were waiting for an opportunity to pounce. Their eyes and taut jaws followed Dr. Aslan's movements as she bustled around the small office.

The office was pristine, the off-white walls in stark contrast to the office space. The large mahogany desk took up a third of the room, piled high with books, loose sheets of paper, and stacked manila files. The one she held in her hand had *Alice Avery* scrawled across the front in messy handwriting. If I never saw another *Alice Avery* folder again, it would be too soon.

Three of her walls were covered in frames. They housed medical procedures, in-depth charts and graphs, and body parts labelled down to minuscule details. They hung haphazardly, some frames closer together, some frames crooked and off-centre. My eye twitched the longer I stared at them.

The fourth wall housed a door, plain white with a silver handle and a sign entitled 'examination room.'

Dr. Aslan snapped my file shut, placing it down on her unorganised desk as she rubbed her eyes; the smile that had been so prominent minutes before now twitching and drooping.

"Come," she said, waving her hand at me, her voice flat as she swung open the door to the examination room.

The room was less than half the size of the office, the walls bare except for small, coloured buttons installed across them.

I hovered awkwardly to the left side of the room. Dr. Aslan sighed and took a seat, clicking buttons and tapping on her computer.

"Change and take a seat, Alice," she said, without turning around, her voice flat and expressionless. It was as if she had flipped a switch and become this sad version of herself.

I nodded to her back out of habit, grabbing the plain pink gown off the chair. I held it up to see a strange clear panel sewed across the midsection.

"So you don't have to pull the dress all the way up," Dr. Aslan said, raising her eyebrows at me as if the gown was her very own brilliant innovation.

My eyes caught the stirrups and a soft groan escaped from my lips. I still hadn't recovered from my last experience in stirrups.

Dr. Aslan swivelled around on her chair, watching me pull the gown on and fidget with the fit. She waved me over to the exam chair as she scratched at the back of her head.

"Is something wrong?" I blurted as I sat down, swinging my legs onto the chair in one fluid motion, my eyes locked on her.

She gave me a smile that tugged at the corners of her mouth.

"No, Miss Avery," she said, letting out a deep sigh and shaking her head. "First, we are going to do a normal ultrasound," Dr. Aslan continued. "This will tell us whether the pregnancy is viable. Correct growth, strong heartbeat." Her mouth twitched. "The basics."

I fumbled to unzip the clear window that lay across my stomach. Dr. Aslan turned away, returning a few seconds later holding a bottle and a white, square hand-held contraption that looked like a wand.

"A transducer," Dr. Aslan said, holding up the wand as she squirted cold liquid onto my stomach.

I flinched, and my skin broke out in goosebumps, sending a shiver down my spine.

The transducer pressed hard against my stomach. The cool gel fused with the wand as Dr. Aslan moved it up and down. She stared at a screen bolted to the side of the chair, her eyes unblinking as she continued to twirl the wand around.

I stared at the screen in awe, the flicker of black, grey, and white images glimmering and changing.

"There," Dr. Aslan said. Her kind smile returned, and she turned the screen towards me. A loud, whooshing beat filled the room. I had never expected to *see* an ultrasound of a pregnancy, let alone be the person in the hot seat. It was an odd feeling, knowing that a little clump of cells was inside me, doubling and growing—on the verge of being human.

"The heartbeat?" I whispered it as a question and pulled myself up onto my elbows to stare intently at the screen. The whooshing beat was strong and fast. It felt for a moment as though it was pounding in my own ears, as if I could hear it both internally and externally.

"The foetus is healthy—see here." Dr. Aslan pointed at the screen. "This is the head." Her finger circled a large, grainy white area as she spoke.

I leaned back, half-listening to the words she was saying, half-frowning and wondering why I felt so uncomfortable—maybe it was the fact that I wanted to roll my eyes because she assumed this was a wanted pregnancy.

"This test is only used to confirm you still have a valid pregnancy," Dr. Aslan said, looking back at me as she pushed the screen away.

"I can confirm everything is as it should be at twelve weeks, three days," she went on matter-of-factly, scribbling notes into my file and printing off small, grey-scale pictures to attach.

"Here." Dr. Aslan handed me a copy of the ultrasound. "A memento." She pushed the photo into my hand and gave it a squeeze.

I crumpled it up, stashing it inside my bra. Unsure of what to say, I grappled with finding the right words, the polite words.

"Can I ask you a question?" I eventually said, feeling the prickly edges of the sonogram pressing against my breast.

Dr. Aslan stopped writing, snapping the file shut and looking into my eyes.

"After this is over," I said, choosing my words carefully, "can I come back and see you about permanent measures to…" I tried to search for the words and frame the question eloquently; instead I trailed off and hoped she would piece it together.

"You don't want to be sitting here again?" Dr. Aslan asked, her eyebrows slightly raised as she watched me. Other people's surprise always took me by surprise.

"No," I said firmly, shaking my head.

Dr. Aslan stood up and placed her cool hand on my shoulder.

"I promise we'll talk." She nodded and gave my shoulder a tight squeeze as she circled around, coming to a halt in front of a small, red button. "Now." Dr. Aslan pressed the button in a sharp movement. "Phase two."

The plain, white wall vibrated, and a secret wall compartment opened. It grew in size by the second, spitting out a square, black device full of cords.

I could feel my face scrunching up, eyebrows rising, my mouth turning into a strange shape as I stared at the device Dr. Aslan now held in both hands.

We were both silent as she unwrapped the warped cords from around the device and threw them into haphazard piles on the floor.

Dr. Aslan's eyes flashed as she pulled out a copper coil, the thread so thin I could only see the glint and its shadow. "Lay back," Dr. Aslan said, her eyes meeting mine for the first time since the wall spat out this new device.

"Could you talk me t-through what you're doing?" I asked, my voice cracking as I spoke, my stomach flipping wildly the moment I finished. Even I couldn't tell if it was fear or curiosity running the show.

Dr. Aslan smiled at me. Her hands remained still for a few seconds.

"A scientist at heart?" She phrased it as a question with raised eyebrows, but didn't give me a chance to do more than nod in response. "This technology is the *Oculus Origins*." The device vibrated as Dr. Aslan spoke, three distinct lights flashing rapidly from red to orange to green. "The short answer is that this wire connects to the foetus's brain."

I could feel my mouth drop open, my jaw hanging by barely a thread as I stuttered and spluttered.

"You are correct, Miss Avery," Dr. Aslan continued. "Impossible? Is that the word you are looking for?" She sighed, tapping the side of the black device three times. Two of the lights extinguished, leaving only a single green light to flicker.

"This technology..." I could hear the awe in my voice. "It will *change the world*."

My words came out in a hushed, jumbled whisper. My mind couldn't keep up at the range of scientific possibilities.

"It *already is*," Dr. Aslan said, her words a little tenser than I was expecting.

I rubbed my hands together, alternating between clasping them and fidgeting with my fingers. When her words clicked, it sent a shiver down my spine; but my own morbid curiosity was still piqued.

"Tell me more." I was breathless as Dr. Aslan pushed down on my shoulder, laying my body back into an inclined position against the examination chair.

The chair cranked out a loud ringing noise, and I felt my body stretching out. My head tilted backwards and my feet rose.

"This technology allows for growth reports, structural imaging, and neural connectivity imaging," Dr. Aslan spoke as she bustled around the examination chair, pulling a plain white table to her side. The floor protested with a loud, scraping sound. "We can plot forward a child's development." She stopped to catch her breath as she huffed and puffed at my side.

"That means…" I blinked. My skin prickled as I stared at Dr. Aslan. I was teetering on the edge of disbelief as she continued.

"We can map the future." The doctor's real smile returned. "Let me be clear," she said, putting her hand on my arm. "After six-hundred and fifty-seven tests, I've yet to map one that wasn't terminated." She was softening the impending blow.

"I asked for a termination," I said, my shoulders tensing. As exciting as the technology was, I still didn't want to be pregnant; and I certainly didn't want Dr. Aslan in a position where she felt she needed to comfort me when I didn't need comforting.

"You're an interesting woman, Miss Avery." Dr. Aslan pulled out a white sheet and placed it over my bare legs. She gently laid a second sheet over my upper torso, breasts, and neck, forcing my head to lay back flat. It was as if she was blocking my view on purpose.

"You'll feel a sharp, stinging pinch," she continued, her standard doctor voice returning. She prodded my stomach, the transducer pressing into my rib cage and then down into the pit of my belly.

I closed my eyes, focusing on the pressure on my stomach that came with each movement. I sucked in a breath before a sharp prick made me twitch.

Dr. Aslan pulled the white desk towards her, connecting a single cord into the screen that sat perched on top. She tapped a button on the opposite side, and the screen flickered to life, multiple windows springing open as her eyes darted back-and-forth. Her gaze and attention on the screen alone was fascinating.

I tilted my head up, watching Dr. Aslan intently as she pulled each of the four windows into their own space on the screen, the overlapping corners making my eye twitch again. Everything here was haphazard and messy.

Jagged lines appeared on three of the four windows, the lines jutting upwards rapidly. Each line was a different colour, now showing similar but different patterns.

The window in the bottom right-hand corner stayed blank. My eyes kept flicking back towards it, waiting for what would appear there. Even though I had no idea how to read the data, I was entranced.

Dr. Aslan's eyes narrowed. Her mouth pressed into a taut line as she stared at the screen.

I laid back and stared again at the ceiling. My neck ached from trying to hold it at an awkward angle for too long. *What a different world we would live in if only those with extraordinary potential were born.* The thought shot ice into my veins as I put the pieces together.

Three long, loud beeps broke through my musing, and I pulled my head up again, craning it above the white sheet.

Dr. Aslan was on her feet, hands clasped against her chest.

"Are you *crying*?" My eyebrows raised as I stared at her. "It's okay, I wanted a termination, remem—" I started, trying to console the doctor and feeling that familiar awkwardness trickle, then flood, through me.

"*No*," Dr. Aslan breathed, her eyes flashing towards me. They may have been filled with tears, but they were wide and manic. "There will be no termination today," she said. "This foetus, your *baby*..." Her voice choked up. "...is *extraordinary*." She dropped into her seat, her eyes locked onto the screen, fingers turning white as she gripped the mouse.

Unanswered questions swam in my head and I couldn't get my voice to do more than let out a confused croak.

"W-wai—" I stuttered as Dr. Aslan jumped out of her chair, slamming her open palm against a large, green button that rested at eye level in the middle of the wall.

CHAPTER EIGHT

PRODIGY

THE DOOR OF THE SMALL ROOM SWUNG OPEN, SMACKING AGAINST THE white wall behind it.

I counted four, five, six doctors streaming into the room, each carrying a large wooden clipboard clutched tightly against their chest.

"*Off the charts,*" Dr. Aslan was breathless and completely ignoring me now. She glowed as she barked directions. "One, two." She pointed at the first two female doctors who stepped forward at her command. "Prepare the bloodwork. Three, four," Dr. Aslan continued, barely stopping to inhale. "Prep the room for a full medical. Five, six," she said, turning on her heel to face the final two doctors. "Get everything ready to sound the alarm, and then *wait* for my order."

A trembling smile crossed onto Dr. Aslan's face as the doctors bustled around her. I watched her gaze at the screen, her finger tracing the lines across the three different windows.

I jumped as icy hands gripped my left arm from behind me, pulling underneath my bicep.

"We're going to run some tests," the female doctor said, patting my arm. She placed a pillow underneath my elbow, then looped a tie around my wrist and started poking at my veins with a focused frown. Without hesitation, she pierced my skin with precision. The small tube filled vial after vial of blood.

"Alice." Dr. Aslan hovered at my head, her hot breath sending a weird shiver down my spine. "We have to run tests to make sure *you* are healthy now. The baby is off-the-charts. Nothing short of a prodigy," she gushed, wiping her hot fingers across my face to move a stray hair. "But you won't win unless *you* are perfect."

"W-win?" I twisted my head to gaze at Dr. Aslan.

"The lottery." Dr. Aslan squeezed my arm before sliding away, returning to stare at the computer screen.

My lips trembled while the other doctor replaced the needle in my arm with a band-aid; the two blood doctors immediately moved at a measured pace as they carried the six large vials of my blood carefully out the door.

With a soft *click*, the door shut, leaving me alone again with Dr. Aslan.

"I don't want to compete in the lottery," I said matter-of-factly. A cold feeling of dread dropped into my stomach. The idea of taking the chance away from a woman who yearned for this burned in my chest.

That got Dr. Aslan's attention. She looked up from the computer, a deep frown creasing her forehead. Then her mouth twitched.

"Dr. Aslan?" I said, my voice trailing off as she stared straight through me, her eyes vacant.

"Alice," she said, blinking rapidly, her focus returning to me. "The lottery is a privilege. Only a select few even get to *begin*..." She trailed off. Her lips trembled and turned down as she spoke. Women rarely openly spoke about the lottery; it felt almost taboo. "And only a handful of babies are born every year," she added, the twinkle in her eye apparent.

"Most to the rich and famous," I chimed in. "They can afford top quality eggs and sperm for insemination, they can time everything *perfectly*." I rolled my eyes, laying my head back against the padded examination chair. "I empathise with every single woman out there who wishes to have children, and can't." I chose my words carefully as Dr. Aslan's eyes welled with tears. "But..." I sighed, repeating a conversation I'd had many times in the past. "That does not mean I should be forced to carry a pregnancy that I do not want. My choice in termination does not correlate with or cause your inability to have a child," I said, my voice even. I wanted to add that this was the government's fault—but that was another day's argument.

I kept my eyes locked on Dr. Aslan's as a cascade of tears spilled down her cheeks.

She hurriedly wiped them away and cleared her throat. "Personally, I respect women's right to choose," she said. My frown returned as I waited for the brutal reality check. "But this—" She swung the screen towards me and traced her fingers across the lines again. "—is bigger than all of us. These lines..." She moved her shaking fingers across the screen. I leaned forward, staring at the three windows that were full of jagged lines, trending upwards and off the screen, their arcs harsh and unbroken.

"Will this child make the world a better place?" My eyes now fixated on the three labels on the screen.

"Without question." Dr. Aslan smiled, turning towards me. Her mouth poised to say more, but the door behind us swung open.

I turned and shrank into the table. The door bounced back to reveal three new figures, and I curled my legs up against my chest.

The three men wore identical suits, tailored and ink black.

I felt Dr. Aslan's hand on my shoulder as she rose to her feet. Her manicured nails dug into my skin, and her quick demeanour change made my heart race.

"Dr. Aslan." The man in the middle spoke, his voice booming and bouncing off the walls in the small room.

"Councillor," Dr. Aslan nodded her head slightly in stiff greeting.

I stared between them, my head rotating back and forth as they stared each other down.

"Congratulations," the Councillor said after a pause. He tipped his head forward, no hint of a smile portrayed on his stern face.

Dr. Aslan nodded back tersely, her ponytail hardly moving at the gesture.

"The testing is incomplete," she stated. She let go of my shoulder and walked around to the front of the examination chair. Her movements felt almost protective, as if she was putting herself between the men and me.

"Phase three will begin *immediately*," the Councillor stated, handing Dr. Aslan a white sheet of paper.

The paper shimmered, and all I could see was typing and a curled signature at the bottom. Dr. Aslan stumbled to the side. Her eyes were glued to the letter. She took a few steps away from me, her feet wobbling as she moved, before dropping to her knees.

She stared up at me from the floor, her eyes welling with tears. She managed to mouth "*sorry*" as the three men that stood in the doorway moved towards me. The Councillor gave the signal to his flanks.

Without a word, the two men stepped forward, lunging at me. Grasping the edge of the examination chair, I swung my legs back and stumbled down, pressing myself up against the screen behind me.

"Miss Avery," the Councillor said, putting up his hand to the two men who were now only centimetres away from me. "Allow me to formally introduce myself. I am Councillor Matthew Constance." His eyes were hyper-focused on me, his stare severe and fixated, his nostrils flared wide.

"What do you want with me?" I asked, my voice sounding stronger than it felt when it left my body.

"The Speaker will meet you at our next location and explain the details," the Councillor drawled, his eyes flicking between my stomach and my face for a nanosecond.

"This is about the foetus." My hands automatically reached to protect my body, curling around my curvy frame. I felt strangely protective of the blob of cells hidden within my belly—especially from men like Matthew Constance.

"Correct, Miss Avery," the Councillor said, the sides of his lips twitching, as if he might smile.

"I'd like to have the remainder of the tests done here," I said. My throat felt like acid as I swallowed.

The Councillor barely let the final word slip from my mouth before speaking. "That is no longer possible."

He nodded at the two men that were lingering on either side of me, turned his back to us, and raised a cell phone to his ear.

I kept my eyes locked on the Councillor, trying to read the back of his head as two rough hands gripped my arms; dry fingers curled around each bicep and pressed down hard. I knew I had no chance, but I wasn't going to go down without a fight.

I jerked back, twisting and pulling my arms, my body lurching until I hit the wall. The cool, uneven concrete pressed into my back sharply.

I hissed as I wriggled, my arms still clamped tightly by the two men who looked at me but didn't see me.

"Subject is in custody," the Councillor sneered, and I stopped struggling for a moment to listen. He faced me, talking about me as if I wasn't there, a harsh smirk etched across his face.

I ducked down, pulling my arms with me. The men's grip loosened enough for me to wiggle their hands down to my wrists before they roughly pinned me and pulled me back to my feet.

"Feisty." The Councillor walked forward until his face was inches from mine, a smile quirking the edge of his lips.

I flipped my hair back out of my face, whipping him as I moved, refusing to break eye contact as he looked me up and down and clicked his tongue.

He swivelled on his heel, his shiny black shoes emitting a loud squeak. Then he raised his hand behind his head to beckon the two men forward.

The grip on each wrist loosened slightly before tight hands gripped my shoulder and left arm. The men swiped at my feet, pushing my body down and catching me before I hit the ground.

"Where are you taking me?" I pulled at my limbs, unable to move them as a hand traced the line from my left arm up to the back of my neck. It gripped hard, sending waves of cold shivers down my spine.

A loud gasp escaped into the air as a needle pressed into the back of my neck, the pressure causing me to let out a scream, muffled by a wad of fabric shoved into my mouth.

The Councillor laid the large silver needle on a tray on the examiner's table. The two men let me go, their grip leaving my skin to pulsate.

I pushed myself to my feet, stepping back towards Dr. Aslan, who was stoic and silent, still crouched on the floor, her arms now wrapped around her slender frame. Her tears felt as if they were my own.

As I took another step, my knee buckled. My leg dipped down and wobbled, and I caught myself against the wall. Dr. Aslan bounded to her feet and caught me, steadying me as I sank down; she whispered something calm and soothing into my ear that my addled brain couldn't quite understand.

"You'll know soon enough..." the Councillor said, kneeling down and clicking his tongue in my face.

Blinking rapidly, I tried to clear my vision as my eyes pooled with water. I sucked in a deep breath, my body wedged between the wall and Dr. Aslan's strong arms.

"What...that?" The words jumbled up in my mind and tumbled out in the wrong order. The Councillor rose and stalked away, waving his hand towards the other suit-clad men.

I placed my head in my hands, sinking down to a semi-seated position with Dr. Aslan's help. My body leaned backwards, my hands gripping at my knees and missing, instead splaying onto the floor.

I sprawled out, falling against the cool concrete.

"Help," I mouthed as I shut my eyes, unsure whether the words manifested outside of my head. My last vision was of a sobbing Dr. Aslan, stroking my hair, before she too was pushed aside by the men.

I could feel my body jostling and my limp limbs knocking against a cold tray. Wheels clunked underneath me, the tyres worn unevenly.

The black beneath my eyelids felt like a prison, my eyelids too heavy to lift, and my mind too clouded to force my body to move in anything more than twitches.

I was suddenly a prisoner in my own body.

CHAPTER NINE

THE LAB

A SIREN BEEPED SO LOUDLY I SAT BOLT UPRIGHT. SOFT BED SHEETS wrapped me up in a tight cocoon. I fought against them; their vice-like grip felt like I was trapped in a coffin. My heart raced as I wildly looked around the empty room, suddenly unsure of where I was. I clawed my way out of the sheets.

The noise stopped as quickly as it started, disappearing after three more loud *dings*.

"Good Morning, Miss Avery." A chirpy, robotic voice echoed into the room, causing me to whirl around wildly. I was lost until my groggy memories slowly flooded back, and ice seeped into my veins.

"Please put on the clothes provided and be ready for collection in thirty minutes," the voice said, its cheerfulness making my stomach curdle.

My feet hit the floor and my body involuntarily shivered. The room was small, the wooden bed tall and solid. Padding across the cold wooden floor, I grabbed the pile of clothes that sat inside the door and threw them onto the bed. They scattered as I flopped down beside them, only slightly creeped out that someone had been inside my room to leave them. The five blinking cameras directed at the bed were more disconcerting.

I turned my attention to the clothes—the choices were all plain black, and consisted of a t-shirt-skirt ensemble, a dress, or pants and button up t-shirt—all with my surname embroidered on them.

Scratching the back of my head, I ran my fingers across the embroidery, the letters perfectly connected in cursive writing except for a capital A.

Undressing seemed surreal. It felt like yesterday I had been in my tiny city apartment, and today I was wondering about the other women that were competing in *the lottery* with me—*against* me. I knew more time had passed, but I had no way of knowing *how much*. The thought was lost as the one-size-too-small underwear cut into my skin no matter how much I pulled at it. I sighed and pulled on the black, fitted dress. A dress seemed like the least effort and fuss, but as I adjusted the shoulder and tugged at the hem, I stared down at my protruding stomach. The too-tight underwear drew a tight line across my hips, making my stomach poke out further.

"Let's play a game." I rubbed my face again, a yawn escaping my mouth. "It's called *foetus or food.*" Normally that kind of black humour would make me chuckle, but today it felt morbid, especially when I realised *I was hungry.*

I looked around the small room properly now. Other than one closed red door, the bathroom was the only feature. The door slid open to welcome me as I approached.

Standing in front of the mirror, I picked at the new dress, pulling at the sides to smooth the fabric. The material was thick, the bump barely visible if I continued to tug at the hem. I was staring at my reflection when a sudden craving for hot wings hit me. I shook my head. It was definitely my DNA growing in there.

"Ten minute warning." The robotic voice broke into the room, making me jump.

I sighed as I stared at my curly brown hair. It frizzed and flopped in different directions, the knots from my knock-out sleep clearly visible. But instead of brushing, I just stood there and stared at the face of an unfamiliar woman, a woman who had forgotten to fight.

Without meaning to, I had done *exactly* what I was told since becoming a prisoner, a science experiment, a captive.

The anger in my fingers boiled over and I tossed the brush aside to pull fistfuls of my unruly hair into a tight, messy bun.

As my hands shook and the realisation sunk into my face, the anger burning in my eyes flared. It wasn't too late to do something. *Nothing* had been decided yet.

A loud rap on the door echoed through the room, jolting me back into my body. With one last nod to myself in the mirror and tug at the dress, I walked out.

"Game face, Avery," I whispered as I squared my shoulders and stood up straight; it was time to greet whatever was coming.

I didn't bother to smile as I approached the door and it slid open. I came to a halt in front of it.

"Good morning, Miss Avery," the woman in front spoke, looking up briefly from her tablet to catch my eye.

"Morning," I said back. If she had been in my position she might not think the word *good* deserved its place.

I stared at the immaculately dressed woman and her two side-kicks. All three women were dressed in all black, each wearing a variation of the same dress-skirt-pants ensemble provided to me this morning. That in itself was unnerving—a uniform for all women here.

The woman in charge wore the same black dress as me; although I would guess it was at least three sizes smaller, tailored to hug her slim figure, accentuating every tiny contour on her rail-thin frame.

"Follow us," she said, her smile small but seemingly genuine.

Swivelling on the toes of her high-heels, she clicked away, her slim frame swaying back-and-forth as she walked. The other women stared at me, waiting for me to move.

I hesitated for a moment, and then quickened my pace to close the gap, matching her step. My bare feet pressed into the hardwood floor.

Throwing a glance backward, I noted the other two women were walking a few paces behind me. They both held tablets, their fingers clicking manically as they tapped and typed, glancing at me and then looking down again and repeating the action. Clearly, I already had a reputation, and for that I must have done something right.

I swallowed, my frown sinking deeper into my forehead with each step; they were keeping very close tabs on me, and it made my skin crawl.

I kept pace with the woman who was leading the way, opening my mouth every few seconds to ask a question. She never glanced in my direction, and I wasn't able to force out the words as we stalked down the long corridor. Doors just like mine were spaced every few metres. Large glowing lights lit the entry above every door, flickering red, orange, or green.

My eyes ached as I stared between the bright lights and thought about the women behind the doors. We turned left into a new dimly lit corridor and the doors disappeared, replaced by blank white walls.

The woman in front of me didn't stop walking or turn to face me as we wound through the winding hallways. She turned right then left, again and again, until we reached an unadorned red door at the end of a maze of segregated corridors. I tried to memorise the pattern, to remember the right-right-left of the way we had just come, but even for my puzzle-oriented brain it was impossible. We were inside a labyrinth and the leader's tiny smile told me she knew it.

As if she had heard my thoughts, she swivelled on her toes again, this time turning to face me. Her tablet dangled in her right hand, her left hand on her hip.

She nodded at the two women, stepping aside to allow them to open the red door and enter the room hidden behind. Their movements were fast and calculated. The door opened for a fraction of a second, emitting only a soft, white glow and giving nothing else away.

With a click, the women disappeared, leaving us alone.

"Welcome to phase two, Miss Avery," the woman said, deadpan. As she spoke, I was calculating. There was no-one behind me, and I wondered for a fleeting second if I could make a run for it.

"I am Dr. Stella Hidalgo." She paused, allowing me to return to reality and nod, "And *you* will want to see what is behind these doors," she added with a small smile. I had expected a lecture, a reminder, anything to put me in my place. I could tell she was smart, but she instead played on my true weakness: *curiosity*.

I blinked and raised an eyebrow. She had my attention—until I was distracted by the loud scraping and banging noises coming from behind the red door.

"My assistants are preparing the room," Dr. Hidalgo explained, her brow furrowing as the loud banging rang out into the deserted corridor.

"Can you tell me what testing will take place?" I asked, surprised at how even my voice exited my body while my heart hammered in my chest, filling my ears with a dull, thumping ring. I was imagining being dissected and pulled apart like an animal, and hoped she would tell me the truth.

Dr. Hidalgo tore her eyes away from the tablet to meet mine. When she spoke, her voice bordered on bored. "Standard procedure, *lots* of questions." She said as if she knew that would make me squirm. "*If* you pass *phase two*, we will continue onto more invasive questions in *phase three*." Her voice snapped off as she dropped her head again, fingers tapping at the flashing tablet.

I could feel my jaw hanging open as I stared at Dr. Hidalgo, waiting for her to continue speaking. Her silence was only marred by the loud noises escaping from behind the red door. Using words like *phase two* and *phase three* only sparked my curiosity, and as I started to ask for more details, she cut me off and asked me to share more personal information.

"We'll also need to contact the father of…" Dr. Hidalgo's eyes rose to bore into mine.

"The father?" I questioned, raising my eyebrows. I didn't want Mason pulled into this disaster.

"Do you know who the father is?" The genuine curiosity in Dr. Hidalgo's gaze unbalanced me. Whatever she had read in my file, she clearly didn't think very highly of my personal choices.

"Yes," I said, staring back at her, wanting to say 'no' if it would mean this would all be over, but knowing it was futile with the advances in genetic technology.

She gave a slight nod, her eyes dropping back to her tablet. The noise of her nails against glass grated on my nerves.

The door behind Dr. Hidalgo swung open. The two women scuttled out and scooted around behind us, bowing their heads before coming to a standstill.

"After you," Dr. Hidalgo said, looking at me as she snapped the cover over her tablet. I had missed my chance to run, but deep down I knew I would have only gotten lost in the maze of corridors and doors—caught, drugged, and returned to isolation as my prize.

I took a few tentative steps forward, a shiver snaking down my spine. I heard the door click shut, followed by three loud *clacks* as the two women spun a large wheel and fastened a padlock. The security here was excessive, or maybe it was just for me—the 'runner.'

The room I stood in was separated into two sections. To my left was a large, white, rectangular bench. Glass beakers flooded the surface, joined by petri dishes, bubbling chemical mixtures, scales and microscopes. It was a scientist's *dream* workspace.

I stared down at the incredible amount of expensive equipment. "Wow," I murmured, unable to help the awe that escaped my lips.

Two large screens took up the opposite side of the bench; their wires twisted down onto the floor and tucked up out of sight. A single chair sat to the side, empty and waiting.

"We are well funded, Miss Avery," Dr. Hidalgo said with a radiating, proud smile. The awe on my face must have been palpable. "Generous benefactors provide everything you see."

I nodded, my brows pinching together as I turned, facing the opposite side of the room. I was sure that *generous benefactor* was code for rich families who wanted children, but I said nothing.

My feet wandered in a slow circle, taking it all in.

"You were a scientist, correct?" Dr. Hidalgo spoke matter-of-factly beside me, making me jump. We both knew she had access to all my personal information, but she was being kind by asking.

"I *am* a scientist, yes," I retorted, smiling sweetly. It was an important distinction, and one I wanted to make abundantly clear.

"You should appreciate *this* technology," Dr. Hidalgo stated, not acknowledging my correction or that I had spoken at all. Her eyes were fixated straight ahead.

I took a few steps forward, my feet grinding to a halt. A glass tank took up over a third of the room's floor space. Inside, a single examination chair sat waiting.

"What is this place?" I asked breathlessly, mostly to myself, as I stared at the metal instruments hanging down from the ceiling, each arm of the equipment holding a different medical tool.

"This is the Epitome Lab's crown jewel." Dr. Hidalgo's voice echoed high and girlishly—excited for the first time since I met her. "*This* is the human benchmark."

"Human benchmark?" I repeated, my voice full of curiosity as I stole a glance at Dr. Hidalgo. Her tight ponytail pulled her forehead back, leaving her cheeks full, and the top of her head squeezed. I watched as her mouth curled into a tight smile.

"Come," she said, taking two-steps backwards to separate us before turning and stepping away. She walked only a few steps, skirting the side of the glass tomb and stopping in front of a blank wall to the left side.

As I took my place next to her, I scratched the back of my head, fiddling and twisting my hair while I waited.

"There's nothing here?" I finally said to break the silence that hung between us, and it felt as if she was *waiting* for me to say those exact words.

"I *hoped* you would say that," Dr. Hidalgo said, quickly opening her tablet and typing furiously.

Her fingers swiped off the edge of the screen several times, the images contained within shooting up and landing in perfect squares and rectangles on what had been a blank wall a few moments earlier.

"Welcome to the Echo," Dr. Hidalgo said, her tablet hand now hanging down, eyes fixated on the wall above.

I followed her gaze as she flicked her head back, and without a word, the lights around us dimmed. The projected images shone black, white, and yellow.

"The human benchmark chamber collects the data," Dr. Hidalgo said. "Then the Echo lets us access it, understand it, map it, project it, create *understanding* FROM it..."

"Is this..." I puffed, the air I sucked in stuck in my windpipe. I was in awe before Dr. Hidalgo had begun to explain.

"With this technology, we can all but *see the future*," Dr. Hidalgo said without acknowledging my breathless recognition.

I exhaled, staring at the seven screens in front of me. My eyes passed over the different images: brain activity and waves, both adult and foetal, a full female body that spun in circles, blood work, genetic markers, and spinning chromosome mapping.

"This is—" I was at a loss for words, which happened so rarely it stunned me.

"Innovation, Miss Avery," Dr. Hidalgo said before I could manage anything. Her eyes were wide as she stared up at the screens. "And soon, these screens will hold *your* images."

"*My* images?" I gaped, pursing my lips as I watched the large brain spin on the screen, the inner waves moving and connecting. I had forgotten for a moment that this was about *me* and the reminder sent a cold, crippling shudder through my body.

"Come, Miss Avery." Dr. Hidalgo clicked her fingers near my ear to snap me back to reality—but this *was* reality, and I was forever altered knowing this technology existed and was determining the next generation. This was the future the government was angling for.

I pulled my eyes away, spinning on the spot as the two silent women approached me. One unlocked the glass tomb, while the other ushered me in, pushing on my back and shoulders to make me move. I let her lead me, my need to fight or escape gone, at least for now. I needed to know more about the Benchmark, more about the Echo, more about *myself*.

Walking up the metal steps, the tank gave a slight groan under our collective weight until I crossed the threshold of the door, alone. The glass door clicked shut and locked me inside.

One of the women flicked a small, silver switch that poured cool air into the tank, making me break out in a rash of goosebumps.

"Sit, Miss Avery," Dr. Hidalgo instructed through a small metal speaker. Her voice echoed as if inside my head. She hovered a few centimetres away from the enclosed tank, close enough that I could see her hands fidgeting with the tablet she now held close to her face.

I took a few tentative steps forward, my eyes cast to each side of the large, white and metal contraptions that hung on either side of the examination chair. Each arm held a different instrument. From needles, scalpels, scissors and tweezers; to gadgets I didn't recognise. It made the saliva stick in my throat, my voice trapped as I stared at the triple-jointed arms. I hesitated at the edge of the chair. I loved science and innovation, but it was a lot scarier to *be* the experiment rather than the one in charge.

With a knot tightening in my gut, I took a few steps away from the chair. Dr. Hidalgo coaxed me with a pointing finger from the other side of the glass; it unnerved me further the way she cooed at me as if I was an unreasonable child.

"Would it be possible to eat something first?" I said, as much stalling as I was thinking about all the food I desperately wanted to inhale.

"Not until after this testing is over," Dr. Hidalgo said with a sad shake of her head. "It's better on an empty stomach."

That made my stomach churn, both in hunger and fear.

"We'll start easy with a basic body scan," Dr. Hidalgo pressed on, a bright red light shooting over my body as she spoke. The light ran from head to toe, scanning me three times before disappearing. My skin prickled with each flash of colour and movement. Nothing hurt, but I knew that scan would give them more information about me than anything I had provided so far.

"Good," Dr. Hidalgo said, her eyes glued to the lit up screen in her hands. "Please take a seat now." Her eyes rose up to meet mine and she gave me a hard look and a nod.

I stood rooted to the spot, torn between fear and curiosity. My limbs and muscles spasmed as I slowly sat down on the edge.

As soon as my skin touched the leather, two thick, black bands shot out, weaving and wrapping around my forearms and chest, and yanked me backwards. Within a second, my back was against leather and a myriad of cords latched me in place.

"What the fuck?" I yelled loud enough for the entire room to hear. I thrashed my arms, the black fabric tightening with every movement. Then I stopped dead, staring at Dr. Hidalgo. A strange, sympathetic smile appeared on her face as she stared back at me, waiting. By her body language alone I knew it was futile to struggle; they had me in their grasp, figuratively and literally.

For a few extra seconds, I tore at the cords. Hot, angry tears prickled in the corners of my eyes before I forced my body to remain still. I tilted my head back, positive I didn't want the doctor to see me sob; that would only make things worse.

"Next, we will administer a blood test." She tapped multiple times on the tablet, the arm with a large needle moving with each tap until it was perched above me, hovering a few centimetres away from my immobilised right arm. "I suggest you sit still and *don't tense*," Dr. Hidalgo said, her finger tapping one last time against the tablet screen.

The arm jolted forward, stopping less than a centimetre away from the curve of my elbow. The latching tightened at the last moment, making my arm throb and veins protrude, snaking up my arm in a bright blue spider web. It would have been incredible had I not been so aware of the approaching sharp object about to stab into my skin.

The needle hovered for a few seconds, the arm gliding back and forth. It sized me up before stopping and darting forward in an instant.

I let out a strangled breath as my blood flowed up the length of the mechanical arm, twisting and turning until it was deposited into three waiting vials. It had been so smooth I had barely felt the prick.

Disengaging, the arm moved away at the same time the tight, black fabric released my arms slightly—still holding me in place but no longer cutting into my skin.

The three vials rocketed down from within the machine, landing gently against the window of the tank. Three small grooves had been drilled into the windowsill waiting to catch them.

Dr. Hidalgo moved forward and reached towards the tank. The

windowsill where the vials sat moved upwards, flipping a full 360 degrees before settling on the opposite side of the glass.

I blinked a few times. I couldn't make out so much as a line where the join would exist.

"Well done, Miss Avery." Dr. Hidalgo grinned as she lifted the first vial of blood out and jiggled it, staring at it as though she might sense or see something within. "The *Human Benchmark* takes human error out of the equation for simple procedures," she continued, handing one blood vial to each assistant before they hurried in opposite directions. "And yet people always squirm, shake, shiver, and wiggle." She rolled her eyes, giving my blood a last shake before slipping it into one of the large metal fridges that sat only a few feet behind her.

"Technology *is* innovation," I parroted, my voice sounding dead as I spoke. I believed the words, but this had rocked even my murky ethics and beliefs; to be strapped to a chair without consent sent a shiver down my spine.

"Right you are," Dr. Hidalgo said, staring down at her tablet again, not catching even a hint of my sarcasm or discomfort.

I wasn't sure whether she was commending me on my statement, or simply wanting to get the next test underway.

"Sit up straight." With a click of her fingers, she returned to the business at hand. The bindings wrapped around my shins and thighs as quickly as they released my arms. The sight of large, welted red lines stitched across my arms from the bindings unnerved me, even if they didn't hurt. "Head back, Miss Avery." Dr. Hidalgo clicked her tongue as if to scorn me for daring to look at the marks they had etched into my skin.

I pushed myself to the back edge of the examination chair, glaring at Dr. Hidalgo as I rested my head against the bottom of the headrest.

Pressure jolted me as the black bindings returned, this time wrapping tightly over my shoulders and under my breasts like an infant car seat.

"Are *all* these restraints *really* necessary?" I called. But Dr. Hidalgo's tablet-wielding presence was now gone from my line of sight.

"Yes," her close voice shot back. A jolt of surprise shot through me as the door to the tank slammed shut. My eyes shot to her as the two assistants locked us in together. "This next test is the last one for today," she said, almost apologetically; but as she got to work, it was clear whatever she felt about the testing was outweighed by her need for answers, a job, or morbid curiosity.

I stared back at her, unsure what to say. My heart hammered against my rib cage. *One more test,* I repeated to myself over-and-over like a mantra as Dr. Hidalgo bustled around.

"Is this phase three?" I finally dared to ask. She hadn't said anything about the end of phase two, but I could only *assume* I had passed.

Dr. Hidalgo looked at me for a few seconds. Then she nodded, and without a word, her eyes dropped to her tablet. She got to work. She walked around me, her shoes echoing against the metal floor of the tank before the room was filled with small noises, movement, and ripping fabric.

"This is the Oculus Sensorimotor," she finally whispered in my ear, her hot breath sending a tingle down my spine. "Now, head forward."

Dr. Hidalgo hovered above my head, gripping a large black helmet. Wires protruded from multiple places, intertwining with each other and knotting together at the back.

The helmet pressed against my skull; Dr. Hidalgo pushed with more force than I was expecting. I lifted my head awkwardly forward, and the helmet encased my face and shrouded me in darkness for a second before blinding me with dancing lights.

My eyes wandered around the inner dome. Compact disc-chips glistened, imbedded every few centimetres, interspersed with long, loose wires that dangled down, their splayed edges barely missing my face.

Dr. Hidalgo peered over me. Her hands pressed and pulled at the outer layer of the helmet. My head rattled as she tapped, pushed, and prodded, the helmet shaking with each movement.

"Look straight ahead," she said, her voice sounding muted.

I leaned my head forward and stared up. The helmet pressed into the back of my head, slicing into the gap between my neck and spine.

Pain shot through my veins as tiny robotic arms clawed at the titanium stitches in my neck, prying them out one-by-one. A tiny thread snaked into the open wound, winding itself tightly down my neck, and a scream ripped from my throat.

I could hear the thrum of Dr. Hidalgo's voice, but her words were only a faraway jumble, as if she was speaking but my ears couldn't compute the words to my brain.

"Initiating launch sequence," a small, robotic voice pinged inside my head.

The stabbing pain emitting from the nape of my neck left me breathless, my skin prickling as I instinctively tried to claw my way out of the bindings. My arms and hands trembled, my whole body jerking and violently shaking. The threads spilled and spiralled into my skin, rippling deeper, the sharp edges like a knife against my insides as it seeped further down my spine.

"Phase one complete," the voice rang inside my ears. An involuntary shiver wracked my body. I fought back the rising bile, the thread now prickling outwards, spreading across my back and up over my shoulders towards my chest.

I barely registered the large pop-up box that suddenly flickered to life across my visor, the white background and black writing distorted by the curve.

Initialising was scrawled in strangely messy handwriting, replaced almost immediately by a large blue loading bar, inching from right to left. If I hadn't been sure it was experimental technology before, *I was now.*

I squeezed my eyes shut. Fear crept into my gut, seeping into my chest and limbs. I could feel myself breathing shallow, on the edge of hyperventilating. The loading bar reached halfway.

Tears spilled out of the corner of my eyes, and I could feel the threads slithering into my skin, threading through my sinew and muscles, the tiny claws piercing my biceps and thighs.

I stared at the blue bar. It inched closer to complete with every second that passed.

"Phase two complete," the voice echoed again, as a shiver snaked up

my throat. The nape of my neck throbbed, sending waves of pain up into my skull. I barely had time to suck in a breath before the voice echoed again.

"Phase three complete," the voice rang out as the pain intensified. The dull throb was taken over by a constant sawing pain, ripping through my skin. If this is what Dr. Hidalgo had meant by three phases of testing, I would have argued her explanation was deliberately disingenuous. But I couldn't concentrate on anything but the scorching pain for longer than a second as my body slowly unravelled at the seams.

"Initiate."

A small scream escaped my lips, and my body thrashed uncontrollably. Something sliced deeply into my skin, causing a ripple to snake down my spine. With a wracked breath, I went limp. Tiny gashes crawled and clawed across every inch of my skin, sending sharp pain throbbing down to my bones.

With one final pinch and twist below the skull, the pain dissipated.

My whole body was clenched tight; my muscles spasming from my curled toes and taut thighs, to my clenched fists and hunched shoulders. My jaw clamped together so tightly that my teeth ached. My body continued to shake violently.

"Upload complete," the voice echoed.

"Full immersion in three, two..." The voice trailed off. My brain warped and the world spun. My hands dug into the black leather as the bones in my back ricocheted backwards and forwards, cracking under the pressure before everything went black.

CHAPTER TEN

FULL IMMERSION

I SUCKED IN A DEEP BREATH AND GASPED, SUDDENLY AWARE THAT EYES were boring into me from all around.

"Am I boring you, Miss Avery?" a booming voice jolted from the front of the room. I struggled to swallow, horrified as my mouth gaped open. My eyes darted around the university lecture hall. The professor stood with his arms crossed, staring directly at me. His large platform stage was filled with scribbled on whiteboards and three off-centre screen projections.

"N-no, sir," I stuttered, my voice sounding meek and croaky.

He frowned and shot me a raised eyebrow before swivelling back towards a whiteboard half-filled with words and diagrams.

I shivered as the professor's voice filled the room again, loud and monotone. I stared down at my notebook; in my left hand, I clenched a pen. What had I just been doing? I must have zoned out completely. The only thing worse than falling asleep during lecture was being called out in front of the whole class because of it.

I hunched my shoulders and slid down in my chair. My body felt strange and tingly; one too many late-night cram sessions must have caught up to me. I lowered my head into my hands and pressed them hard against my eyes, a starry black populating my field of vision.

"Miss Avery?" The professor's voice rang out, shattering my internal confusion.

I looked up. The students in front of me stared at me, their faces kind and etched with sympathy. I stared at the board, where the professor had written a brain teaser. He stood beside it, arms crossed, tapping his index fingers against his stiff, starched white collared shirt.

"Could you provide the class with an answer?" A small smirk danced on his lips.

A weird squeak escaped from my mouth. Written on the whiteboard was a long row of numbers in thick, black ink. In the centre hung two large, red question marks.

19, 20, 21, ?, ?, 26, 28, 32, 33, 40

Replace the question marks was written underneath, in beautiful cursive handwriting.

"Well, Miss Avery?" the professor prompted again, his voice almost excited at the prospect of my impending failure. It was almost as if he was *waiting* for it, shaming me for not being fully present in his classroom.

"Wait." I scrawled the numbers down onto my notebook.

My brain fluttered, the cogs finally turning as I wrote the final number and stared at the sequence.

"Twenty-two and twenty-four," I blurted, my heart racing. "Sir," I added, ensuring my answer was final and didn't sound like a question.

"Correct," the professor said dryly. "Explanation for your classmates." He looked almost bored now as he picked up his coffee cup.

"Isn't that your job?" I frowned. He took a long sip of coffee and raised his hand to tell me to hurry up and speak. "There are two interwoven sequences within the puzzle. If you start with nineteen, the numbers progress two, three, four, five. If you start with twenty, they progress two, four, six, eight." I felt my face flush as I lowered my voice, the echo disappearing.

A nod from the professor was the only acknowledgment that I was correct.

"Well done," a whisper came from beside me, sending a jolt down my spine. I turned my head, coming face-to-side with a mop of curly black hair. I smiled, not wanting to make it obvious that until this moment I had no idea that I was sitting next to another human being.

"Puzzle two," the professor called, setting a large, black timer on his desk. The numbers ticked down from ten minutes.

The silence in the room was palpable as every student stared at the whiteboard, their eyes fixated on the new puzzle.

What number is logically missing from the sequence below?

*348269, 284315, *****, 8438, 4811, 842, 86.*

I stared at the asterisks, their edges bleeding where the whiteboard markers had been pressed too hard. My eyes watered, and I was unable to force myself to blink, my body feeling weirdly wobbly and light.

I gripped the side of the lecture chair, my nails digging into the hard plastic until they ached.

Out of the corner of my eye, I could see my seat-mate furiously scribbling, ambidextrous enough to rub out her answer with her left hand while rewriting with her right. She flicked her pencil back and forth, hitting her notebook in a slow, methodical way. She tipped her head towards the board and her notebook, looking up and down. Her motions were unnerving and robotic.

With a twitch, I wrote the sequence of numbers down, dropping my head into my left hand to stare at them. My eyes fixated on them each in turn. My mind put together the sequence piece-by-piece as I doodled a small picture of a house, crooked windows and door included.

"Miss Avery," the professor said, his voice loud enough to feel as though he was speaking directly into my ear. Instead, he stood in front of me, perched awkwardly with his leg up on the chair one row down from where I was sitting, his body hunched forward.

"Y-yes, professor?" I asked, stifling an uncomfortable giggle as I tried to figure out *exactly* what was causing him to pick on me so incessantly today.

Without meaning to, my eyes flicked to the countdown clock that shone red behind him.

It read 4M 39S.

"I assume if you have time to doodle and stare off into the distance, you have already solved the equation?" His voice was grating.

"Yes, professor." I nodded, even though the hairs on the back of my neck prickled and my stomach churned with a touch of uncertainty.

"Who else has completed the riddle?" His eyes bored into mine for a few seconds before he stood up straight and did a quick spin to look at the other students. "Well, Miss Avery. It appears you are the first one finished." He raised his eyebrows. "Why don't you come up to the front of the class and walk us through it?" He smirked as he spoke, as if he was in on a joke I had missed.

I nodded, my face burning red hot as I stood up, notebook clenched in my hand. I hesitated, feeling unsteady on my feet. The only thing worse than getting the answer wrong in front of the class would be falling down the stairs first.

"Second guessing yourself, Miss Avery?" The professor's smirk turned into a gleeful grin.

"No," I said, frowning at him and clearing my throat with a few lacklustre coughs. My feet finally seemed to remember how to walk, and I approached the whiteboard. The professor stepped graciously aside, sweeping his arm to invite me in.

Without looking at him, I rolled my eyes, grabbing a whiteboard marker and turning to face the lecture hall. Staring out, the students' faces seemed distorted by the bright lights beaming down from above.

I swallowed past the lump in my throat. "Each number is the sum of the last two digits of the previous number," I said, my voice echoing. "Preceded by the remaining numbers in reverse order." My voice shook as I turned to face the whiteboard. "As you can see, six plus nine is fifteen, and then in reverse order is three, four, eight, two." I underlined the maths in my sloping, scrawled handwriting. "This means the asterisked number is 34,826." I spoke quickly, struggling to write the number on the whiteboard legibly. "One plus five equals six, and the three, four, eight, two remain until the next calculation." I half underlined numbers as I went, not quite in sync with my own hand movements. With shaky fingers, I clicked the cap back onto the whiteboard marker and set it down, glancing at the professor, whose face had turned from a smirk into a more genuine smile.

With a brief nod, I turned, walking quickly off stage to a soft, slow clap from the professor. "Class dismissed," he said, just as I reached my seat, barely missing a beat before he added, "Miss Avery, a moment." The rest of the class was gone before I had a chance to look up.

I stepped back up on the stage, closing the gap between us. I averted my eyes, staring at the black wooden stage. My legs felt strange; my skin itched and prickled as I approached the professor. Up close, he looked older—the crow's feet around his eyes more pronounced and the lines at the edges of his mouth deeper. He leaned back, placing his body weight against his almost-overflowing, wooden desk. He crossed his arms as he looked at me. But then he smiled, small dimples appearing, his face kinder now.

"I won't keep you long, Miss Avery." He pushed his floppy, dark-brown hair out of his eyes with his black-rimmed glasses.

He paused for a moment, looking thoughtful. The longer he stared, the more my ears burned red and my cheeks flushed pink as the silence between us grew. I didn't want to be rude, but I hated the long-stretching silence.

The professor broke first, standing up and dawdling around his desk. He flipped through papers, shuffling things from front-to-back and side-to-side. Discarding multiple things before leafing through a stapled booklet, he skimmed the pages as I waited there awkwardly.

Holding the booklet out, he shook it at me, the pages falling apart as I reached to grab it.

I half opened my mouth before his hand cut me off, the professor's words drowning mine out. "Have you ever taken an IQ test?" His eyes gleamed from across the desk.

I shook my head, staring down at the paper he had given me.

"Instead of a final exam, I want you to take this."

His voice felt distant. My eyes cast down on the paper, which read *Advanced IQ Tests: 10 of the World's Toughest Questions*.

"Sir?"

He held his hands up in the air, as if to shoot down my objections.

"Miss Avery, the two problems I put up on the board today were from another advanced IQ test booklet." His words jumbled up and ran together in his excited state. "Do you know how many students I have taught over the years?" he asked, his thoughts changing tracks mid explanation.

"Thousands," I said, without thinking, my unease growing.

"Thousands and *thousands*." He nodded, putting both of his hands behind his head. "And do you know how many solved the two mathematical equations I used today?" he asked, eyes wide.

"Hundreds?" I shrugged.

"Four," he retorted, unblinking.

"Four?" I repeated, sounding like a parrot and not someone with a high IQ.

A grin tore his face in half. "To be clear, *you* are number four."

"Four?" I said again. I stared at the IQ test that I now gripped in my left hand.

"I will speak with your other professors," he said. "This will be your final exam for each of your four subjects this year,"

"Wai—" I started to say, my heart thumping as I read the few sentences underneath the title. *'These types of questions measure the most advanced levels of verbal and spatial ability, numerical ability, logical analysis, lateral thinking and problem-solving.'*

The professor put his hand up like a stop sign once again.

"Ignore the titles. And I promise, if you cannot complete these tests, we will allow you to take each of your finals as scheduled next week."

"I-I..." I stuttered, unsure how to argue with the professor. How could I have argued; this was essentially a free pass. I had nothing to lose and everything to gain. Instead, I nodded, a deep knot forming between my eyebrows as I wondered how to prep for IQ tests.

"Go," the professor said, waving me off as if suddenly my lingering was annoying him. "Fuel your brain." He took the papers back from me. "Please be back in my classroom in three hours."

His deep brown eyes bored into me, and I nodded, a few too many painful seconds of intense eye-contact before his eyes returned to the piles of paper on his desk, giving me the chance to swivel on my heel and hurry out of his classroom.

CHAPTER ELEVEN

AN UNUSUAL LUNCH DATE

My mind raced as I clicked the lecture hall room door shut and hovered outside. I stood and stared at the wooden door for a few extra seconds, my mind weirdly empty except for the overwhelming feeling of impending doom.

With a deep sigh, I realised most of the anxiety about what was to come had settled in my stomach. I tried to take a few deep breaths and closed my eyes. "It's just a few tests," I whispered to myself. I sucked in and held my breath.

"Avery?" An airy, light voice broke through my deep breathing, causing me to cough as I exhaled in surprise.

I turned and pressed my back up against the door, the handle jabbing into my skin.

I stared at the girl with black curly hair that had been sitting next to me in the lecture hall; she looked back at me expectantly and I was mortified that she had heard me talking to myself.

"Food?" Her foot tapped as she clung to a handful of notebooks and textbooks. I couldn't tell if her kindness at not mentioning my weirdness was a good or strange sign about our possible friendship.

I stared at her blankly. Her face looked familiar, but I wasn't able to place her.

"Come on," she said, her voice almost a whine now.

My stomach answered for me, letting out a loud, gurgling scream as if on cue and pushing me to follow the bouncing curls.

I fidgeted as we walked, tucking my hair behind my ears and picking at the edges of my notebook. I knew where I was, but also felt like I didn't. Everything was exactly as it should be, but somehow still out of place.

The curly-haired girl walked fast; soon we rounded the corner, and the lunch hall sprang into view. My stomach let out another loud gurgle, the nervous butterflies suddenly overpowered by hunger.

The glass doors opened and we made a beeline for the food, grabbing white plates and waiting patiently for the lunch-lady to reappear from behind the food stacks.

The lunch hall was almost empty. The stacks of tables and chairs were laid out in perfect symmetry. As we waited, I eyed a table in the far back corner that sat in full sunlight, and made a mental note to shoot there as soon as I had food on my plate.

"Next," a loud, irritated voice called, snapping my focus back to the present.

The lunch-lady stood with her arms crossed, her white apron covered in flecks of brown and green muck, squashed in further by her crossed arms.

I rushed forward, realising my companion had already been served and was waiting with her plate full of food.

The lunch-lady slopped a bit of everything onto my plate without conversation or enthusiasm, each food running into the other, the edges melting together. It was a gross kind of beauty.

"Let's sit in the sun?" I flashed my classmate a nervous smile and jolted my head towards the back corner at the sunny table.

Once settled, we dug in. The food was average, but my stomach didn't seem to mind. It happily accepted the greasy mess.

"Phew." I let out a loud, exhausted sigh.

The curly-haired girl watched me, her body perched forward with her elbows on the table. The intensity of her unblinking stare unnerved me.

I swallowed, searching for a conversation starter, unable to stand the tension of unspoken words anymore. At the same moment, she ducked under the table to rummage through her jam-packed backpack.

"I made up a game." She re-emerged from the depths holding a large stack of cards. "Can we test it out?" Her eyes lit up as she smiled.

"Tell me about the game," I offered cautiously, trying not to frown or raise my eyebrows as she spoke. This girl was a bit quirky, and I was still figuring out *how* we knew each other—and if I liked her.

"It's a best-friend, get-to-know-you-game," she said, her words running together, her grin growing larger as she spoke. She gripped the stack of cards too hard, bending them.

"Like an ice-breaker game?"

"Yes!" She clapped her hands together with the cards held in the middle. She was far too excited and I was far too sceptical. She split the deck in half and handed a pile of cards to me. "We can take turns asking and answering questions."

I fidgeted with my half of the deck, which was comprised of about fifty cards, their laminated edges still sharp.

She looked at me expectantly and I nodded, thinking that three hours was a long time to kill. "You go first, seeing as it's your creation and all."

"Can I ask all of my questions first and then we switch?" she asked, her eyes dropping. I might have thought she was embarrassed, but when she looked back at me, I saw nothing but a gleam of excitement.

I shrugged, shifting in my seat. I felt a strange tingle in my hands and feet, like the first sign of pins-and-needles, only softer. The same strange sensation had been plaguing me all morning. I would have worried, but living on coffee, chocolate, and no sleep was bound to catch up with you eventually.

"Sure," I said, conceding as the weird tingling overwhelmed my fingertips.

A beaming smile shot onto the girl's face and I wished I could ask her name, seeing as we were about to play an intense round of get-to-know-you. She shuffled the cards for a few seconds, before saying,

"Come on, just for fun." Then she stopped, holding up and reading the first card. "What is your major?"

"Bachelor of Biology, focusing on the Natural Sciences."

Flashbacks to the first day at University crossed my mind. The memory of awkward introductions and being forced to share 'one interesting fact about myself' swirled in my head. Who would have guessed I would be sitting here, playing this game of my own free will?

She flipped the first card down, the plain red backing shooting a few red square reflections across the glass window.

"What do your parents do for work?"

This question made me grit my teeth behind my closed mouth, the pit in my stomach returning and deepening.

"My mother was a teacher," I said slowly, dropping my eyes. "And my father was a scientist. He specialised in immunology..." My voice trailed off, the life sapped out of it. Even now, I missed them profoundly.

"Was?" the girl prodded, and I didn't feel like elaborating so I simply nodded without speaking. She smiled sympathetically, patting the back of my hand. Her warm, soft skin sent a strange tingle up my arms.

The girl flipped the parent card face down and cleared her throat. I tried to make my face blank as she read the next question to herself.

"Okay, these are easy ones." She leafed through the next four or five cards. "Siblings?" she rattled off.

"Only child," I retorted with a smile.

"Where did you grow up?"

"Australia."

"Middle name?"

"None."

"Religious?"

"No."

"First kiss?" The girl's words hung in the air as she asked that last question. She looked up expectantly as if she knew she'd caught me off guard. Her widening smile told me she enjoyed my squirming.

"W-well," I stuttered, my face flushing, my ears turning hot. "My first real kiss… I was thirteen, at the bottom of the school field." I tripped over my words.

"Thirteen?" Her eyebrows raised high, and she laughed. I let my shoulders drop and I giggled, too. "I guess I know the answer to the next one. But I'll ask anyway. Introvert or extrovert?"

"Introvert," I said, barely leaving a one-second gap between our words. It was as if suddenly the game also involved how *fast* you could answer.

"Last book you read?"

"*Memoirs of a Geisha.*" I smiled, conjuring up the pristine image of a Japanese Geisha and their brilliantly coloured kimonos in my mind. The ache in my chest about not being able to travel was ever-present.

"First serious boyfriend?" She stacked the used cards into a pile in the middle of the table in rapid succession.

"Rodney Carroll," I said almost dreamily, a dorky smile creeping onto my face as my eyes lost focus. "A bad boy, if there ever was one." I giggled. "We dated through the end of high school. Inseparable—*almost*…He was my *first*," I whispered, my face pulling as I smiled and cringed at the same memory. A strange flicker shot through my body, as if my memories were running on a loop inside my head—replaying the moment I met Rodney and all of our firsts that followed. It felt weird, as if my memories were on display to someone other than me.

I blinked a few times to refocus and shook my head before meeting the eyes of the girl across the table. She smiled, her crooked, bright white teeth poking through her lips.

"Other serious love interests?"

"Two." I shrugged, a ball suddenly jammed in my throat. "Harry, four years…Gorgeous, successful, and a serial cheater." My grimace grew before I sighed wistfully. "And Mason." I smiled more genuinely now and cleared my throat. "A dorky scientist just like me. In one night I felt more connected to him than—" I dropped my voice, my smile faltering. My cheeks flushing as I lifted my eyes. I realised I had been rambling about a man I'd slept with once to an almost stranger. What's more, he had immediately come to mind at the mention of 'love interests' and *that* was a bad sign. I blinked rapidly again, trying to reorient myself. I somehow felt like I was back-in-time and lost-in-time at the same moment.

The girl wore a sympathetic smile, her eyes soft and kind, and she gave me a little nod letting me know she understood.

"Tea or coffee?" She powered on, kindly changing the subject. She spoke slowly, letting me take a few shallow breaths.

"Tea." I shrugged, feeling suddenly worn out from all the questions.

A sharp pinch in my bicep made me jump and grab my arm, rubbing it vigorously. "Ow." I pulled up my sleeve to reveal a tiny, red bump. "I think something bit me," I said, frowning. My head cleared and calmed as I stared at my arm, the tiny bump disappearing as quickly as it had appeared..

I shovelled in some of my dessert—a now rock-hard brownie—for a brief reprieve from question time. It tasted like nothing; its blandness seeped down my throat, the dryness catching in my windpipe.

I pushed my plate away, rolling my eyes in irritation. I wasn't hungry, just an odd combination of on-edge and bored. The silence was growing again, even the questions were better than the growing quiet.

"Any further questions?" I asked, lifting my head to meet the girl's eyes. My fingers continued to trace over the tiny, raised dot on my bicep.

"Children?" she asked, her voice sounding hesitant, as if this was the first question to be prying.

"No, none." I shook my head, a weird twinge shooting through my stomach. "I don't want children." My words were followed up with a forced smile, hoping she wouldn't pry too deep. Other women never seemed to understand my lack of maternal longing.

The girl just nodded, her eyes glassy, and asked, "Organ donor?"

"Yes."

"Allergies?"

Her thumb fidgeted with the edge of the laminated card, the plastic peeling under the heat of her hands. The cards brushed against each other, making it obvious there weren't many left.

"Bees and latex."

She barely paused. "Birth control?" Her face flushed but otherwise stayed still.

"Always," I said matter-of-factly, trying to keep my face blank but frowning internally. As I looked at her, she met my eyes, her eyebrows raised as if to say "go on." "The pill." I shrugged. "Latex allergy, remember?" I felt as if I had to explain why I was on the pill and didn't have a huge stash of condoms in my top dresser draw.

"That's an unusual one," she said, peeling the laminate down, her arm shaking slightly.

Without meeting her eyes, I stared at her. Her body had begun vibrating. Her hair had turned to a strange frizz rather than curls; her face was pallid and pale.

"You okay?" I asked, biting my bottom lip. Her unused arm shook from the shoulder, vibrating oddly in three-second bouts as she squirmed in her chair.

She gave a grunt and a rough nod. "Last two questions," she said, her voice cracking as she spoke, the words coming out barely more than a wheeze. "Generational illnesses?" She coughed a few times to clear her throat.

"Generational?" I asked, puzzled. She seemingly fought off another bout of the shakes. "My mum died from breast cancer," I said, my voice now the one to crack as I swallowed the golf-ball sized lump that had appeared in my throat.

"Breast cancer," the girl repeated, her voice robotic. "Mental illness?"

I shook my head, words failing me. My stomach twisted; my insides knotted up and twisted themselves into kinks, tightening and loosening as the girl's lips moved.

"How many sexual partners have you had?" she continued, her eyes blinking rapidly.

My eyes ached with how wide they were, unblinking and incredulous. "I have to go to the bathroom," I said, gathering up my few possessions and standing up. The chair pushed back with a loud creak, scraping against the linoleum floor. I left my food tray and quietly backed away from the table.

The girl didn't look up, her blinking eyes fixated on the last card she held in her hand. I scooted back and stumbled away, my eyes darting back four times as I crossed the large lunchroom. The girl didn't move; her body stayed frozen in that position, staring at a single red-backed card. Was the University testing out some kind of new AI robot and thought this was the way to do it? I didn't know, but I had to get away.

I ducked out into the hallway, almost jogging as I rounded the first corner. I looked back one last time, the hallway behind me completely deserted.

Breathing heavily, I stopped and pressed my back against the wall. The cool brick made the back of my bare arms tingle; the paint was a little bumpy against my skin.

My feet moved painstakingly slowly, and I barely lifted them as I shuffled towards the end of the hallway. I contemplated what had just happened. I had just taken the oddest and most invasive questionnaire, *willingly*. If they were testing students on making dumb decisions, I would get a zero on this one.

I kept my eyes cast down, only looking up enough to ensure I didn't crash into oncoming traffic or smack into a piece of furniture. My mind was somehow both muddled and buzzing.

Tugging at my clothes, I sat down on the toilet—I blinked, not remembering opening the door into the bathroom or locking the stall door. But the silver latch was pushed across, locking me in.

I sighed, staring at the back of the off-yellow door. The metal was speckled with dirt and grime, the brown flecks making my stomach turn. I groaned, dropping my head into my hands and resting my elbows against my knees. My wrinkled pants had bunched up, and the fabric rubbed against my arms, scratching my skin and subsequently my forehead as I crumpled into a ball.

I sat like that for a long while, my jumbled thoughts unable to catch up with my increasingly foggy mind. My body turned stiff as the minutes ticked by, my muscles slowly turning to stone.

CHAPTER TWELVE

ADVANCED IQ TESTING

I SHIFTED BACK AND FORTH FROM MY LEFT FOOT TO MY RIGHT, ALMOST hopping while I waited outside the professor's large wooden door.

Checking my watch for the sixteenth time, I took a long, drawn-out breath. Finally I pounded three loud, clear knocks. I took an unsteady step backwards to wait.

I had barely moved out of the way before the door swung open and the professor stood in the doorway. His dimpled smile was gleeful as he graciously waved me in.

I stepped across the threshold, itching at the back of my neck. A strange prickly sensation crept down my spine—the tingle crackled through my limbs, my fingers and toes electrified.

"Come, come," he said, overtaking me, the spring in his step obvious. He was clearly thrilled with today's turn of events as he bounded up onto the small stage, crossing to his desk within a matter of seconds. He turned to look at me expectantly.

I had barely taken the first step; my legs were heavy and uncooperative.

His eyes sparkled while he waited for me to catch up.

All I could manage was a weak smile in return. I leaned against the desk laid out for me, hands shaking.

"Take a seat," he said. I leaned on the desk for support, and a slight frown appeared on his face.

Wiping my sweaty hands against my jeans, I pulled the chair back, sitting down with an audible groan. I bent my joints, and my body creaked weirdly, a dull ache developing in both knees as I positioned myself at the slightly too-small desk.

My hands hovered, coming to rest in my lap. I flicked my eyes between the professor and the four piles of paperwork that were stacked on my desktop.

"IQ testing is completed in different categories," the professor said, answering my arched brow. His voice ripped through my muddled mind and cloudy thoughts. If I hadn't been as interested, I would have struggled to keep up.

"Let's begin with logical-mathematical." His head tipped forward to the right-hand corner where a neat stack of paper sat, the edges almost flush. I stared at the four piles in turn as he talked. "Linguistic, or *the study of languages.*" He stepped closer, pointing now. The second stack had been printed on light blue paper.

"Third category," he said, clearing his throat. "Naturalistic, or the study of the earth." A wistful smile crept across his features.

"Professor?" I asked, blinking a few times. "Do these tests really measure a person's intelligence?" I stared down at the labels on each of the four tests, aware that the categories weren't enough to make up full human capacity.

"Yes and no," the professor said, a grin breaking out across his face as he shrugged his shoulders. "IQ testing is a funny beast." His eyes drifted away from the classroom and landed on the ceiling. "Think of IQ testing as a narrow scope." His eyes returned to meet mine, sparkling and thoughtful. "It tells you when someone is intelligent in one specific way. But remember." He closed his eyes. "It doesn't tell you everything,"

I nodded, somehow knowing exactly what he meant.

"Sorry, sir." I bowed my head and bit my lip. Asking questions I already knew the answer too was a waste of both of our time.

"*Never* be sorry for your curiosity, Miss Avery," he chided cheerfully, continuing without missing a beat. "Last," he said, "and, in my humble opinion, the most important aspect of all..." He paused for a second, the words almost spilling out as I tried to think what an academic lecturer would consider *most important*. "Emotional IQ."

I felt myself frown and my eyebrows raise, unsure if I was shocked or if I agreed with his assessment.

"You seem surprised?"

I chose my words carefully. "Not...surprised." I exhaled. "More..." I paused, searching for the right word. "Impressed?"

The professor smiled, his dimples re-appearing in an instant. He clasped his hands together—his hands almost instantly turned white from the pressure. "Final questions, concerns?"

I stared up at him, surrounded by the four different IQ tests. As I sat here, it seemed I had become as curious as he was about my own aptitudes; and I was ready to get started.

I smiled and shook my head.

"You will have three hours." He swivelled around and pulled a giant clock with vibrant red numbers out from behind his desk.

The clock was placed front and centre, barely a metre away from where I sat. Its red, ticking count was clearly visible.

"You may use a dictionary if you don't understand the definition of a word." A thick, brown leather dictionary was waved at me before being placed down next to the clock. "But everything else must be your own work."

I nodded, trying to keep my hands and feet from shaking and tapping.

"Start and finish wherever you please." He waved at the array of tests. "And *good luck*." He smacked a button atop the clock. The numbers flickered and began descending from the three allotted hours.

He bowed his head to me before exiting the stage and leaving me alone in the giant lecture hall.

I watched the clock tick down for a few seconds, the red numbers almost mesmerising. My hands and feet tapped to the rhythm the descending numbers created.

2H 57M 25S flashed on the screen, and I shook myself. I had work to do.

Staring down at the desk, I piled three of the tests on top of one another, leaving only one in front of me. I hadn't consciously picked, but I was glad to see *Advanced IQ Tests: 10 of the Toughest Questions Available: Linguistic Edition.* I took a deep breath and opened the first page, quickly scanning the questions.

Questions one to six came easily, and I answered them one-after-another as my eyes continued to flick to the clock, the number descending in what felt like slow motion. It had only been eleven minutes when I turned the page, and the seventh question made me pause. I blinked a few times, staring at the jumbled letters of six potential words. Their lack of sense irritated me; my body itched and tingled as I squirmed in my seat. It was like a visceral pause; my body forcing me to slow down and breathe.

"Only one group of six letters below can be rearranged to spell out a six-letter word in the English language. Identify the word," I re-read the question, whispering the words to myself as if that would help.

"NITLAF IFCLEA AHGOLI OLKECM FITRAB RNUMLA." I read the letters aloud, twice. My brain felt like it was swishing around in my head, continuing to throw out partial words like FLEA, FIT, RUN.

I stretched my arm out and laid my head down to the left, staring at the muddled letters from a different angle.

The letters danced across my vision, which was foggy and distorted from this angle, before rearranging themselves over and over inside my mind.

Squeezing my eyes shut, I took a deep breath as the word FACILE shimmied across my blackened vision.

My eyes shot open, and I sat up, re-reading the letters and realising that I was indeed correct. In big block letters, I wrote the word, underlining it twice for emphasis. I basked in my glory for a few celebratory moments before rubbing my face, checking the clock again.

2H 26M 35S

I let myself watch the clock for ten seconds, taking the opportunity to breathe before finishing questions eight through ten with ease.

Tucking the *Linguistic Test* at the bottom of the pile, I shut my eyes.

I grabbed at the other three tests haphazardly, my fingers shaking as I shuffled them, settling on my next test before opening it to read the title.

Advanced IQ Tests: 10 of the Toughest Questions Available: Naturalistic Edition.

I put down the papers and opened the pages, only to groan.

Within the booklet were multiple pictures of trees, flowers, and plants, all with little blank labels beside them. I leafed through the booklet, labelling the planets and answering two questions about pollution and climate change before tossing it aside, unable to answer more than a third.

It was clear my intelligence didn't lay in the naturalistic realm. But instead of wallowing, I grabbed the logical-mathematical booklet with a smile. I knew in my heart if I was going to shine, it would be within these pages filled with rhymes and riddles.

I stared at the cover; the title was subtly different from the others.

Advanced IQ Tests: 25 of the Toughest Questions Available: Logical-Mathematical Edition.

My mouth dropped open. The professor had given me *fifteen* additional questions in this test compared to all the others.

I quickly examined the final test, beyond grateful to discover it was back to the original ten questions.

I returned to the mathematical booklet. I knew he had done this on purpose, and I was strangely grateful. The pages were packed with numbers and riddles.

My pen tapped against the first page itching to begin. The anticipation roared through my veins making my fingers and toes tingle.

My fingers moved with ease, scribbling answer after answer as I completed the first three questions in a matter of minutes. When I opened the third page and looked at question six, the first hint of a frown pulled at the edges of my lips. The page contained nine boxes full of small black and clear circles, their patterns irrelevant and confusing the longer I stared at them.

The black boxes blurred and twisted. I realised two boxes equalled a third, the little equals sign straight, narrow, and symmetrical.

A deepening frown embedded itself across my forehead, the lines sinking into the skin with each passing second. The more I stared at the dots and patterns, the more they blurred together, any hidden pattern lost in my eyes.

With a huff, I lay back in my chair, letting my head drop backwards. The chair pressed into my neck and shoulder blades, pushing against the strange tingle that lived there now.

I stared up at the ceiling, and my eyes ached and twitched as I wrenched myself forward again, my elbows landing softly against the wooden desk. I used my left hand to cover question six, pretending for now that it didn't exist. This trick always served me well in tests.

Scanning the next two questions, I let out a sigh of relief.

"Well, well," I mumbled to myself. "*We meet again.*" With a smirk, I stared down at the list of numbers, a few of which now containing decimal places, and the same allusive question mark.

Instead of thinking, I looked up at the red-lettered clock.

1H 49M 20S

"Time flies when you're having fun," I said, realising more than a third of my allotted time had already passed.

With a sigh, I wrote the numbers out on my working paper, staring at them.

100, 99.8, 99.2, ?, 92, 75.8

I read them backwards and forwards, the number dancing before my eyes..

With a sudden internal click, I wrote the number 97.4 neatly in the small answer box. I loved it when puzzles clicked for me like that; it was one of my favourite things.

I moved on, completing the rest of the booklet with relative ease. Questions about fractions, number patterns, odd-ones-out, and equations filled my mind and spilled over onto the page.

As I wrote the answer to question twenty-five, I felt a smile dance across my lips. I had crushed it, but as quickly as I thought that, the smile slipped and the frown returned.

I flipped back, landing on page three again. Question six remained blank, the dots still dancing across my vision.

With a sigh, I closed the booklet, making a mental note to ask the professor to explain that one question in great depth to me once this was all over.

My eyes snapped back to the countdown clock.

1H 12M 40S

"An hour," I breathed, nodding. "I can work with that." I shrugged my shoulders and stared at the final booklet's front page. The title alone was enough to make me balk.

'Advanced IQ Tests: 10 of the Most Thoughtful Questions Available: Interpersonal (social) and Intrapersonal (self) Intelligence Edition.'

I twitched while studying the title, my sweaty fingers pressed up against the paper.

I flipped open the booklet and turned to the first page.

Describe yourself using five words. I immediately stood up and left the last test on the table. My legs wobbled as I paced back-and-forth across the small, wooden stage.

My shoes clipped against the wood, the sound like a drill in my head, banging against the sides of my brain. I *hated* self-evaluation and self-description. In my opinion, these questions were too subjective to be called science.

But I sat down again, slipping into the chair and missing the edge. I wobbled, catching myself just in time.

"What is *wrong* with you today?" I snapped, the frustration in my voice ringing out into the empty room.

I stared back at the test paper and the ever-ticking clock.

1H 1M 32S

I closed my eyes for a few seconds, holding my breath before letting it go in one sharp burst and writing the first words that sprang to mind.

Independent, adventurous, persistent, spilled out the end of my pen. "All true," I nodded to myself, my stomach giving a strange, twisting kick as I sat there, wracking my brain for two more words that I thought suited me.

Passionate, I wrote with a nod, before letting my head fall backwards. I tapped my pen against the desk, the noise filling the room as I drummed a familiar tune that I couldn't quite put my finger on.

"Curious," I said with a startling click, knowing I had to move onto the next question. My eyes blurred and ached.

With a few sharp blinks they cleared, a single tear rolling out of the corner of each eye and smudging the first word of the next question, which read: "Introvert or extrovert: explain why."

I could feel a frown embedding into my forehead. *This is not science,* I wanted to scream, but instead I put pen to paper.

Writing *introvert* was the easy part. I held my pen poised above the paper, hoping the *why* would come spilling out of the pen tip. When nothing came, I forced myself to start writing.

I believe in science, not people.

I grinned and then grimaced, knowing this wasn't the answer anyone was looking for, but I didn't care. It was true.

I wrote brief answers for the next two questions—a few words about my favourite fictional characters, and the quote I relate to most in life. I was barely able to fill a paragraph between all the answers in this booklet. I hoped it didn't make me a tragic person, but I had a feeling this would explain some of my well-documented flaws.

With a heavy sigh, I looked up at the ticking clock.

29M 56S

I forced my eyes down. The red numbers of the countdown clock burned into my skull. My heart beat faster as I read the final question.

Describe what true love is.

The words sat neatly typed without a question mark or apology for their difficulty.

I felt my mouth go dry, my lips parting as if to independently scream. Staring at the dancing words on the page, my mind went blank—except for floating images of my parents.

True love is, I wrote, my hands trembling, *honest.* The tell-tale prickle in my eyes came out of nowhere.

True love is genuine and emotional. It's laughter at 2pm and tears at 9pm. Joyous celebrations and sad work nights. Shared joy, pain, happiness, and sorrow. It is everything.

The words stuck in my throat like a giant lump, but I swallowed and wrote the next sentence.

When my mother got sick—the tears swelled to the surface—*my father never left her side. He would sing to her, read to her, and hold her tight.* The words now came faster in my mind that I could write them. I could see my parents' faces perfectly.

They would talk and laugh, cry together, cling to each other, and that didn't change until her last breath. My father stayed with her, even though it broke his heart.

I took a deep breath and leaned my head back, the tears spilling out the side of my eyes; I rushed to wipe them before they fell. I had to write one last sentence about true love.

True love leaves us broken, but grateful for every single second.

I put my pen down. The tears that filled my eyes blurred my vision as I watched the red numbers on the clock slowly ebb down to zero.

When the tears stopped, I snapped all the tests closed and stacked them neatly in a pile. I fidgeted with their corners as I straightened and re-straightened them, waiting for the professor to return.

My eyes hopped back to the zeroed out clock every few seconds. The six red zeros taunted me—my eyes out of tears, my stomach swirling and fluttering.

The wood made a soft creaking sound as I jostled my leg against it, wondering if this was another test.

Cautiously, I pushed my chair back, lifting it so it didn't scrape against the floor.

Just as I was about to stand, the door swung open. I jumped and turned back to face the front, awkwardly shoving my chair in.

The professor bounded up onto the stage, a strange half-smile, half-frown etched onto his face.

He held out his hand, gesturing to the four booklets that were stacked against my desk without saying a word. With shaking, almost vibrating hands, I handed them to him.

He nodded and immediately marched back to his large wooden desk.

Out of sight, he pulled out his black-rimmed glasses and a large, red marking pen. With a knowing nod, his hand moved fast, marking and scribbling notes against my tests.

I scratched at my skin. My wrists and ankles were blisteringly irritated, the skin turning red with the little raised bumps that had appeared. My skin bristled against my t-shirt, the tag suddenly the most annoying piece of material in the world.

My fingertips brushed against the misshapen and uneven bumps, and I struggled not to scratch like a maniac.

"Miss Avery," the Professor finally said, clearing his throat, his presence suddenly feeling too close. His face looked almost happy, except for his eyes. "Do you have the capacity to discuss your results?" His voice was calm and kind.

I nodded, the skin on my wrist bubbling and itching as I tried to focus, not fidget.

"Very well." He nodded, his eyes trailing to my red-raw wrist with raised eyebrows. "Follow me."

His body drifted past me, the fabric of his suit jacket passing so close I thought it would touch my skin. Everything felt too much, too raw and wild, as I followed in the professor's footsteps, my feet knocking awkwardly against each other.

He walked quickly and disappeared behind the first bend in the corridor. I leaned against the wall slightly. I forced my legs to move; my muscles felt like lead, each movement sending a weird ache into my thighs. But I painstakingly followed after him.

CHAPTER THIRTEEN

RESULT

THE PROFESSOR WAS ALREADY SEATED WHEN I ENTERED HIS OFFICE. THE door swung open with a slow, painful creak.

The dust from the hinges of the door clung to my nose and mouth made me rub at my face.

By the time I looked up, the Professor was staring at me quizzically, his expression a cross between impatience and excitement. He indicated for me to sit.

The office was cramped and small, jammed with overflowing bookshelves. The books were stacked high and mismatched, spines in different orders and directions, facing both inwards and outwards.

I cringed internally at the disorder as I navigated around stacks of scrawled paper, too-many half-full coffee mugs, and yet more haphazardly and distinctly unorganised piles of books.

I sunk into the vacant chair, the stiff padding holding no bounce or elasticity at all.

The Professor sat back in his chair, his hands clasped near his mouth with his head tilted and waiting. His intensity unnerved me.

I looked away, letting my eyes wander the room. Even the posters hanging on the wall were chaotic—their corners lifted, the paper crinkled. My eye twitched as I noticed they were all hung at a lopsided angle, the left side higher than the right.

When I looked back at the Professor, his expression was still quiet and contemplative, but this time, he was staring directly at me.

Shifting in my seat, I felt the uncomfortable sensation of being watched creep down my spine. The longer the silence stretched on, the further the discomfort expanded, looping into my stomach and down the tops of my thighs before the professor cleared his throat. Had I done so horribly that he felt the need to make sure I was seated first before personally consoling me?

"Aptitude tests are a fickle thing," he said, a small smirk crossing his face. "They are always seeking more than just what is read and written, asked and answered." His hands unfastened, now rubbing against his rough stubble.

I desperately wanted to ask if I had passed *any* of the tests. My curiosity was clearly leaking out through my contorted expression. He was torturing me.

"Let's go through one at a time." He waved his hand at me. "Logical, mathematical," he said with a nod and a smile. "As I am sure you know, *this* is where your aptitude truly lies."

I nodded, not wanting to say anything that may make me seem conceited or cocky, but also wanting to acknowledge that I already knew this about myself.

"You sit in the top tier of the logical-mathematical aptitude." His eyes bored into me, unnerving, unblinking.

"Thank you, sir." I fidgeted with my hands before shoving them between my legs and clamping them shut to force myself to sit still. I wasn't sure why I was thanking him; it was my aptitude after all, but somehow it felt like the normal thing to do.

"It's not a matter of thank you or congratulations…It just is."

I nodded, frowning, wishing I'd just kept it to a quiet, acknowledging nod.

"Next, linguistic, or the study of languages," he continued without missing a beat. "Did you ever learn or study another language, Miss Avery?" the Professor asked curiously.

"No, sir," I said, wishing I'd taken up language studies after the travel lockdowns and mandates.

"Regardless, your linguistic ability is also far above average…" He paused for a second and then added, "Although not as high as your mathematical abilities."

"Thank you, sir," I said, cursing internally that I had said thank you again. I dropped my eyes for a few seconds and fidgeted with my t-shirt collar as my skin prickled.

"Unfortunately, your naturalistic ability is laughable," the Professor continued with an airy voice, delivering the bad news in one swift, harsh blow. He waved his hand at me, his shoulders shrugging a few times.

"Most people are not both mathematical and linguistic, let alone *also* high on the ability spectrum for the natural world," he said simply. "Asking you to take four sets of IQ tests was, *in other words*, outrageous and unrealistic." He spoke with a calm, vibrant air about him, his voice soft and melodic.

"So why *did* you ask me to take all four tests?" I felt my mouth purse as I crossed my arms and stared at him. It shouldn't have annoyed me to be below average at something outside my skill set, but it hurt to see my shortcomings recorded on paper.

"Curiosity, Miss Avery. All outstanding scientists have it," he said with a wink.

"I can understand that, Professor," I said and laughed, uncrossing my arms and laying them back in my lap, as my brief flare of annoyance disappeared.

"And finally…" He picked up the few sheets of paper that he had hidden in his lap. "...what I like to call Emotional Intelligence." He held up my written test, my name scrawled in messy, cursive handwriting across the front page. "You write beautifully about love, Miss Avery." He opened my test and hovered over the words on the inside pages. "How long were your parents married?" His eyes pulled up to meet mine.

"Thirty-six years," I said, the corners of my eyes itching. "They died within a year of each other. It was as if the universe knew they couldn't bear to be apart." My voice cracked. He could hear the sadness in my voice, but no one could see the crater in my heart.

He nodded, once again his head bowed and his eyes focused down. "A love like that is rare."

"Once in a lifetime, if we're lucky," I said, smiling weakly. Mason's face flashed into my mind for a split second. I fidgeted, pushing the thought away. My hands ached at the joints, and I flexed them and tightened them back into a fist, repeating the movement multiple times as the Professor stared down at the test papers.

"You didn't finish the test," he said—a statement, not a question.

I shook my head, although I could tell the question was rhetorical.

"Did you know thirty-three minutes elapsed between when the clock struck zero and when I re-entered the room?" the Professor asked, raising his eyes to meet mine.

I shrugged and shook my head again, only knowing that the wait had felt *really* long.

"I assumed you were busy teaching or dealing with students." It was true, and also not. The thought *had* crossed my mind, but I had wondered if I was being graded on my patience too.

"No, Miss Avery," he said, pressing his hands to his lips in a strange shushing move, his arms wobbling. "The wait at the end of the test was to determine another part of your personality," he continued, his voice distorting at the end.

I blinked a few times as his body squiggled, his voice turning high pitched and then dropping incredibly low.

"Rule follower." The words came out distorted and uneven, and my senses scrambled.

I squeezed my eyes shut, forcing myself to take four deep breaths. The bile in my stomach swayed and swirled as my body twisted in on itself, like I was collapsing from the inside out.

Gasping for breath, I struggled to open my eyes; all I could see was black.

I tried to move my arms and realised I couldn't—they jiggled, my fingers wiggling as something held my arms at my side.

I could feel restraints wound around my shoulder and collarbones, snaking tightly under my breasts. With another shallow breath, I felt a soft chair pressed against my back, the leather touching every tiny piece of exposed skin. The sweat pouring out had pooled and stuck me to my clothing.

Minutes passed as I laid there, the darkness compressing in on me, my heart hammering in my chest and ears. My brain scrambled to desperately piece itself back together.

"Welcome back, Miss Avery," a kind, familiar voice spoke. "You are alive and well." I could feel multiple presences in the room—bodies bustling about. The restraints that had been pressing and cutting into my skin loosened, and my shoulders dipped down into a more relaxed position.

I took a few deep breaths, flexing my sore muscles and stiff joints, my stomach swirling.

"Three, Two, One." The voice came through, and my head lifted as the large, black helmet was pulled off. A breeze struck my face, the air cold against my hair, which I could now feel was ringing wet from sweat.

My eyes burned as I rubbed them, wiping away the stream of watery tears. I looked around the room and tried to pull myself up into a seated position.

The room swam at the movement. My vision disappeared, replaced by blackness and little stars. I lurched over the left side of the chair, my stomach emptying its contents into a waiting bucket.

When I looked up, I frowned, making eye contact with a young, dark-haired girl. She held the full bucket of my vomit, her face nothing but sympathetic.

I shot her a grimacing smile, my stomach settling.

"Welcome back, Miss Avery," the familiar voice repeated. It was as if she was reminding me of where I was.

I sat back up, my body feeling disjointed, as if my brain didn't quite recognise my limbs.

"Dr. H-Hidalgo," I said, my brain putting the voice and the face together. I stared at her as I laid back and pressed into the cool leather chair.

"It feels a little like sea-sickness, doesn't it?" She gave a sympathetic smile as she walked towards me and pressed a cold compress to my head, gently wiping it across my brow. "This is why I said not to eat." She waved the catcher away and I was grateful the lingering smell of vomit went with her.

"Almost everyone throws up," Dr. Hidalgo continued. "Hence the catchers."

I could feel my eyes closing, my body rebelling against the old but now unfamiliar sensation of being alert and alive. "You will feel exhausted for the next twenty-four hours." Her words were slow and echoed within the glass walls and inside my mind.

My brain felt rattled, as though I was shaking my head, even though I wasn't moving.

"You lasted in the simulation for thirteen hours, twenty-eight minutes."

I opened my eyes. I tried desperately to concentrate, but the world kept spinning.

"We planned for twelve hours, and you *exceeded* all expectations." Her words bounced around my mind, not sinking in or making any sense.

I opened my mouth to speak and then closed it, letting my eyes shut again. My world swam in black, the stars behind my eyes coming in waves and then disappearing, leaving me in the dark. Time must have been different inside the simulation.

A loud click made me jolt; my eyes fluttered open long enough to make out a bright light.

"Wha—" I slurred, my mouth dry and sore. I swallowed hard, running my tongue against my teeth and cracked lips.

"Sip." Dr. Hidalgo's voice felt close but echoed in my ears.

A hard poke at my lips made me groan. Water trickled out.

My body jostled as I sipped; my abdomen tensed and my legs wobbled.

"We'll be taking you back to your room to rest." Dr. Hidalgo's hot breath blew against my ear.

A groan was my reply, and nausea rippled with each movement as cold hands moved me. Seconds later, the plastic wheels clunked against the floor, not entirely soft and round, causing them to bump and shake my body every few seconds.

I grabbed at my knees and pulled them tight against my chest. The cart made its way along corridors and around bends, turning multiple times at too sharp an angle, causing me to grab onto the side out of instinct.

"Three, two, one," came an unfamiliar voice from my left-hand side. I felt icy hands against my neck and lower calves. Their firm grip pressed against my skin, spreading a trickle of cold down my spine and up my legs.

I felt my body hit a mattress, this time soft, warm, and still. The cool air from the spinning fan above hit my skin, causing me to shiver and break out in goosebumps.

Groping at the bed, I heard the door shut with a loud *click*. I struggled to turn, my body heavy and fluid as though I was made of both feathers and concrete.

My hands pawed at the blanket, grabbing a handful and pulling it towards me. I covered my top half, leaving my legs bare from the thigh down.

Swimming and swaying, my hands groped my face, my fingers fumbling and poking and prodding my skin.

I let out a loud sigh, my hands falling away, landing on the fluffy pillows that took up half the bed.

"Curious," I whispered, my body unclenching inch by inch until only my toes remained curled. "Very curious," I murmured, snuggling into the fluffy pillows and letting my mind switch off and the darkness consume me.

CHAPTER FOURTEEN

THE FINAL, FICKLE STEP

A DEEP, RACKING GASP RIPPED ME FROM SLEEP. MY CLOTHES CLUNG TO me, the fabric drenched in sweat. The room was dark and quiet other than my own laboured breathing.

My tingling hands pawed at my face, groping their way from my forehead, down to my nose and across my cracked lips before heading down and grabbing at my collarbones, breasts, and stomach. I was in one piece—even if every inch of my body ached.

With an almighty groan, I pushed myself up to a seated position, my muscles crying.

I sat for more than a minute, taking deep breaths, one after the other—each time a little easier. On shaky legs, I hobbled towards the bathroom, each tiny step causing an ache to sear through my body.

I hovered over the sink, gripping the side as I stretched out my legs. I had a hell of a lot of questions for Dr. Hidalgo, and I was sure she had no plans to answer them.

I rubbed my face, then stared at myself in the mirror. I looked as tired and awful as I felt, which was both comforting and horrifying. Giant welts ran down the length of my neck and chest, the dark stripes now a blotchy, angry red.

With an eye-roll, I turned around, stripping my clothing off piece-by-piece. The fabric was crinkled and stuck to my body in places. I had a feeling I smelled as bad as I looked; a hot shower had never sounded so good.

"Good Morning, Miss Avery," a distorted voice crackled through the room. I quickly grabbed the nearest towel and wrapped it around myself, scampering out of the bathroom in less than ten seconds. The movement hurt, but I crossed the bedroom, coming to a stop in front of the intercom.

"G-good morning," I stuttered breathlessly. Dr. Hidalgo was right about feeling tired after the simulation.

My body stiffened as I lingered near the intercom, hopping from foot-to-foot every few seconds to stop the deep ache in my ankles.

I opened my mouth a few times, my voice letting out a quiet squeak before closing it again and staying silent. I had a lot of questions, but none for the automated voice.

"In front of the door, you will find a change of clothing." A loud click reverberated and the door popped open. "Please wash, dress, and be ready in one hour." The static prickled in my ears, making me squirm. I stood frozen, listening for a few more seconds, but all that remained was silence.

Gripping the towel, I took a few steps and pushed the door open.

Outside the door lay a package wrapped in brown paper and tied with a red and white ribbon, along with a small tray of bland, hospital-grade food that made my nose wrinkle. It might not have been this particular food's fault, but this morning I felt more nauseous than ever.

I grabbed the package, looping the ribbon over my forearm before shooting a look down the corridor. It was dark and empty, the air still and quiet.

My feet still planted in the open doorway, I could hear the distorted voice coming through the intercom again. My fingers tensed around my towel, the ligaments and bones aching with the tightness. It was the first tiny chance I had been given to make a run for it—and foolish or not, I was going to take it.

I flung the package into the room as the voice crackled, but I didn't catch anything it said. Instead, I found myself running through dark corridors wearing nothing but a towel.

I had opted to run the opposite way from where Dr. Hidalgo had led me yesterday, hoping that the messy labyrinths of corridors, twists, turns and doors would be less—or at least less confusing.

Five minutes in, it was clear I was wrong. The underground bunker was a complex maze filled with an entangled network of looping dead ends and corridors that led back to the same places.

As I spun around, at the end of *yet another* dead end, I knew I was lost. I groaned and leaned against the nearest wall. My heart was racing and my stomach curdled in waves. Everything ached from yesterday's testing, and now I could add sweaty and starving to the list of discomforts I felt.

More mortifying, I was now basically laying on the ground in nothing but a white, too-short towel, waiting for someone to find me.

I should have at least gotten changed and put on underwear before running off.

Clawing up the wall, I pulled myself back to my feet, panting a little too hard at the effort, when Dr. Hidalgo appeared at the end of the long corridor.

Her red high-heels announced her every step as she closed the gap between us. She walked with purpose, but didn't look irritated or concerned that I had tried to escape; instead, I would have guessed she looked *amused.*

She was as pristine and perfect as yesterday. Dr. Hidalgo looked me over and clicked her tongue, and I tugged at my towel.

"Good Morning, Miss Avery," she said, her smile soft and genuine. She didn't seem angry or put out to be standing here. I watched as she instead looked me up and down and let out a reverberating sigh.

With a little shake of her head, she handed me a tiny packet of dry biscuits before she turned her attention to the tablet in her hand. She tapped against the glass, her nails creating a strange symphony of sounds. "Follow me, Miss Avery." She clicked the tablet shut and let it swing to her side. She said nothing about my escape attempt, or the fact I was wearing only a bath towel. She simply swivelled on the spot and walked back the way we had both come.

I hurried to keep up, shuffling along behind her, trying to eat my biscuits while keeping a tight grip on the towel.

"I've been reviewing your case notes," Dr. Hidalgo said, ignoring everything that was happening off-script.

I was behind her, but I nodded, gnawing at my lip. Silence fell between us as we rounded a corner, hugging to the left side of the room, before turning left down another corridor. The hallway was dimly lit, the lights above flickering as we passed.

Dr. Hidalgo moved quickly, her high-heels echoing against the concrete floor. I hurried behind her, my bare feet ice cold, making my body break out in a rash of goosebumps.

I caught fleeting glances of myself in the glass window panels that lined the hallway, each a different size, each distorting my body in a different, unflattering way. Unfortunately for me, I was still wearing a towel in each version.

"Miss Avery," Dr. Hidalgo said, taking the empty packet from me, her smile now strangely forced. Her eyebrow harshly arched and her lips pursed. I hadn't managed to pay attention to where we were going as we walked the long, winding hallway.

"Y-yes?" I stuttered, strangely breathless.

"Please remember this is the final test you need to pass," she said coyly, a little nod directed at me.

I frowned and nodded, adding, "Do I have to do this *in a towel?*"

She smiled and said nothing as the light above us flickered, bathing the hallway in warm, bright light.

A second light switched on, illuminating the glass-window room we stood in front of.

Dr. Hidalgo stared into the glass before stepping back.

I stood still, rooted to the spot for a few seconds.

"No," I whispered, shuffling forward and staring inside. *"Not like this."* I pressed my face up against the glass, my forehead leaving a dirty smudge. Relief flooded me momentarily, before dread took over.

He was here, and all I could do was tug the towel tighter against my body and hope this would be over quickly.

CHAPTER FIFTEEN

THE FATHER 2.0

THE SILHOUETTE OF A YOUNG, BLONDE MAN SAT IN A STIFF METAL CHAIR behind a long metal table. His hands were wrapped together, fingers intertwined and fidgeting, his head bowed.

"Miss Avery," Dr. Hidalgo's voice broke through my whirling thoughts.

I turned, swivelling on the spot, my bare feet now sweating against the floor.

"Come." She pulled open a camouflaged door, the handle and hinges springing out as she pressed something on her tablet.

I shuffled forward, feeling my gaping mouth turn dry and cracked.

Clumsily, I crossed the threshold, Dr. Hidalgo stepping in behind me and letting the door shut with a loud click.

"In you go," Dr. Hidalgo motioned to the sliding door a few steps away.

I shivered; her casual voice shot goosebumps down the back of my neck, and my back instantly broke out in a cold sweat.

Dr. Hidalgo's nails pressed against my shoulder, pushing me forward.

"This is the last hurdle, Miss Avery," she said, squeezing my shoulder. The inset sliding door opened with a soft *swish*.

Dr. Hidalgo gave me one last push, and I realised I was going to have to face him in nothing but a towel.

"Alice?" came a deep, soft voice whisper, swallowing a giggle.

Two loud clicks rang out as the lights dimmed overhead.

My eyes watered as a stubbled face pressed up against mine.

I took a few steps back, Mason's face coming into focus, his dorky smile wide.

"Are you okay?" I whispered, stealing a sideways glance at Dr. Hidalgo, who was tapping a long nail against the tablet she always gripped. Her gaze on it was intense.

Mason nodded. "Are *you*?" His smile faltered as he looked me up and down with wide eyes.

I cringed and nodded. "Other than this." I gestured to the towel. His face cracked into a grin, and even though I felt silly, I somehow felt comfortable with Mason.

The room felt smaller from the inside, the three metal chairs divided by a metal table, all bolted to the floor.

"Miss Avery," Dr. Hidalgo's voice broke through the awkwardly long look Mason and I were sharing, finally giving me an excuse to break eye contact.

"Can you confirm, *for the record*—" She was closer than I expected, her eyes never leaving my face. "—that Mason McConnell is the father of your unborn child?"

I fidgeted, moving from my left foot to my right foot.

"Is that your last name?" I whispered, turning to face Mason and raising an eyebrow. I was desperate to keep things light even in this wild situation.

He snort-laughed, running his hands through his hair, his cheeks flushing a vibrant shade of red as he nodded.

"Yes," I said, snapping my head back to face Dr. Hidalgo.

With a taut face, Dr. Hidalgo tapped her tablet, and I could have *sworn* she was struggling to hold back a smile.

"Please sit." She waved her hands towards the two vacant chairs, then slid her body into the waiting metal chair on the opposite side, simultaneously smoothing her pristine dress.

I shot a quick look at Mason, who was already plodding over to the far seat, pulling at the top with a little frown.

"Bolted? *Really?*" I huffed as I slid in, the cool metal pressing against my bare thighs. Dr. Hidalgo said nothing. I tugged at the towel, trying to pull it down to cover more of my naked body without success.

Mason casually slid into the chair beside me, making us barely inches apart. I tried not to make it obvious as I breathed him in, relishing the tiny touch of familiarity.

"Mr. McConnell," Dr. Hidalgo said, staring at Mason before her eyes crossed to me. "Miss Avery."

I tucked my hands under my thighs, both to get a break from the cold and try to stop myself from squirming in my seat.

"Individually, you have both passed your intelligence testing." Her fingers swiped across the tablet, a wistful smile crossing her face as she looked down at multiple slides full of graphs and figures. "Phase one is complete." She discarded the tablet on the table. Her hands sat clasped together, her knuckles turning a strange shade. "We must now understand more about your sexual and personal histories." She spoke matter-of-factly, but her lip twitched, giving her discomfort away.

"I'm sorry," I blurted, putting my hand up to stop Dr. Hidalgo from speaking. "But what if we decline to answer your questions?"

I could feel Mason looking at me, his eyes boring into the side of my head.

"Termination," Dr. Hidalgo said, a strange sadness dancing across her face.

"Perfect," I said deadpan, not daring to hope it was *actually* an option. "I choose that."

I stared at Dr. Hidalgo as her sadness turned into a deep, sinking frown.

"Do you not understand your privilege, Miss Avery?" Dr. Hidalgo spoke low and slow.

"Privilege?" I repeated. My eyebrows pushed together in a long scowl. "This may come as a surprise to you," I spoke, forcing myself to keep my voice even, "but not all women want to have children." I could feel my jaw clench. I was tired of other women not understanding how I felt.

"Whether you recognise it or not," Dr. Hidalgo said quietly, her eyes focused directly on mine, "to carry a child *is* a privilege." She stared right through me, her eyes flashing with a kind of frustration I didn't understand. This wasn't the same as the countless arguments I'd had with friends; this ran much deeper.

I unclenched my hands, pushing them down onto the cool metal surface. I dropped my head, letting out a deep sigh as my fingers returned to fists. Dr. Hidalgo wasn't the person I was angry at. This mandate went all the way to the top and ensnared people at every level on the way down.

Suddenly the metal table beneath me shook, and four small, square hatches opened up, two on each side of my arms.

I scooted back, my back smacking into the bolted-down metal chair behind me, unaffected by my sudden jerking movement. Thick black threads shot out from within the table, wrapping their coarse fabric around my wrists before snaking their way up both of my arms and jolting me forward.

The black threads reeled me in, tugging at my arms until they were pulled tight against the metal table. The pressure cut deeply, the tightness of the cords causing my arms to bulge in some areas and flatten in others.

Dr. Hidalgo watched me with sympathy, her mouth pursed. Her long fingernails tapped against the metal as the chains pulled me forward. My back arched at my struggle, unable to reach the bolted seat with the tethers holding me firmly in place.

A low growl escaped my lips. My arms turned red and ached from the pressure.

"*Or…* I could tie you down until you agree to discuss the final questions," Dr. Hidalgo said with a shrug; she didn't look happy, but she had a job to do.

"Alice," a soft, deep voice spoke gently.

I turned my head, and my eyes took in Mason's bound wrists and carefully placed smile. It was clear his cords weren't as tight—the restraints were really meant for me.

"We could just answer the questions," he said, his eyes darting between Dr. Hidalgo and me with alarming speed. His eyes were wide, his back stiff, his body twitching slightly. *He was scared* as he looked me up and down.

My anger flared and I rolled my eyes. At that moment, I wasn't sure if I was more angry at Dr. Hidalgo, Mason, or myself. Mason was scared and I was making things worse. Even as the thought crossed my mind I couldn't hold my tongue.

"We could," I said, my stomach bubbling. "But *why should we?*" I pleaded, wanting someone to fight on my side. I bit the inside of my cheek, the waves of pain keeping me somewhat in control.

He shook his head, and shrugged. No trace of a fake smile remaining when his eyes met mine again.

"We fucked once," I said. "Don't pretend you know *anything* about me." I wrenched my arms and grimaced, whipping my face away from him and pressing my forehead down against the cool metal table.

"Casual sexual partners," Dr. Hidalgo said, her voice chipper and upbeat. "You must have had *fantastic chemistry*?"

I pressed my forehead harder against the steel, the cool surface disappearing, replaced by heat burning from my skin. She was right—of course—and that made me angry in a whole new way.

"We knew of each other," I heard Mason try and explain, his voice shaky. "Same circles, friends-of-friends." He stumbled over his words, his voice cracking on the final word. He was going to talk *and lie* whether I liked it or not. I hadn't so much as heard his name spoken before we met.

"Did you date?" Dr. Hidalgo asked.

"No," I said, my head still pressed against the warm steel, eyes cast down to look at my bare feet.

"No," Mason echoed. "We did meet once for coffee afterwards."

"That wasn't a date," I said, scrunching up my face. I looked up at Mason. "That was *me* telling *you* that I was *pregnant*." I knew I was being mean and condescending, but all I could feel in the moment was a deep, simmering rage.

"I know." Mason's voice dropped. "But you did call, and we did meet up." His eyes were fixed on mine now, widening as he turned his body away from Dr. Hidalgo. What was he doing? Trying to impress her?

"*Ten weeks later*," I hissed. "It hardly counts." Why wasn't he trying to impress *me*? As soon as the thought crossed my mind, I cringed. Why did I *care*?

I could hear Dr. Hidalgo tapping her tablet incessantly. The sound irritated me, and I clenched my teeth to not snap.

"So why did you call me then?" Mason said, his cheeks flushing pinker the more he spoke.

"You had the right to know," I shrugged my shoulders in an awkward, bound way.

"Miss Avery," Dr. Hidalgo cut over the top of our weirdly intimate conversation. "You clearly believe fathers have rights in pregnancy?" She phrased her words as a question.

"To a certain extent," I replied, choosing my words carefully. "Although the government apparently has more rights than both the mother and father combined," I snapped, huffing and puffing. I was just being petty now, but I couldn't stop.

"The government regulates the population, Miss Avery," Dr. Hidalgo said, her voice low and controlled. "We have seen the devastating effects of overpopulation in other countries."

"We have," I shot back, pulling my head up from the table and forcing myself to look Dr. Hidalgo in the eye. "And yet, before *this*, I saw *twelve* doctors for sterilisation…and yet *here I am*. Because women are *still* not trusted to decide the future of their reproductive health." I wanted to throw my hands in the air or smash my fists against the table, but I couldn't do any of that tethered and in a towel.

"I'm sorry, Miss Avery," Dr. Hidalgo said after a long, silent pause. "It's clear the system has failed you." She smiled weakly, her eyes welling and on the verge of spilling over. I had been right. Dr. Hidalgo had a hidden story—but didn't we all?

"This entire experience," I whispered, "has been mind-boggling. I never intended to *get* pregnant, let alone wind up with a genius baby growing in my womb." I laughed at my use of the words *genius baby*. I stared down at the tiny bump that lay beneath my towel, a pang racing through my heart.

"But here we are," Mason said, interrupting the strange sensation of longing that had washed over me.

"Here we are," I said, sighing. I looked at Mason's face, and gave him a forced smile. This wasn't his fault, and I was just as guilty of making this mistake as he was. My anger at him was ebbing, guilt taking over as we stared at each other.

The black cords released my arms, winding down and shooting back into the table. They disappeared with four loud clicks.

Immediately, I scooped my arms off the table, rubbing at the deep indentations where the cords had pressed into my skin. The mottled redness spread as I scratched and rubbed them, holding them close to my chest.

I felt a gentle arm wrap around my shoulders. Mason's warm breath tickled the back of my neck. I stiffened, dropping my arms and head, my heart thumping. He squeezed my shoulder three times before backing off as if I might bite.

Clearing my throat with a loud growling cough, I turned to Dr. Hidalgo, who had been sitting silently, watching us.

"What happens now?" My hands fidgeted in my lap.

Dr. Hidalgo rose to her feet. "Fortunately, or unfortunately, Miss Avery," she said, "with paternity confirmed by testing and both of you today, you pass."

I nodded, stunned and questioning if the rest of the personal questions had been for Dr. Hidalgo's own morbid curiosity.

"You will return to your room for the next fourteen days. Until we can carry out the final testing on the foetus."

For the first time I felt thankful that she had used the word foetus and not baby.

"Everything will be provided for you. If the foetus passes their final test, you will officially enter *the lottery*." The words hung on Dr.

Hidalgo's tongue like liquid gold. She spoke them so carefully, so gently, that they seemed on the edge of magic.

I nodded again, unable to put my feelings into words.

"Mason," Dr. Hidalgo said, turning away from my vacant stare. "You will return to your life outside." My body stuck in place, I could see a flicker of movement out of the corner of my eye.

With a jolt, my mind came back into my body as Mason crouched down in front of me. His pale arms were covered in red welts from the black cords.

"Hey," he said, looking up at me, his light brown eyes full of concern. "I know this isn't what you wanted...I wish I could trade places with you." His twitchy smile was endearing.

"Mr. McConnell," Dr. Hidalgo said, standing in the doorway.

Mason gave her a nod before turning back to me.

"I hope after this is all over, you'll let me take you on a proper date," he said, a cheeky grin and wink following his words, along with an on-cue flush of his pale cheeks.

"Maybe I will," I said, winking back at him. And I meant it.

"Mr. McConnell," Dr. Hidalgo said again. This time her voice was firm, almost curt.

With one last look, Mason rose to his feet, kissing my forehead on the way up before he spun away. He hovered in the open door for a few seconds, a little shake of his head visible before striding out.

Dr. Hidalgo let the door close behind him, and then turned to face me. She slid into the chair opposite me, shoulders now relaxed.

I dropped my eyes; Dr. Hidalgo's face was now parallel with mine.

"He's a good man," I whispered, breaking the silence between us.

"He is," Dr. Hidalgo confirmed with a soft nod.

"I'm not such a good woman," I said, lifting my head, my eyes meeting Dr. Hidalgo's as I gave her a sad smile.

Dr. Hidalgo shrugged, then reached out and put her hand on mine.

"You don't have to be a good woman, you only have to be a good person."

I smiled weakly, feeling the edges of my mouth twitch. My eyes itched, tears welling from somewhere deep within But I refused to acknowledge them.

"I tried to be a good woman," Dr. Hidalgo said in a whispered tone, "and all it got me was eight forced terminations and divorce papers." Her voice was low and sad.

I put my hand on top of hers, giving it a quick squeeze before clearing my throat and looking away. I tilted my head back, blinking a few times until the tears that had reared their heads disappeared.

"We don't all have to want the same things, Miss Avery," Dr. Hidalgo said, standing up and picking up her tablet again.

"And yet, the world expects all women to be the same," I said. "Regardless of our feelings about children."

I stood, stretching one handed as I kept a tight hold on the towel. I paused for a few seconds while Dr. Hidalgo composed herself and tapped on her tablet. I felt almost sorry for her when I suddenly realised I hadn't properly processed a critical piece of information.

"Did you say *fourteen days in isolation*?" I turned to look at her.

"I did, Miss Avery," Dr. Hidalgo said without looking up; to her, this detail seemed perfectly normal.

I stood rooted to the spot, a beat of sweat dripping down the back of my neck as my stomach lurched violently.

Lunging, I grabbed the nearest trashcan and threw up. The vomit burned my throat and bubbled in my stomach. With a second heave, more hit the plastic with a soft *thump*.

A third heave came and then disappeared, my body stiffening and then relaxing. I slumped against the wall, my hair stuck to my forehead with sweat as I fanned myself.

"Isn't morning sickness supposed to be the first twelve weeks?" I barked at Dr. Hidalgo as if she was at fault.

I spat into the garbage can, my mouth feeling furry and acidic.

"Usually," Dr. Hidalgo said, peering at me and looking me up and down. "Should we check on the foetus? Measure its growth?" Her words were phrased like a question, but before I could answer, she was on her feet, heels clicking across the floor. She wrenched open the heavy wooden door and held it open, nodding for me to follow.

I stayed a few paces behind, both watching her and allowing my eyes to dart around the barren facility. I still hoped I would be able to map this level, even as we twisted and turned through the tunnels. A few minutes later, we entered a small area filled with interview rooms. Each room had a tiny window that allowed you to watch the person within. A pulse of relief washed through me when we reached the last door. Every room was empty.

We turned off the main laneway and into a small corridor. This corridor was plain, with three different coloured doors on each side.

Dr. Hidalgo stopped in front of a green one, swiping something at the side before it swung open with a soft *swoosh*. My eyes lingered on the amber and red doors further down the corridor for a few extra seconds before I turned and followed Dr. Hidalgo.

The bright lights flickered on, and I blinked a few times before blurting, "Why are the doors different colours?"

Dr. Hidalgo clicked her tongue and sighed, her back to me. She was dragging a small machine forward. She said nothing, and that only fuelled my curiosity.

"Hop up," she said, eyeing the chair.

With a frown, I complied. I could hear Dr. Hidalgo's laboured breathing as she dragged the machine into place beside me. I sunk down, and the chair reclined back. Within seconds my feet were almost level with my shoulders.

I squirmed, trying to get comfortable. Dr. Hidalgo pressed a rapid series of buttons.

A whirring sound filled the room, followed by a flash of light as the screen flickered on next to my head. It was white for a few seconds, before turning a deep black. Dr. Hidalgo pressed a wand up against her arm.

Movement flickered on the screen, a few blob-like shapes appearing momentarily.

"Shall we have a look?" Dr. Hidalgo waved the white wand in my direction, tapping the edge of the chair right across from my stomach.

I groaned, realising *again* that I was wearing nothing but a towel.

I draped the towel across myself, trying pathetically to cover everything and wishing I had at least put on underwear.

Dr. Hidalgo stifled a chuckle by clearing her throat. She stared at the machine and pushed down on my stomach. I watched the black screen flicker, different shapes coming to life, a grainy white blob appearing on the screen.

Shifting in my seat, I raised myself up to my elbows, squinting at the screen, trying to emulate Dr. Hidalgo's narrowed eyes and head tilt so I could see what she saw.

A soft drumming filled the room—the sound emanated from the screen. I stared at it for a second before looking around, trying to find the source of the noise.

"The heartbeat," Dr. Hidalgo whispered, a soft, sad smile planted on her face.

"Is everything..." I whispered, staring back at the small screen in front of me. My eyes widened at the odd circles and flickering parts. I was suddenly breathless waiting for more information.

"*Perfect*."

She clicked a few more buttons, and I exhaled and laid back again.

Dr. Hidalgo's wand hand disappeared from my stomach. With a side-ways glance, I watched her fiddle with the screen, her eyes glued to it, her fingers moving between the buttons.

I looked away, pulling the towel back around myself as the noise of the machine being dragged away filled the small room. It all felt so surreal.

"Here," Dr. Hidalgo said, waving a small photograph back and forth in her hands before handing it to me.

My hand shook as I took the photograph from her: a printout of the little white dots that looked almost alien to me.

"Could you..." My words fell back into the pit of my stomach. I was half-embarrassed and half-desperate for her to help me.

Dr. Hidalgo closed the gap between us; gently placing her hand on top of mine. She leaned in close to look at the print with me.

"Head," she said, pointing her long, red nail at a misshapen circle to the upper-left side of the photograph. "And here's the torso." Her hand moved down to trace another part. "And here at the bottom are ten toes." She gave my arm a little squeeze and stepped away, her back turning to me.

"Dr. Hidalgo?" I said, my voice shaking. "Does the baby have ten fingers, too?" I stared down at the photograph. I didn't know why I asked, why I used the word *baby*, why I was asking so much of the doctor who had been forced to have multiple terminations.

With a loud sniff, Dr. Hidalgo returned to my side, this time wrapping her arm around my shoulders. "Right there," she said, clearing her throat and pointing to tiny shadows on the print. I could tell she was hurting and heartbroken, and somehow that shattered part of the wall I had built up.

"Thank you," I whispered, closing my eyes, the tears welling up and spilling down my cheeks. "I know I shouldn't ask," I said through quiet sobs, my body heaving and sighing.

"Ask, Miss Avery," Dr. Hidalgo said, her chest heaving beside me, her voice crackly and strained. She held me tight and close, and I had never been more grateful for another woman's comforting arms.

"Can you tell gender this early?"

"I have a hunch," Dr. Hidalgo said, her voice sounding happy for the first time. "But no, officially it is too early." I nodded, trying to wipe the tears away, but they fell as quickly as I tried to hide them.

"Seems I've opened the floodgates now," I said, half-laughing, half-crying as I looked up at Dr. Hidalgo. "I'm going to blame the hormones," I added with a shrug, following it up with a genuine grin as the tears continued to stream down my face, cascading off my cheeks. It felt strange to cry tears that were both happy and sad; joyous and heartbroken.

Dr. Hidalgo laughed and pulled away, wiping her own face before turning back to me. I frowned at her, half-annoyed that her make-up seemed undisturbed, but mostly purely grateful for her support.

"Now." She cleared her throat and looked down at me. "We need to get you back to your room." She smiled, her eyes still glazed.

I hopped down from the bed, fidgeting and tugging at my towel. Dr. Hidalgo pulled open the door.

"Next time, make sure to dress first before you attempt to escape," Dr. Hidalgo said. She still smiled, but her voice had snapped back to its professional tone, no hint of the tears from before remaining.

"Thank you." I wiped away the last of the tears, my face feeling hot underneath my fingers.

"You will be isolated in your room from today for fourteen days," Dr. Hidalgo said matter-of-factly. Her steps were too long and too quick as we walked back the way we came, and I struggled to keep up. "All food and water will be provided, although no unlocked doors this time." She glanced back at me with a raised eyebrow. "In addition, a nurse will attend to you every 72 hours."

"A nurse?" I interrupted.

"Yes, Miss Avery, a nurse. They will check you over, check your blood pressure and pulse, and ensure that you and the foetus are healthy."

I nodded, a deep pang pulling inside my chest. I was nervous about isolation. That kind of time alone could send anyone mad—being stuck with only their own spinning thoughts.

"On day fourteen of your time in this facility, you will be sixteen weeks pregnant," Dr. Hidalgo continued. Her voice was almost robotic, and I could see the pain etched on her face. She was just as much a prisoner in this place as I was—just in a very different way.

"Day fourteen is the day we administer the final test to determine your suitability to officially enter *the lottery*." Dr. Hidalgo's last two words hung on her lips, enunciated in a strange, strangled way. It was the way women had said it for years, as if it was somehow a secret-club and a life-long goal.

We rounded another corner, and I watched the rooms zoom past. Her feet moved fast, the click of her heels louder with each step as she practically jogged, and I hurried to keep up.

A huge sigh of relief escaped when Dr. Hidalgo rounded a final familiar corner, coming to a halt outside my room.

I hobbled down the long corridor, pawing at a stitch on my left side.

Dr. Hidalgo stood there, waiting. She looked as desperate to get out of here as I did. As I tried to formulate a question, the door swung open and Dr. Hidalgo caught it gracefully. She held it open, and I stepped across the threshold. She nodded at me before letting the door go as soon as possible.

"Wait," I grabbed the door and stuck my head back out. "I'll need to make a few phone calls." The words jumbled out, as much of a mess as I was. "Work doesn't know…and my friends were waiting when I came in." The words were panicky and rushed. "I-I had forgotten with everything else going on." I dropped my head into my hands. The weight of my new reality threatening to crush me as Dr. Hidalgo brushed me off. It felt as though I had been living in a strange twilight state, and by the doctor's explanation, it was two weeks ago that Kit and Darcy sat in that tiny waiting room—and I never came back.

"Everything is taken care of, Miss Avery. Your office has been notified of your advancement. Your rent and bills will be paid by Epitome Lab." Dr. Hidalgo swivelled on her heel and took a few steps before I called out again. She'd made no mention of Kit and Darcy, and I had to try one more time for my own conscience.

"Can I *please* make a phone call?" I said, my voice pathetically soft and choked up.

Dr. Hidalgo turned to look at me, her hard eyes softened momentarily.

"Not tonight, Miss Avery. I will see what I can organise in the coming days." When she let her guard down, in those tiny moments, she was kind and caring. "Good night, Miss Avery," she added gently. She pulled the door shut behind her.

A shiver ran down my spine, and I wrapped my arms around my shoulders, my fingers tracing across the newly replaced stitches at the nape of my neck.

Hands falling to my sides, I stared up at the ceiling, and the tears came again. Every emotion came pouring out, and I stood frozen for a long time, just letting myself *feel*.

For the first time, I acknowledged that I was in trouble, and *no one was coming to save me.*

CHAPTER SIXTEEN

DAY THIRTEEN

THREE LOUD RAPS ON THE DOOR MADE ME JUMP AND SCRAMBLE OUT OF bed. A second ago I had been half-awake and trying to stay asleep, and now I was desperate for any human contact.

"Hello?" I said, my voice high and hopeful.

"Are you decent, Miss Avery?" Dr. Hidalgo's familiar voice echoed through the wooden door—still matter-of-fact, but kinder than other days.

"Yes," I said, stepping back from the door. I checked the top button on my pyjama top to be sure.

The door swung open, and Dr. Hidalgo glided through. "Good Morning, Miss Avery." A gentle smile swept across her face.

"Good morning." I stared at Dr. Hidalgo, eyes wide, jaw agape. "Y-you—" I stammered, staring at the doctor who was dressed in a casual black t-shirt and a pair of tight-fitting blue jeans. But most shocking: no tablet was attached to the end of her arm.

"It is technically my day off," Dr. Hidalgo said with a sharp curl of her lip, fidgeting ever-so-slightly with her black t-shirt before continuing. "But I wanted to give you *this* before testing tomorrow." She held out her hand, a folded white piece of paper outstretched towards me. "Open it," she said as I gripped the paper and tore it open.

"A phone number?" My eyebrows furrowed. I had a talent for remembering numbers and this one was unfamiliar.

"Kit and Darcy are waiting on the other end of that number," Dr. Hidalgo said, her smile changing to an almost smirk. This was the kindest gift anyone had ever given me, and I couldn't hide my excitement. My eyes traced the number again, the edges blurring as tears welled in my eyes.

"Thank you," I choked out, furiously wiping the tears away and smiling at her. Just the idea that I would soon hear their voices was almost enough to send me into hysterics.

"The room phone has been switched to outgoing for the next forty-five minutes. The only number that will work is that one in your hand." Dr. Hidalgo gave me a hard look. Her eyes darted between the phone and me, brows creased. *Message received.* I didn't have anyone else I wanted to talk to anyway—except maybe Mason.

I pushed that thought away and smiled. "Thank you," I said again. She turned her back to me and pulled open the wooden door with one swift flick of her wrist.

She shot me a last warning look as the door clicked shut. With trembling hands, I picked up the old corded receiver attached beside the door and punched in the numbers.

The piece of paper fluttered from my hands, looping in the air as the phone rang loudly in my ear.

"Hello?" came two loud, high-pitched, jumbled voices after a single ring.

"Hello?" I said after a brief pause.

Shrill squealing was all I could hear, followed by loud, muffled movement.

"Hello?" I said again, pulling the receiver away from my ear as the rustling quietened down. All the fear and uncertainty of the last two weeks vanished in an instant, and I felt like I could finally breathe again.

"Is it really you?" Kit whispered from the other end of the phone.

"The one and only," I said back with a laugh and a giant sigh of relief.

"That sigh could only be Alice Avery," Darcy said, laughing. Her soft voice rushed through the phone, music to my ears.

"What the hell is going on?" Kit and Darcy said in unison, their tone of voice a combination of worried, curious, and excited.

"How do I even begin to explain?" I said, chuckling at the strange, breathless panting that was on the other end of the phone.

"Last we heard—" Kit started.

"You were brilliant," Darcy finished.

"And then they kicked us out," Kit said, her voice sounding almost sad now. "But we didn't go without a fight," she added, and I smiled, imagining how that would have gone.

"That was *weeks* ago," Darcy continued, her voice switching to almost whiny, which happened when she was upset. I had been right before—I *was* losing chunks of time. "And then, out of the blue, this perfect specimen of a woman showed up while we were having beers, and told us you would call."

"She handed us this really old phone and then disappeared," Kit said with a strange scoff. The realisation that Dr. Hidalgo had gone, *in person*, to see Kit and Darcy almost caused me to drop the phone. While she was all tangled up in what happened here, it was hard not to be grateful for Hidalgo in that moment. I didn't know what to say, where to start.

"Sixteen weeks tomorrow," I finally said. "If we pass the next lots of tests, it will be official."

"*The lottery*?" Kit and Darcy cooed, that same tone in their voice—full of half-questions, half-realisations. None of us knew what it really meant, to enter *the lottery;* it felt terrifyingly real now.

"You'll be a superstar!" Kit blurted, her voice quickly shifting to excitement

I groaned, my cheeks flushing red and my heart hammering in my chest with those four simple words. I had no interest in being in magazines or writing a dull and over-exaggerated biography for booksellers to hawk to hopeful young girls.

"Will they let you out?" Darcy asked, her voice breaking through over Kit's chatter about fame, red carpets, and movie star premiers.

"To do press maybe?" I tried to sound brave and matter-of-fact. "But I don't think so, not really." Kit finally quieted down with that last sentence. They both followed the winners trails more than I did, and in that moment it seemed to click that while those girls won and lived 'happily-ever-after,' there were heartbroken women left in their wake, picking up the shattered pieces of their lives. No one ever released *that* memoir, and I had a swirling hunch on the why. I cleared my throat, forcing my voice back to cheerful. "What's happening in the real world?" I asked, beaming, my voice showing no hint of sadness. I needed an escape—anything to change the subject.

"Kit met a guy!" Darcy's excited voice shot through, followed by some muffled movement and rustling. I giggled, imagining them tussling for the phone—Kit's mop of red hair bouncing around, and Darcy overpowering her with her super-strength.

"I-it's not important," Kit squeezed in before Darcy's voice returned.

"He's tall, dark, and handsome," Darcy said. An audible soft groan followed in the background.

"Come on, Kit," I said, laughing and feeling the swell in my heart. "I need some new gossip."

"Ask Darcy about how her competition went!" Kit's voice was high-pitched and muffled, having had the phone yanked away from her.

"Darcy!" I squealed, pacing back-and-forth as far as the corded receiver would let me go.

"Fucking second," shot Darcy's haughty voice. I could just imagine her standing there, head pushed against her shoulder to hold the phone, arms crossed against her chest, eyebrows furrowed in deep annoyance. It was a picture-perfect vision.

I laughed, feeling my entire chest and upper torso shake while I listened to them bicker, their voices coming and going as they fought to keep the phone and share more news with me. The ache in my chest tightened. I missed the women who had been like sisters to this sad, parentless, only-child.

"Can I switch back to me for a moment?" I blurted, whilst in the middle of laughing at Darcy's expense. "What *the hell* happens if I succeed tomorrow?" I let the air fall out of my mouth in a loud huff.

Muffled silence came from the other side of the phone.

"Well," Kit finally said, "I guess you had better decide which of us will accompany you on your world tour." She giggled.

"Oh, and you mean *when*?" Darcy interrupted.

I groaned and laughed, causing myself to snort loudly. It was nice to talk about the silly aspects of this nightmare, Darcy was the *queen* of keeping things light.

I sat down on the edge of my bed, clutching the phone to my ear, sure it was red-raw.

"You would both come, right?" I said, my voice overlapping the chatter between them.

"YES!" they yelled down the phone in unison.

I clutched my hand to my chest, my heart beating against my fingers.

"What is the next test?" Darcy asked.

I paused for a second, a frown imprinting itself on my forehead. "Honestly, I'm not sure," I said. "I know it is a test for the foetus, but that's it. The technology here is next level, though." I quickly followed that with: "If I didn't have concerns about the ethical standards they meet, or *don't* meet, I would love access to it."

"Wait," Kit asked, her voice coming into focus. "Have you experienced any of the tech?"

I rolled my eyes in a loving, frustrated way, realising that someone who works in the IT field would be fascinated with what was happening at the Epitome Lab.

"Yes," I said, trying to keep my next description of the Oculus Origins' technology succinct. "It's a deep dive. It's everyday life, but—" A beep sounded loud and blaring in my ear—a warning. As the receiver cut back in, I could hear Kit's rambling questions, but I knew I couldn't answer any more.

"But how dotheygetyou in, and howdotheykeep youunder, and howdothey gatherdata?" Her questions all ran together, her words crashing into each other as they tumbled out of her mouth at a ferocious speed. She was as fascinated as I was, just from a different perspective.

"Whoa, whoa, take it down a notch," Darcy laughed, wrestling the phone away from Kit for a second time.

"Honestly," I said, pinching the bridge of my nose, "all I know is what I lived through, and I promise to give you every detail I remember the next time we see each other." My words felt heavy, partially because I wasn't sure when that would be, and because I honestly didn't know if it was true. The warning tone was enough to remind me that this was a privilege they could snatch away.

"When will that be?" Kit mumbled sullenly in the background. I was unsure if she was upset about not seeing me or not getting more information about the technology available here.

"When *will* we see you again?" Darcy asked.

"Another question I don't know the answer to." I shrugged, my index finger now tangled in the receiver cord.

"Maybe you'll find out more after the next test?" Darcy said, her voice soft.

"Maybe." I didn't want to sound too sad or too hopeful.

"THIS IS YOUR 10 MINUTE WARNING MISS AVERY," Dr. Hidalgo's voice blared over the speaker in my room, the sound echoing through the small space and into the phone.

"Ten minutes left already?" The feeling of dread settled deep in my chest.

"His name is Harry," Kit said. "And tomorrow we are going on our *third* date." The not-so-subtle emphasis on third made me laugh.

"You haven't slept with him yet?" I yelped, clapping my hands and then clasping them together, almost dropping the phone. She always waited, and it was almost always a disaster. All I wanted was to be able to hear about that tale tomorrow.

"She's nervous," Darcy's loud, muffled voice yelled in the background.

"Are you?" I asked, sure she would hear the surprise in my tone.

"I'm a little nervous, *but* it's because I actually *like* this one," she said, and I couldn't tell whether those words were pointed at me or at Darcy, who was sure to be making fun of her out of earshot.

"Where, how, when?" I blurted, needing just a little more of their lives before I hung up. I needed a little more *real* before I returned to the closed-in walls.

"You'll *love* this," Darcy's voice pierced through obnoxiously.

"You know it's just been Halloween," Kit said, after a long pause. "This year I dressed as Luna Lovegood."

"And her *Harry* was there waiting for her," Darcy swooned in the background.

"They don't end up together in the books," Kit snapped, her voice pulled away from the phone. I imagined her glaring at Darcy, her piercing stare hot and focused.

"Kit," I said, trying to bring their attention back, while acutely aware the phone was going to cut out any minute. "I think that's perfect for you." My cheeks ached as my face broke into another smile —it was as if they had forgotten what smiling felt like.

"You'll have to tell me every detail when I see you..." My voice trailed off.

"Soon," Kit and Darcy said in unison.

"Oh, and don't forget—" Darcy's voice cut off abruptly.

The receiver went dead and silence rang in my ear. Not even a dial tone remained.

I dropped the receiver, and it swung back-and-forth, dangling in the air.

"I love you, too," I whispered, my hands trembling. I clasped them together to stop them from shaking. The nervous jolt relocated to my legs instead.

With a huff, I began to pace again. My horrid, now-stained pyjama shirt fell below my knees as my bare feet carried me back and forth down the same small pacing track I had followed every day for the last two weeks.

"PLEASE CHECK THE DOOR FOR YOUR DAILY PARCEL," Dr. Hidalgo's voice boomed through the room, replacing the usual automated voice. It was as if she had turned the speaker to full volume.

I cringed, covering my ears even though her voice was gone as quickly as it had interrupted. I wanted to call out to her, to thank her, to ask her a hundred questions. Instead, with a sigh, I moved to the door, hovering until the package was squished through the hatch that had been installed after my escape attempt.

A smile, then a frown creeped across my face as I stared down at today's delivery.

Dr. Hidalgo had come through again. The dress for day fourteen was beautiful.

Dress in hand, I sunk down onto the bed. Ready or not, tomorrow would come, and this would end in one tragedy or another.

CHAPTER SEVENTEEN

DAY FOURTEEN

A LOUD RAP AT THE DOOR MADE ME JUMP. I HAD BEEN READY FOR HOURS, pacing and waiting for day fourteen to begin.

Dr. Hidalgo stood in the now-open doorway, flanked by two male nurses, both in full blue scrubs and matching face masks.

"Good morning, Miss Avery," Dr. Hidalgo said with a full-blown grin. I had never been more excited to see her. I had missed human contact and leaving my room more than I cared to admit.

"Good morning." I grinned back at her.

Dr. Hidalgo waved her hand at me, then snapped her fingers at the nurses.

"Final weight and measurements before we officially start phase two." The two nurses bustled around me as Dr. Hidalgo juggled her ever-present tablet.

With a sigh, I consented, pushing my shoulders back. I stepped forward, and the two male nurses swarmed me on either side.

"As of today, the foetus is the size of an apple," Dr. Hidalgo said with a nod. A piece of tape threaded around my midsection by a pair of warm hands. Within seconds, they were gone, and Dr. Hidalgo was talking again.

"Twelve centimetres," she added matter-of-factly.

"Do you mean my stomach has grown *twelve* centimetres?" I didn't mean to sound shallow, but the quiver in my voice gave me away.

"Yes, Miss Avery." Dr. Hidalgo didn't lift her eyes from the tablet.

"Step," instructed a deep, male voice to my left.

A small, black, portable scale now sat in front of my feet. The scales and I had never gotten along, but it seemed in pregnancy people were fine with the number going up.

I stepped on, and the numbers ticked in a steady journey upwards. I closed my eyes, deciding at the last second I still didn't want to know. Normal or not, weight was a tricky subject.

"Good," Dr. Hidalgo said. I stepped off with a sigh halfway between relief and exasperation.

"You're gaining weight slowly," Dr. Hidalgo said. "Why the sigh?"

I smiled at her, knowing she was being kind, and shook my head. My brain was still catching up with the fact that I was pregnant, and this was real.

"Come," she said, waving me over. "Sit." One of the male nurses set a chair down in front of me. "Last thing," Dr. Hidalgo said when I didn't move.

I walked around the bed, lowering myself down into the flimsy chair.

Warm hands touched my arms on both sides, tugging up my sleeves. One wrapped something around my left arm and the other straightened it out before poking a few times. I looked back and forth between my two arms, impressed at the quick ease of the two men at work.

"Thank you," I said awkwardly as they both stepped away, my blood drained and my throbbing arm returning to normal. I wasn't thankful for the circumstances, but their hands were kind.

"Go," Dr. Hidalgo said, turning her back on me to talk to the nurses. She barked a few mysterious orders, and they bowed and backed away. They waited until she turned back to face me before they sprinted away.

The frown carving its way into my forehead was overtaken by a giggle as I watched them run.

Dr. Hidalgo smiled at me—a soft, genuine smile.

"All looks good from a medical standpoint," she said. "Within half-an-hour, we'll have the blood tests back and I can medically clear you to compete in the next portion of the preliminaries." But her voice seemed to waver as she spoke.

"I can feel flutters now," I whispered. The words came out before I could stop them. "I can *feel* backflips in my stomach." My eyes grew wide and brimmed with tears. I felt more emotional saying this aloud than I had every time I had felt the movements in the last week. It wasn't like me—but even I was losing track of who I was through all of this.

"The foetus is hitting all milestone markers," Dr. Hidalgo said, coughing and clearing her throat. "It is to be expected." Her voice was nonchalant, but her eyes brimmed with tears as well. She smiled, giving me a little extra nod.

"Time to get ready, Miss Avery," she went on, stepping backwards over the small lip that signalled the beginning of my bedroom. "As soon as the bloods arrive, we will go to a new location."

I nodded, keeping my face blank. I fidgeted with the dress I had been wearing for hours. The fabric scratched against my skin, and I pulled at it, wishing the long sleeves were short and the high-neck was lower.

"Are you going to do your hair?" Dr. Hidalgo was pacing in the doorway; a deep frown crept onto her face, unaccompanied by frown-lines, which left me wondering if she'd had anti-aging injections.

I scratched the back of my head. "I did try…" I shrugged. "I'll tie it up." I reached up to tug my hair into its signature messy bun.

Another loud, exasperated sigh followed, unmatched by the soft smile on the doctor's face. "Sit," she clicked, motioning to the chair left behind by the nurses.

She walked past me, letting the door close behind her. She returned with a handful of ties, clips, and bobby pins, which she dumped into my hands.

We sat in silence, Dr. Hidalgo pulling the brush through my hair, stopping every few seconds to tease out a knot. I tried not to grimace too obviously.

"Pin," Dr. Hidalgo said, after what felt like three hours of brushing.

I held up my hand, unsure exactly what she wanted.

Her taloned fingers ran through my hair, pulling out strands and pinching and prodding at my scalp.

With a flurry of pins, twists, flicks, and the snap of a hairband, Dr. Hidalgo proclaimed she was done. "Perfect," she clapped, before promptly sticking another three bobby pins into my head, deep enough that I let out a whimper.

She walked around to my front, leaning over me and fiddling with the tiny hairs that had escaped and hung down over the right side of my face, another pin saving the day.

"Enough, enough," I said, throwing my hands up at her. I tried to smile, so she knew I was appreciative, but my skull couldn't handle another pin.

She looked me up and down, her eyes running over my hair for longer than anywhere else, before giving me a nod.

Standing inches apart, Dr. Hidalgo gave my shoulder a squeeze. "Miss Avery—"

A loud tap at the door interrupted her. She cleared her throat and turned away from me, then threw open the door. I wished she'd had another thirty seconds; instead, a lone male nurse stood in the doorway, clutching a tablet with a green case in his hands. He panted, sweat dripping down his brow, as if he had just been sprinting before he arrived.

"Results?"

He nodded curtly, then held out the tablet to Dr. Hidalgo.

She took it, veraciously swiping through pages of graphs, tables, charts, and blocks of words. When I tried to sneak a peek, all I could see was a blur of colours.

With a nod, she handed the small green tablet back. The nurse turned his back and scurried away.

Dr. Hidalgo stood with her back to me for a few seconds. She said nothing, and her silence unnerved me.

"Is everything..." I said after a stretch of awkward silence.

"Yes," Dr. Hidalgo cleared her throat, then ran a hand across her face and into her hair before she once again turned to face me.

"Your bloods are *exactly* where they should be," she said matter-of-factly, choosing not to elaborate any further on her weird pause. "And now," she said with a heavy sigh, "it is my job to explain to you what happens during the final pre-lottery test. Sit." She waved her hand softly at the bed.

My stomach fluttered as I perched myself on the edge of the bed, inches away from Dr. Hidalgo. She remained standing, her tablet cast aside on the chair, her arms crossed against her chest.

As I pulled myself up onto the bed properly, I watched her as she drummed her fingers against her arm. Whatever was coming, I was glad I was sitting, even if I wasn't ready.

"Until now," she said, "you have competed alone." Her fingers tapped more rapidly against her arm, and my heart followed suit, banging in my chest and hanging on her every word. "Today, that changes in more than one way."

CHAPTER EIGHTEEN

ECHO VR

I SWAYED FROM FOOT-TO-FOOT IN A LINE FULL OF SILENT WOMEN. EACH wore a different dress—but just as beautiful and elaborate as mine—in three distinct colours: green, orange, or red. Each stood perfectly still, and it was clear I was the only one struggling to keep my hands and feet still.

After a beat, the last woman in a red, billowing dress was called forth by the lone male figure. She walked with wobbly legs towards the dark-suited Gatekeeper with a tablet and an uneven smile. His harsh warning to *remain quiet* was still echoing in my ears as he ushered through the women one-by-one.

He tapped a few buttons before the woman was asked to hold her fingerprint on the screen. Within moments, he ushered her inside. She followed in the footsteps of the other red-dress clad women that had disappeared before her. I tried to keep count but was distracted by their blank faces and wide eyes. I swallowed hard as the first woman from the orange dress group was called forward. Her dress hung too big across her shoulders, and watching her stumble up the stairs left me shaken and unsteady.

My body swayed and my mind slipped into repeats of my conversation with Dr. Hidalgo. Everything and nothing played on my mind as it drew closer to my turn. I hated the way they categorised the women who had given up everything to be here; I wondered fleetingly if other women felt like I did, or if I was a strange anomaly. I didn't have time to think as the woman directly in front of me ascended the short set of stairs. She hovered at the top, hushed words rocketing between woman and Gatekeeper, before she pressed her finger onto the tablet. The black door opened seconds later to usher her inside.

"*Good luck*," a cold voice slithered from behind me. The woman's breath against my skin sent a shiver down my spine, and I resolutely stared straight ahead.

With a small wave of his hand, the Gatekeeper looked me dead in the eye.

I took the few steps forward, placing my feet carefully as I climbed the stairs, not wanting to stumble.

At the top, I looked into the warm hazel eyes of the Gatekeeper.

"Miss Alice Avery," he said, swiping through the screens on his tablet, his eyes narrowing to meet mine. He gave me a brief nod, and then tapped through a few prompts, the lack of sound off-putting after listening to Dr. Hidalgo's fingernails *click* on the screen for weeks.

"Right hand index finger please." He turned the tablet to face me.

With a slight quiver, I placed my finger against the cool glass. The lines and swirls of my fingertip turned red, then yellow, and finally green.

"*Good luck*, Miss Avery," the Gatekeeper said. The black door swung open.

With lead feet, I stepped through the doorway. It snapped closed behind me as soon as I crossed the threshold.

I stood in almost darkness, the only light coming from the end of a long, narrow hallway.

"Miss Avery," barked a short, stubby figure from the end of the corridor, shrouded in light. She gave me no chance to answer. "Come," she snapped at me, her short frame scurrying away as I hurried to keep up.

"What is this place?" I broke into a jog, swiftly closing the gap between us. My eyes widened as we turned the corner.

The once shining light at the end of the corridor now illuminated the top of a winding set of stairs descending into darkness.

"Welcome to the testing centre," she said matter-of-factly, already three steps down.

I stood at the top for a few extra seconds, my jaw hanging open. A large, round room was carved into the earth, the harsh concrete walls perfectly round and smooth.

Each of the fourteen women that had entered before me were below. The colour of their dresses were the only colour I could see on the entire floor.

They had each been taken into small bays, separated by thin concrete walls.

The woman who had led me in cleared her throat, her arms crossed and an unimpressed scowl imprinted on her forehead when I tore my eyes away to look at her.

I opened my mouth, and she waved me away, turning her back to me and descending a few more steps. She clearly wanted me to hurry up, but I was in awe of the view from this vantage point.

The wooden banister was cool and smooth under my fingers. My feet moved slower than ever as I followed her down into the depths of the testing centre.

Each woman had multiple people in the bay with her; threading this tube and inserting that needle. Each lay flat on a small metal bed with a blue mattress, feet bare.

We reached the bottom of the staircase, and I stumbled, my foot reaching for another step. I had never felt so curious and simultaneously full of nerves.

"You are in bay fifteen, Miss Avery," the woman said. Her scowl imprinted so deeply on her forehead that it looked like a scar. She clicked her fingers, both towards the bay and at me.

With an awkward nod, and a distinct lack of words, I walked towards my bay. The concrete wall to the left had *Bay 15* scrawled in messy handwriting on the wall.

There was no door, just a narrow, open space.

Hovering, I peered into the room, the same small metal bed and blue mattress as in the other bays positioned in the middle.

The air smelt of clean towels and hospital grade sanitiser. The combination burned my eyes and nose as I inched through the narrow doorway towards the bed.

My fingers clipped the blue plastic, and a loud voice rang out from behind me, causing me to jump and swivel.

The woman from behind me in line stood in my doorway, hands firmly placed on her hips. She looked me up and down a few times, a strange, condescending smirk on her face.

"Good luck," she echoed, her eyes wild and lit up. "*Commoner,*" she whispered, so only I could hear her.

"Mrs. Astley," the harsh bark of the short woman who had shown me in cut through the tension. "You should know better than to speak to the other contestants." Her harsh voice was loud and commanding, and I was glad I wasn't on the receiving end.

"I was just wishing her good luck," the woman called Mrs. Astley said, softening her eyes and putting on a fake smile before turning away from me. I rolled my eyes. If she wanted to make an enemy, she had immediately succeeded.

The woman waved her away, pushing her towards the final bay.

"Shoes off." The short woman snapped her fingers at me. She hadn't looked at me at all. I was only a number in a bay.

I looked down at my bare feet, realising I hadn't put shoes on.

"No wonder she knows I'm a commoner." I sighed and grimaced, wishing Dr. Hidalgo had made me put on shoes before letting me out in this new world.

"Lay down," the woman snapped, her eyes narrowed at my jumpy movements. The nerves were getting the better of me, so I bit my cheeks and swung my legs up. The cool plastic of the mattress crinkled and pressed against my exposed skin. I wriggled, pulling myself further up towards the top so my feet wouldn't dangle over the bottom of the bed.

It was hard to believe I was here, laying on my back in a sterile room, just panicking and waiting for my fate.

"Miss Avery?" A new, kind voice came from the foot of the bed.

"Yes?" It sounded far more like a question than an answer. "Yes," I corrected myself. If nothing else felt right, familiar, or comfortable, I could at least be certain that I was Alice Avery.

In the doorway stood two people dressed in scrubs. They both smiled as they dragged in an array of equipment.

"We'll be looking after you today," the female nurse said sweetly. She came up near my head, her round face young and lineless, the smile planted upon it genuine and kind.

I nodded, my eyes unable to stop bouncing between the two nurses. Their presence instantly made me breathe a little easier.

"Have you been in this position before?" the same nurse asked, her warm hand coming to rest on my shoulder.

"No." I shook my head, remembering Dr. Hidalgo's mention of eight terminations and having a new level of pity for women who kept trying regardless of the tragedies on the inside of *the lottery*. It seemed some women would continue to try, despite their own test scores being low, or their foetuses being nothing but ordinary. This was the pull towards motherhood that I would never understand.

"Well..." Her fingers gripped my shoulder and gave it a tight squeeze. "Nurse Benjamin—" Her eyes swung towards her busy companion, who had stayed near my feet and waved without turning around. "—and Nurse Amy are here to walk you through it."

I looked up at her, my shoulders slackening. Her kindness and sincerity were rare, and I held back tears of gratitude. I was already crying all the time from sadness and frustration; I didn't want to add a new emotion to the list.

"Thank you, Nurse Benjamin and Nurse Amy" I whispered, my hand reaching across and giving hers a squeeze.

She knelt down, her mouth only a few centimetres away from my ear. "Just Amy and Benjamin are fine, sweetheart. Too much of a mouthful otherwise." Amy squeezed my shoulder and got back to work.

"I would love to see a *normal* woman win." She winked at me as she stood up, clearing her throat. I hated the labels–*normal, common, ordinary* but it was the fundamental truth of who I was.

I loathed that even at this stage in the competition, in the throes of all that was about to unfold, it was still clear who was favoured. "Now." Amy clasped her hands together and snapping my attention back to her. "How much of an explanation do you want on what's happening?"

"*All of it.*" No hesitation existed, my head was off the pillow barely a second after Amy had asked. I stared intently at Benjamin, who fiddled with pieces of medical equipment. Curiosity would always outweigh fear, especially when science was involved—and this would be the most interesting distraction.

Amy laughed, squeezing my shoulder again before bustling around to the right side of my head.

"How much do you understand about the brain?"

"Enough," I responded. "I studied Science at University." I kept it purposefully vague, not wanting to sound like I was a know-it-all, but also not wanting them to dumb things down for me.

"Well, well," she said. "A girl after my own heart." She gave me a cracking smile. The room seemed to swell with female comradery.

Benjamin cleared his throat loudly from the corner, making me jump. I had almost forgotten that two nurses were in here with me.

"Let me explain what happens next," he said sweetly. I propped myself up on my elbows.

Amy cut in. "From our brief, we believe you understand today's basic premise. Test the foetus."

"The testing itself is straight-forward," Benjamin said, his words slicing behind Amy's in perfect rehearsed harmony. It was clear they had given this spiel together many times before.

"This is an intelligence test for foetuses," Amy said, her smile dropping with the words.

"Wait," I said, interrupting Benjamin's open mouth. "An *intelligence test for foetuses?*" My frown crept down and tugged at my lips.

"Yes," they said in unison.

When Dr. Hidalgo had told me they were testing the foetuses today, this wasn't what I had imagined.

"You understand where intelligence comes from?" Amy said, giving me a little wink.

"I understand the cerebrum controls thinking, learning, and emotion," I said back, Benjamin held up his hand, and I paused.

"What we are about to do can *predict* foetus's future development," he said, almost too casually, as if this was a normal conversation. As if this wasn't technology the rest of the world didn't know about. As if this shouldn't blow my mind.

"W-what, it—in—what?" I stuttered, the words sticking on my tongue and coming into the world jumbled. My mouth had gone dry and my brain had short-circuited.

"Deep breath." Amy squeezed my shoulder hard before walking over to the back of the room where Benjamin stood with his back to me, fiddling with instruments I couldn't see.

Amy wheeled the small trolley over, pulling with her an array of shiny silver implements, black cords, needles, and velcro straps.

"This technology is ground-breaking," Benjamin said, the excitement in his voice tangible, dulled only a little as he looked at my face.

"Let's talk as we show you," Amy piped in, throwing a heavy black cover over me. The weighted sheet covered my chest, stomach, and the tops of my thighs.

Benjamin fiddled with a small, black clicker, pointing it at a screen rapidly dropping from the ceiling.

The screen flickered on, and black pixels morphed into bones, muscles, and inner organs.

"That's your body," Amy said.

"Anywhere that weighted sheet touches, we see here," Benjamin explained, switching through a few different channels. The image of my insides changed with each click. "And this is what we are really here for." He clicked the button one last time.

The screen faded, the image zooming in on a small, grainy part of the picture.

I squinted a little, trying to bring the image into better focus.

"It's okay," Amy said with a laugh. "Most women need a moment to make sense of what they're seeing on the screen."

The image was now large enough to take up the entire screen.

"This," Benjamin stepped in, talking me through the image, "is the head." He pointed at a large, white-outlined blob. The imaging reloaded and got clearer with each passing second; it was like a lens coming into focus. The view made my skin crawl because on the screen was a *baby.*

"As the sheet uploads more data to the screen, it will become clearer, changing from this old-school black-and-white blob to a photographic 4-D image." Amy's awe of the screen was clear as she spoke, but I struggled to relate. I never imagined this moment or dreamed about children, and the shiver running down the back of my neck left me in a state of unsettled discomfort. It was incredible and terrifying that the tiny body that was rapidly filling in on the screen was *inside* my own body. I couldn't quite get used to the fact that this was actually happening.

"What kind of technology is this?" I was sure that my open mouth would fall off; my jaw ached almost as deeply as the nausea setting into my stomach.

"The secret kind," Benjamin said.

"The still-in-trial kind," Amy murmured.

The image continued flickering, more colour appearing every second. Small blue and red lines emerged on the screen.

"That's the brain filling in," she said, her eyes glued to the screen as if it was the first time she was seeing this. "All the soft tissue, nerves, neurons, and blood vessels are appearing. Mapped one-by-one by the weighted sheet that is covering you." She hovered by my side, her eyes unmoving.

"This is impossible," I whispered. The small red lines filled in as I watched wide-eyed. Even though this technology sent shivers down my spine, I was still in awe of it—it was as impressive as it was terrifying.

"It's almost finished loading." Benjamin tore his eyes away from the screen. "It never gets any less fascinating." He smiled down at me.

"Prepare yourself for the next part." His grimace told me to over-prepare.

I followed suit and tore my eyes away from the screen, consciously attempting to listen to his next words.

He continued, "To trace, track, and then project intelligence, the creators use—"

"—In our opinion—" Amy piped in over the top, still not looking at us.

"A barbaric type of technology," Benjamin finished without missing a beat.

Their repertoire made me laugh despite myself, and a little snort came out of my nose. Their comedy and timing settled my nerves a little bit.

He gripped my wrist, his warm hand sweaty against my skin.

"Once the brain is fully mapped," he said seriously, "we will trace where the cerebrum is."

"Cerebrum," I said, half-asking, half-thinking out loud to myself.

"You rem—" Benjamin got half a word out before my brain caught up and I waved him off, nodding vigorously, not wanting him to repeat himself. "Once we have mapped the full foetus, we will *plug into* the brain," he continued, talking a little slower now.

"Plug in?" I felt the frown creeping back across my forehead, my eyes caught between the screen and Benjamin.

"We want to *future* map the cerebrum and the cerebellum, and we can only do that through the brain stem," Amy said, turning her back on the screen. It was as if they were telling me what they had eaten for breakfast—not that technology existed that could map out a foetuses brain and future development.

They both faced me now, their faces plastered with what felt like soft, fake smiles as they gazed down at me. It felt strange and forced and I wanted to yell at them to stop, to just be honest with me.

"Through mapping, we can tell future intelligence, future balance, coordination, muscle control, and likelihood of incapacity or disability at full term," Amy said again, peering down at me, my eyes unblinking and stinging.

I couldn't help but stare at them with my mouth gaping open. I had put two-and-two together, but hearing it aloud was nothing short of horrifying.

Benjamin gave my wrist another squeeze, his warm hand pressing into my now cold and prickly skin. My whole body had gone cold and clammy, breaking out in a hive of goosebumps.

"You're telling me you can predict *everything*?" My brain fought between the absurdity of the situation and my scientific mind that had already gone into overdrive.

The nurses nodded in unison.

"All of it," Amy said, a sad smile on her face.

"The good and the bad," Benjamin said.

"Many women have walked through these corridors thinking they were carrying a prodigy, only for the *Echo VR* to project that by age two their child would be strikingly normal," Amy said.

"Echo VR?" I asked, the only two words that I didn't recognise in that sentence.

"The name of the technology," Benjamin said, shooting Amy a side-eye.

I nodded, bursting with questions, but not wanting to cause trouble for the nurses who had been so kind.

"How far into the future can the technology predict?" I pushed.

"The general rule is five years." Benjamin's voice softened and his eyes returned to me.

"*Five years?*" I felt my eyes go wide, the words spilling out of my mouth in shock. Every time they gave me more information, I felt more uneasy and fascinated. It has always internally been science versus humanity, but this was a new level of moral discomfort.

"Alice," Amy said, her voice breaking as she spoke. "To predict the future, there is always sacrifice." She spoke with a sudden severity. I didn't dare move. I kept my eyes on her, waiting for her to continue, waiting for her to make the rationale make sense.

I watched her suck in a deep breath before opening her mouth again.

"But," Benjamin interjected, "the next step is dangerous." He paused and waited for me to look him in the eye. "We need to connect a needle and wiring into the brain stem."

His fingers stayed wrapped around my wrist, squeezing every few seconds, as if I needed to be tethered to reality by human touch.

"A needle? Wiring?" I said, biting my lip. "Won't that hurt the foetus?" It felt strange to be asking that question, but everything already felt strange.

"In rare cases, yes. In the most unfortunate circumstances, it can kill the foetus," Benjamin said matter-of-factly. I appreciated his honesty, but it didn't make me feel any better.

"Kill?" I looked towards Amy, hoping she would say something different. She didn't. She simply nodded, her smile gone, replaced by a sad blankness.

"It's rare, but we've seen it happen."

I swallowed hard, nodding as I reminded myself that I had asked for a termination.

"I've never seen it happen with a foetus as extraordinary as yours," she whispered as she leaned over my head to puff up my pillows.

I nodded, firmer this time. If nothing else, I could outwardly be strong. It wouldn't help me or them if I lost my cool. I also didn't want to do this strapped down, but that was hardly an option.

"Let's get started?" I prompted. The nurses eyed each other, exchanging a long, hard look. Both of their lips pressed together before sharing a nod, as if this was the signal to go.

"We'll be laying you down flat," Benjamin said, coming up near my head at the same time as Amy. They both lifted the top half of the bed, and I could hear a soft, cranking grind as my head lowered down, until my top half was on the same level as my bottom half.

I wiggled, tugging at the top of my dress that now rubbed against my skin, the fabric itching me. The beautiful coloured gowns seemed like a strange kind of torture knowing what was coming.

"We wish they would just put you in hospital gowns," Amy said, as if reading my mind. She tugged my dress up and out the way.

I flashed her an awkward smile, but not much else. I could barely string a coherent thought together as we rocketed towards the next phase of testing.

"Are you ready?" she asked, her kind eyes fixated on my face.

I barely saw her. My eyes instead focused on Benjamin, who was back standing in the corner.

He picked things up off the silver tray one-by-one. Each sharp, scary tool he examined made my heart beat faster.

Amy wrapped her fingers in mine. Her hands were hard and calloused, but also warm. She squeezed hard as we sat together, watching and waiting.

"I'm ready." The words stuck in my throat, true and untrue.

But I *was* ready to get this over with.

CHAPTER NINETEEN

THE BIG SCREEN

The large tray now sat inches away from me as Amy fidgeted with the needles, wiring, scalpels, and scissors, rearranging them more than once. Benjamin fussed over me.

"Here," he said, hovering up near my head, holding two white, sticky dots.

I tore my eyes away from Amy.

"What are those?" I looked at him with a frown. Every little thing seemed suspicious.

"It's not *all* about the foetus," Benjamin said with a wink.

"For me?" I smiled, trying to bat my eyelids and play along with the joke even as my insides quivered.

"Here and here." He tapped my chest lightly on either side of where my heart was located.

I did as I was told, placing them under my high-necked, now insufferably itchy dress. The fabric stretched when I pulled it aside, not quite going back to its original, stiff dimensions when I let go. I was relieved.

"Amy will do the procedure," Benjamin whispered in my ear. Amy put the last needle down at the front, closing her eyes and tipping her head forward. "She always prays before." His hot breath brushed against my ear as if he didn't want anyone but me to hear. "She's not religious—she just wants all the help she can get." He pulled away, fidgeting and clipping the two white cords that twisted out from under my top into a small, white machine. I looked back at her with a swell of gratitude.

He fiddled with the dials on top, twisting a few times until he gave me a sharp nod. The lines on my personal screen peaked into soft triangles before falling back down, their repetition transfixing me.

"Sorry to break up the nerd party," Amy called, pulling a glove onto her right hand and letting the plastic twang against her skin. "But we have a competition to win." She winked and grinned at me, the traces of concern I saw before now gone.

I nodded at her, looking between the two nurses.

"Thank you," I said, barely loud enough for them both to hear. I had to say something so they would know how much I appreciated them in this horrendous moment.

"Close your eyes." Benjamin placed his hand in my hair. He stroked my head softly as Amy took charge.

"Sharp pinch." Her words were followed by an immediate poke into my stomach. A searing pain bubbled and burned from my right-hand side.

I held my breath, squeezing my eyes closed as Benjamin continued to stroke my hair, his voice humming a soft tune.

The pain in my right side subsided as quickly as it had come. A strange tingly sensation replaced the pain radiating across my belly.

I opened one eye, looking up at Benjamin, who nodded and flashed me a smile. "The rest will feel strange."

"Am I allowed to watch?" I whispered back, my eyes travelling down to my black-fabric-covered stomach. Amy worked diligently in the small, open holes.

Benjamin laughed. "Watch the screen," he said, raising his eyebrows at Amy. The two of them shared a secret language and connection, and the mere presence of it made me miss Kit and Darcy terribly.

The screen still flickered black and white, the zoomed-in image of the foetus now crystal clear.

The pull in my stomach startled me, and my eyes ached from not blinking. I was enthralled as I watched the picture. Two grey lines slithered in. Their thin, spindly arms stretched outward, enveloping and twisting around tiny nerves, before splitting off in multiple directions to snake through my insides.

My stomach quivered; the strange creeping sensation transmitting from inside my body was akin to nervous butterflies.

Open-mouthed, I watched the screen. The tiny grey lines twisted their way around all parts of the foetus's brain, the little arms embedding themselves at different points.

Amy had her tongue sticking out between her lips, bitten and squashed by her teeth in her concentration. I was in awe of her, in awe of the technology, and somehow not able to feel anything other than pure interest.

Finally, with a loud sigh and a nod, she looked back up at me, her eyes big and beaming. "You did great," she said.

I let a long breath out, my body untensing one muscle at a time.

She gently wiped a small trickle of blood off my stomach; the little black holes that had appeared in the black cloth were already closed. Nothing but the strange fluttering feeling in my stomach remained.

"And you were pretty calm the whole time," Benjamin said, his hand stroking my hair a few more times before taking a seat beside me.

"Curiosity often makes you forget to be scared," I said, almost laughing. I laid my head back against the semi-soft mattress. It was as true as it was silly.

"You see those lights?" Amy pulled off her gloves and pointed to a multitude of coloured lights above my head, each one hanging a few metres apart. "Green means ready," she said with a raised eyebrow.

"When everyone's lights turn green, it's go time," Benjamin said with a wink.

Another green light flickered on across the room, its dull glow slowly heating to a bright, green fluorescence.

"Half the women are ready." I counted the lit green lights, including the one that now flickered on above my head.

"And you are, too," Amy said.

She opened her mouth to speak again when a blood-curdling scream ripped through the room, followed by giant, echoing sobs.

My head snapped sideways, the sound coming from my left somewhere a few doors down. Within seconds, the light above the room four doors down flickered off, relighting a few seconds later to a deep, blood-red. My skin crawled and my pity was palpable. I felt awful that my light was green and hers wasn't.

My nurses shared a quick look, their faces pinched and sad. I knew what they were thinking before they spoke.

"Green doesn't always last," Benjamin whispered, his hand returning to my head and stroking my hair again. I found my hand had automatically gone to my stomach, sitting atop the side where they had implanted the wiring, waiting in full protection mode. It was a reflex I didn't know I possessed. And that unnerved me even more.

"But you—" he said, trying to force my attention away from the red light, "—and you," he said, placing his hand on my stomach, "are doing just fine." The sweet reassurance in his voice placated me.

My eyes ached from the buzzing of the fluorescent lights, their colours changing one-by-one. My eyes leaked over from both sadness and my inability to look away.

Amy pulled up a chair, sitting across from Benjamin on my opposite side. "When the last two lights turn green," she said, her voice barely audible, "the games will begin."

I nodded, having figured that would be the case. Dr. Hidalgo hadn't given me a lot to go on, but I would never have believed her if she had.

"With each passing second, the technology will map your foetus's brain," she said. "By the end of the games they will have enough data to eliminate eight—now seven—women." Her eyes lifted towards the red light a few doors down, and another pang of guilt shot through me. "Alice, they will eliminate eight women in total from the lottery. Here and now."

"Eight?" I whispered, biting my lip. "And what *happens* to them?" I winced, unsure if I wanted to know what their fate might entail; what *my* fate might entail.

Amy shook her head, her face soft and sad, the hint of a frown on her forehead. She didn't speak, but we all knew what fate awaited the losers.

"But at this stage t-they—" I stuttered, shaking my head a few times.

"Foetuses aborted at sixteen weeks can be used—" she said before a terse grunt came shooting out of Benjamin's mouth, stopping her words mid-sentence.

She fell silent and looked away from me, her eyes moving upward to trace through the lights. It seemed there was much more to the Epitome Lab than met the eye; and Amy was bursting to tell someone about it—to tell *me* about it.

"One left," she said, not returning to her previous words, the crease in her forehead more prominent than before.

I stared up, the indent in my lip deepening and aching as I forced myself not to ask questions that they couldn't answer.

"Are you ready?" Benjamin asked. The last light to our right flickered on.

I nodded, my head shaking up and down a few times before I switched over to a shake—no longer sure.

The last light flickered and turned a deep green. The remaining fifteen green lights shone brightly overhead. A few flickered, where mine stayed a brilliant, luminescent green.

"Welcome Ladies," a voice boomed throughout the room, climbing over the small partitions and echoing through the concrete walls.

I looked up at the landing. The thick concrete corridor we had slipped through before we descended to a lower level now filled with five shadowy silhouettes.

The figure in the middle had stepped forward, her dark black clothes hugging her figure, but concealing her. The small, black microphone attached to her face was the only visible feature at this distance.

"Welcome Sponsors," she went on, throwing her arms out as if this was a performance. She waved at the men that flanked her.

Each of the four suited men carried a small briefcase; their black suits and black sunglasses shielding them from proper view.

"We have to leave you now," Amy whispered, her voice squished against my ear. Her words hung in the air as if waiting for me to protest. But I couldn't bring myself to cause them any trouble.

With a soft sadness, she gripped my shoulder. Benjamin did the same on my other side. Their hands pressed against me and then were gone within seconds.

With a quick wave, they were gone, leaving me alone. It felt strange to feel so alone when inches away were hallways, corridors, and rooms full of women having the same experience. I blinked back a few straggling tears before refocusing on the new row of people.

Four men had been ushered out onto the high landing and seated. All but one held their briefcase on their lap. They cradled them as if their briefcase were a layer of protection, a sign of their importance.

"Welcome, welcome," the Spokeswoman said, nodding down at her now seated companions. Her eyes lingered on the man with the briefcase not in his lap.

"Now for the stars of the show." Her voice boomed, echoing and distorted as a large, silver-rimmed television screen descended from the roof.

Four thick, black wires held the descending screen, swinging with the momentum. It stopped below the seated men; the brightness of the screen cast light over the balcony where they sat. They had a perfect line of vision from their vantage point as the enormous screen came to a halt.

The screen flickered, the pixels turning from pitch-black to black-and-white before splitting and multiplying into large, sectioned squares.

One square remained black as the others faded in—and I immediately knew we were about to be a spectator sport. My eyes flicked between my screen and the big screen, narrowing and looking for any details to help me figure out which square I would appear on.

My eyes matched the black number fifteen above my bay to the fifteen hidden in the top left-hand corner of my small screen, barely visible against the other details, and my eyes snapped to the second screen to find it there too.

I wiped my hands against the blanket draped over me, my palms sweaty as I waited for the rest of the screens to load. My breath was stuck in my chest. I wasn't sure if I was curious, anxious, excited, or appalled at what was to unfold.

Curiosity got the better of me as I stared up at the Spokeswoman. She stood still, her head bowed while the screen continued to fill in, her hands clasped together against her chest. The sponsors, oppositely, were now all moving about, their heads close together, the hum of their whispered words knocking against the tense silence of the rest of the room.

As the last individual screen flickered on, I heard an audible sigh of relief from somewhere across the way, shaky and loud. I couldn't imagine the feeling of desperation linked to that sigh. I felt another pang of guilt for all the women trapped here, forced to compete. The pixels within the big screen slowly loaded into focus, and my heartbeat thumped in my ears. The pixels were settling and the blur was clearing. We could finally see the fifteen tiny, baby-shaped blobs. They looked less alien and more human than I was ready for.

I ran my eyes across them, clasping my hands to my chest. Every screen looked similar. A foetus staring back at me, their wired heads the clearest part of each picture.

My eyes hovered on the single blank screen. It felt out-of-place, but full of a deep sadness. I tore my eyes away.

I stared at the square I knew was mine, my eyes flicking back to the smaller screen that hung in my room multiple times—checking and re-checking, wanting to be sure.

"Everyone has connected," the Spokeswoman boomed again, her voice distorted with the increasing volume. I cringed at her echoing voice, too loud for this space.

She didn't seem to notice as she waltzed along the top landing, her figure flitting away from the seated men. The men fidgeted, each opening their briefcase and pulling out large tablets or laptops from within. All the better to take notes with, to judge and score the women who were trapped below.

I scanned the company logos and my stomach went ice cold as I saw the *Aztec Pharmaceuticals* logo emblazoned. My hands tightened their grip on each other. Fingers sweating, I found the logos of more big pharmaceutical companies marked on the back of each tablet or laptop. These weren't individual men with power, but the heads of multinational corporations, and I wasn't sure what was worse.

A strange strangling sensation crept into my throat and down my neck when I read the last label.

The words *Rosalind Institute* blazed across the back of a small tablet, gripped by pale fingers.

"Rosalind—" My eyes narrowed further at the figure who sat still in the chair above. "Venter." My stomach twisted as his face came into clearer focus and the screen lit up the stage. His hands fidgeted, tapping at his tablet, his demeanour more anxious and jumpy than the other sponsors.

With choppy movements, he looked up, eyes scanning the room from back to front. He was searching for *me*.

I held my breath as his gaze came towards me, forcing my eyes to meet his.

My face felt red hot, the veins under my skin bubbled and burned. His eyes lingered on my face. The other sponsors also gawked at the women, wondering which of us would "win."

With a shudder, I realised the actual answer was none of us. No woman in this place was a "winner," no matter how this challenge turned out.

"The foetuses are locked and loaded," she boomed, startling me and causing my eyes to fly back to the big screen. "Let the games begin!"

CHAPTER TWENTY

FOETUS GAMES

THE BIG SCREEN BEGAN ITS COUNTDOWN. THE NUMBER TEN FLASHED before counting down at glacial speed.

I wiped the sweat off my brow, the missed trickles rocketing down my forehead to the back of my neck. The four now-black squares along the bottom of the shared screen stared back at me, their light dimmed and muted.

The soft sobbing coming from the room to my right echoed in my ears and stabbed at my chest, and I tried to steady myself. My whole body tensed as I sat quietly in the uncertainty of the next test, my breath coming in ragged gasps as I tried desperately to catch it.

Right as the countdown timer flashed to two, then one, I gripped hard onto the side of the metal bed frame, my stomach instantly swirling and twisting. The movement from within created a strange nauseous ache I had never experienced.

I held my breath, trying to steady my body, but the foetus in my stomach bounced around and pulled my torso back-and-forth.

A flurry of action on the screen just looked like a blur of black, white, and grey. The shrunken blobs converged as images flashed behind them, too quick for me to comprehend.

The little number fifteen now hovered over my blob's head, fixed to its skull. I let my eyes scan the rest of the big screen, watching the other numbers bump around as well.

I forced my eyes back to the big screen as the individual contestants' displays flung to the edges of the big screen and the center expanded into one big picture. I stared at number fifteen, *my number fifteen,* in awe as it flashed forward, ahead of the pack. I still had next to no idea what was happening on the screen; there had been no explanation, no in-depth run down. All I knew is that the babies were competing, racing each other on the screen in a range of different and utterly confusing games—and most importantly, *we were winning.* Fifteen's blurry, misshapen head and torso rocketed forward and came to a halt at the front. My stomach whimpered, the movement stopping as quickly as it began.

I felt my fingers unclench from underneath the bed frame. My whole body was stiff; my chest hammered hard as I tried and failed to catch my breath.

"Six eliminations have already occurred," the Spokeswoman announced, as if a crowd was cheering her on, her voice so bright and bubbly. I waited for the crowd to erupt, but the only thing I heard were quiet sobs and whispered consolations. The lump that had formed in my throat pulsed, and I forced my eyes back to the screen.

Six of the sixteen once-coloured boxes were now pitch black, their once green lights flickering off. Ten black, white, and grey blobs remained, the numbers surprising, and yet not.

"Sixteen, fifteen, fourteen," I whispered, my eyes shooting toward the room where the strange woman who had walked in as an elite, head held high, now lay. I imagined her body centimetres away from me in the next room. With a jolt, my hand shot to my stomach, the swirling movement returning. "Twelve, Seven, Eight." My eyes ran across the small dancing numbers, now on the second row of the big screen. "Five, Four, Two, One." I blinked a few times, the numbers staring back at me unchanged. A test of unborn babies had seemed impossible, but here I was watching it unfold.

I felt a smile peel across my face as the countdown timer flashed again, glad that one couldn't *truly* buy a spot past this point.

Steeling myself, I gripped tighter onto the bed frame, twisting my fingers up into the latticework that held the mattress in place.

My body must have looked strange as I gripped onto the bed frame. I pulled my knees up, my body tilting to the side and contorting into a half-round ball. I tensed as the numbers flashed in a blur on the screen. Intelligence testing for a foetus; the thought of those words winded me, and yet I found my eyes glued to the screen.

The sudden movements from within left me breathless, forcing me to keep my eyes closed for fear of throwing up. My stomach stretched and pulled internally, sending spirals and waves of nausea through me.

My fingers ached as they gripped against the metal cage. I couldn't figure out the *how* of the technology and it left me with so many unanswered questions. I couldn't switch my scientific brain off. All I could do was *watch and wait*.

"Go," I whispered to the tiny blob, through clenched teeth. "Go." My competitive streak was taking over at this moment and the gravity of my focus on winning and those implications were only tiny flutters in my mind. As tears welled in my eyes, my nausea bubbled over. My head thrust over the side of the bed, my control finally lost as the contents of my stomach spilled.

I gagged at the taste in my mouth, a mixture of breakfast and bile.

A loud scream perforated my self-pity, snapping my head to the left. But the sound stifled and curdled.

The screen was split in two, eight lit with misshapen foetus-shaped figures bobbing strangely along on the top.

The bottom eight screens were a dull black. *It was over.*

"Fifteen, fifteen," I located my number among the lit screens before gulping down a breath to force down the rest of my nausea. I still was at a loss on *exactly* what had happened as I stared up at the big screen; one minute I was being wired up, the next my stomach was contorting as they tested the foetus. Whatever had happened, we seemed to have made it through. Before I could process anything more, a booming voice echoed.

"Escorts," the Spokeswoman's voice ricocheted off every small surface within the open test-room.

I laid still, the sound of shuffling feet and heavy footsteps plaguing my ears. Leaning to the right, I hung the top half of my body off the bed, peeking through the open doorway. Outside stood a blur of figures, their bodies wrapping around red, orange, and green shaking forms.

Unable to make out a single face or feature other than the colour of their dress, my lip quivered. Without truly seeing them, I knew each woman was sobbing, their shaking shoulders proof enough of their suffering.

"Miss Avery." With no warning, the top floor Spokeswoman was standing in my doorway.

The tears that had formed in my eyes shot down my cheeks as I wiped my face.

I opened my mouth to speak, a stammer of incomprehensible sounds coming out before I shut it again, my eyes narrowing at her.

"Congratulations," she said, her loud voice carrying through the tiny room.

I opened my mouth to say *awful*, but realised she hadn't asked how I was at all.

"How does it feel to go into the second test in *first place?*"

She was so bright and bubbly, her arms flailing excitedly at the same speed as her mouth before landing on her hips. Her head tilted towards me like a reporter without a camera.

I could feel my cheeks flush as she looked down at me, her slicked back brown hair so tight that it pulled her eyebrows up into a perpetually surprised position. I chose to say nothing this time, and hoped my face would give her the hint to go away.

"See," she prompted, her body turning to the side to point at the big screen. The faces of eight women were now staring back at me.

My face, a grimace to the other women's shy, soft, half-smiles. My face stared back at me from the top left corner, a small number one bouncing in the corner.

My eyes ran along the lines. Unsurprisingly, women I didn't recognise took up six of the slots, with the woman who started in first now in fifth position.

"W-we came first?" I stuttered, still staring at the screens. It was the only thing I could think to say as the nausea rolled around inside me.

She flashed me a smile before retreating out of my small room without another word. I certainly wasn't the contestant she had hoped to be talking to.

Breathing shallowly, my eyes ran over the other eight women pictured on the screen. The Spokeswoman's voice echoed from behind each wall, the same silly question posed with only the number changing.

Their faces all looked happy and innocent, and my heart ached for the women who had smiled for a lottery mugshot and didn't get to see their photo here.

"Hey," came two whispered voices, breaking through my too-intense stare.

My nurses fluttered into the room, zooming towards me.

"You—" Benjamin started.

"Are a superstar," Amy said, butting in and giving both of us a cheeky wink. We all knew all I had done was hold on for dear life as the foetus seemingly competed on the screen, but we all ignored that for now.

"Wait." I threw my hands up at Amy, and she twirled and side-stepped my vomit pile.

A loud groan escaped my lips, a guttural sound coming from within.

She waved me off, grabbing something off the shelf behind me and sprinkling it onto the vomit, only for Benjamin to sweep it into a small dustpan in one quick motion before dumping it into the bin. They were the perfect duo, standing side-by-side and smiling.

"Feeling okay?" Amy said, breaking the silence and looking me up-and-down with careful eyes.

I nodded. "I feel a bit..." I started, my voice shaking. "Weird?" The word came out as a question rather than a definitive answer.

She smiled down at me, inching closer and putting her cool hands against my forehead. She was both mothering and maternal and in full nurse evaluation mode—and I appreciated all of it.

"Weird is normal." Her gentle smile did the speaking as her hands stroked against my hot skin.

"What happens now?" I whispered, looking at the nurses.

"First, we need to get you untangled," Benjamin piped up, patting the heavy, black, padded rug that was still slung over my stomach. I had almost forgotten the weight of it; it had felt light when I fought to stay seated through the final rounds.

"Each of the mothers-to-be will be asked if they want to find out the sex of the b—" Amy said, her eyes downcast.

"Foetus," Benjamin jumped in. It was one of the only times they had exchanged a hard look. As if they disagreed on this detail.

"Baby is okay," I said, almost shyly. How could I not acknowledge that was what it was after seeing it on the monitor? The two exchanged a look, but pressed on.

"They sell the scan as something to look forward to before the next test." Amy's shoulders hunched forward, a small shrug interrupting her words.

"The scan takes place at eighteen weeks," Benjamin said matter-of-factly, wrapping his arm around Amy and scooting her towards the small holes that housed the wiring inside my stomach.

He plonked her in front of the thick, black blanket that was draped over me, placing her hands on my stomach; the soft, fidgety pressure was obvious against my skin.

"I-is everything okay?" I asked, looking between the two nurses. I knew it wasn't, I knew *none* of this was okay—but I needed them to tell me why it felt like all the air and happiness had disappeared from the room.

Benjamin knelt down near my face, his big head blocking my view.

"Listen." His smiling, prancing, cheerful façade dropped as he spoke in hushed tones. "These tests are grueling." His sympathetic smile returned. "But not just for the contestants." His voice had dropped so low it was barely audible, and his eyes flicked back towards Amy.

I nodded, stealing a glance at her over the top of his head, her vacant expression a little terrifying as she worked on my stomach.

"She's a brilliant nurse." I shot another quick look at her pulling out another string of thin wire from my stomach, sure she would quirk an eyebrow as we talked about her, but she was lost completely in her work.

"She is," he agreed, patting my hand. "The best ones care too much."

He gave both of us a soft squeeze on the shoulder before grabbing the blood-covered pile of wiring that was now stacked up on a small, silver cart with wheels. The sight of blood made my stomach twist. I turned to watch him pull gloves on and peel the thick, black blanket off my stomach. The weight lifted and I inhaled and exhaled normally for the first time since the test began.

With careful manoeuvring, he folded the blanket, stashing it on the second level of the trolley before tugging the handle with force and pulling it out.

"Two minutes." His eyes were stern while facing Amy but then softened when he looked in my direction. His body and the cart disappeared through the small door. He was giving us an opening.

Amy stood still with her eyes closed, her body almost swaying where she stood. Only a matter of seconds passed before she forced her eyes open and turned to face me, her hand still resting on my stomach.

"I'm glad you made it," she said, her voice soft. "So many women don't." A tear fell down her cheek. She cleared her throat, vigorously wiping her face as if she shouldn't cry. Her vulnerability made me like her more.

"There's something you aren't telling me?" It wasn't really a question.

She intertwined her fingers with mine, gave my hand a tight squeeze, and then nodded. A few stray brown hairs fell onto her face, sticking to her sweaty forehead and the remnants of tears.

"So much of what happens here is deceitful," she said, her hand squeezing mine tighter still. "Foetuses lost so they can use their stem cells and underdeveloped organs." Her words were barely a whisper. "This place..." She shook her head as Benjamin returned, loudly announcing his re-entry.

"Ready?"

I wasn't, but I knew I couldn't ask any more of the nurses. Amy's hand squeezed mine and then pulled away, tucking itself back into her other hand.

"Do you have sticky-strips?" she asked him, her voice calm.

Without a word, he held them up, moving them together in his fingers before walking them over. He watched as she stuck them to my stomach.

"All patched up," Benjamin said with a smile.

I nodded, sure my stare was glazed. The view of Benjamin flouncing around to my left side with his hands outstretched didn't register until he was in front of me, snapping his fingers in my face to get my attention.

As I swung my legs off the bed, everything felt changed. And yet I had to focus as my movements were stiff and awkward.

"Up, up," he said sweetly, pulling at my limp hands. "We need to give you the all clear."

With a louder groan than I expected, I pulled my body up and tugged down my dress. My face flushed as only now did I realise my underwear had been on full display for a lot longer than necessary.

My feet tingled with pins and needles; they snaked their way up the soles of my feet and into my ankles, forcing my mouth into a grimace.

"I don't mean to rush you," Benjamin half-said, half-whispered, his demeanour certainly feeling rushed. "But the final eight are meeting and—" He trailed off, letting me connect the dots in my head.

"It's still a test, isn't it?" I whispered back. Everything within these walls was a test, so his nod didn't surprise me. His mouth was almost sympathetic as he shrugged his shoulders.

"Everything is," Amy read my mind. Her fake smile had returned, and her sense of false cheeriness oddly calmed me even though I knew it wasn't real.

I gave them both a nod and flicked my ankles back and forth, the pins and needles subsiding enough to walk. I ran my hands down the length of my deep green dress, fidgeting with the creases that had appeared. I tugged at the velvet collar, smoothing it and re-smoothing it as the nurses pulled the door open.

With a deep breath, I stepped out behind them.

CHAPTER TWENTY-ONE

THE FINAL EIGHT

THE NURSES STOOD BY MY SIDE AND SQUEEZED MY HANDS AS WE STEPPED out together. Only their warm, sweaty grip pulled me forward.

We ascended the staircase to the left, and my eyes darted around the rooms below. Slow movement behind three bays was enough to put me at ease that I wasn't the last to leave.

At the top of the stairs, I cast my eyes forward, the narrow hallway forcing Benjamin to scoot ahead. Amy remained by my side, her hand still intertwined with mine, little squeezes periodically letting me know she was still present.

Benjamin's quick pace forced us to hustle, making me more than a little breathless.

We rounded the corner into another corridor and came to a halt at a second, shorter set of stairs. Benjamin stepped aside, and a glance at Amy made her let go of my hand. She stepped back and folded into Benjamin's waiting arms. I knew this was goodbye before anyone spoke.

"This is it," he said with a smile, his arms wrapped around Amy's shoulders.

I hovered at the base of the stairs. "Any other words of wisdom?" I asked, hoping for a tip or trick I could use as the walls felt like they were closing in.

"Don't hesitate," came the snappy voice of Mrs. Astley from around the corner.

I looked up, and my eyes locked with the older woman who had been kind enough to remind me I was a commoner.

She strode past me, her nurse trailing metres behind her, whose face was a mix of ashen and scared.

"Good to see we both made it." She eyed me coolly. Her shoulder bumped roughly into mine. She stopped at the top of the stairs, giving me enough time to spin on the spot and look up at her as she flattened her velvet collar and smoothed her smile into place.

Hands on her hips, she gave me a little shake of the head as if she couldn't believe she was forced to be in the same room as me. Swivelling away, the loud *click* of her heels followed her behind the door.

"Guess I," I exclaimed as I ascended the staircase, "the *commoner*—" I bowed deeply when I reached the top, acutely aware that I was still barefooted, "—might be permitted entrance." I winked at the nurses, who stood huddled together, wide smiles on their faces. I dipped my head and my fake hat at them before pivoting around and stalking towards the wooden door.

I wasn't about to let another woman make me feel small or out of place—that pleasure all came from within.

As I crossed the threshold, bright light spilled out of the door, making me blink a few times. With a loud *crack,* the door slammed shut just as I took my first step onto the elevated stage.

Five heads snapped towards me, each wearing an expression of either pity or relief. They wore their own version of red, orange, or green dresses. I was on the verge of apologising when I saw *her.* She had entered only a few seconds before me, sitting at the end of the row with three vacant chairs to her right, her grin the size of her entire face.

She gently patted the chair beside her as if to beckon me forward. If nothing else, she was a brilliant actress.

Head held high, I crossed the stage, careful to watch my feet. I took my seat with a straight back without looking at her. The stage was a small part of a much larger, almost bare, room with three doors looming in the distance.

In between us and the door sat a line of six black, padded chairs on a smaller, higher stage, in front of where we sat.

My eyebrows pinched together. A small clipboard had been placed on each seat. I could imagine a line of men sitting in the chairs, scribbling notes about us, judging us—and my stomach turned as I realised who was likely to sit there.

Heels against the wooden floor snapped me back to reality as two young women stepped out onto the stage. The second one was smart enough to close the door softly before scurrying forward.

The first young woman closest to me wore a red dress, and the glitter caught the light when she crossed the stage. She sat, folding herself into the chair gracefully and going about displaying her dress with careful placement of the fabric.

The second wore a green dress already torn at the hem; her fidgeting fingers picked at the fabric the second she sat down. Her bottom lip was stuck in her mouth, and her red, raised flesh glistened as she continued to gnaw at it. The women around me all handled the moment differently, and I had no plans to judge any of them—except maybe those who judged me.

I snapped my head back and turned my attention straight ahead to scan the three-separate doors for movement.

My body stiffened, my nerves getting the better of me. I forced my eyes to follow the same pattern, searching each door for a few seconds before moving on. *Eventually, one would open and the next challenge would arrive with it.*

A loud *bang* in the centre of the room snapped my attention, my eyes scanning the now-busy doorway.

Four people hovered just inside the entryway, shrouded in darkness. A single man squatted down, grabbing fistfuls of paper and shoving them back into his shiny briefcase. As he stood, his face flushed a vibrant shade of red.

The same spokeswoman from the other room scooted around him, her thick heels clicking on the tiled floor of the silent auditorium. She strode forward, leaving a sizeable gap between herself and the four suited men, three of whom now scurried after her. They were quite the sight and even I could feel the tension building.

The man who dropped his briefcase hung back, leaning up against a small table and straightening his things. The red shine of his bald head was visible from here, although his features were obscured.

The Spokeswoman ascended the stage, ushering the men in one-by-one. They squished their chairs close together and stashed their briefcases to one side. Clipboards in hand, they fixed their eyes on the eight women who sat before them.

The dawdling man finally ascended the stage. His briefcase tucked firmly under his arm, his splotchy face scrunched, he took his seat in the far right corner.

I felt my chest tighten as my eyes swept the line until I spotted him. I stared at his face, one eye twitching. The man of the hour; the boss I couldn't take my eyes off.

"*Venter.*" His name burned like acid as it spilled from my mouth. My eyes narrowed and locked onto him. He fiddled with his chair, deliberately fussing and fidgeting to avoid looking at me.

The Spokeswoman pulled a chair from the edge and sat herself front-and-centre. This split the men into two groups, two on each side of the stage.

A single chair remained vacant, towering over the others on a higher platform.

The silence felt awkward. She leaned back in her chair, and her gaze made its way down to the women opposite her.

I watched each woman divert her eyes, dropping them low, their smiles faltering as she stared at them.

With a frown, I cast my eyes to the older woman beside me, her face a strange mix of humbled and grateful as the Spokeswoman looked her up-and-down, her eyes lingering for a few seconds longer.

I felt my eyes roll as my gaze lifted to meet hers. We stared at each other, eyes locked for a few seconds, before a devilish grin broke out across her face, the dimples in her cheeks flashing at me.

I held her gaze while she looked me up and down, her eyes lingering a few seconds too long. Her grin dropped when she looked to my other side. Her eyes returned to mine a few times before she swivelled around in her chair. With her back to us, she fixed her eyes on the watch on her left wrist.

The hard wood of the chair pressed into my spine, and I squirmed in the seat.

We were clearly waiting for someone more important. As the minutes ticked by, the men stared intently at us. Each of them made me uncomfortable in their own way, from beady eyes to vacant stares; from intense gazes at particular parts of my body to copious note taking.

My defiant gaze shifted to one of irritation as I fought the urge to shrink. I refused to cower in front of men who wouldn't stand up to my own scrutiny had our roles been reversed.

They each rifled through sheets of paper, their pens only leaving the paper to stare up at us. Frowns and puckered lips were common as they scribbled notes.

My arms crossed, and I leaned back in my chair, staring at each of the plain men. I wondered what these men could be commenting on, as no one had given us the chance to speak yet.

The men could have been the same person; their lack of distinguishing features were irritating. Their black suits and plain white shirts were identical. Their hair was styled differently, but all in a middle-aged-dad kind of way. Their dull eyes only focused on the women in front of them.

I settled into staring at Mr. Venter. His hand moved as quickly as the other men's as he scribbled notes. He put his pen in his mouth in thought, something I had seen him do a thousand times in the lab. Now, the familiarity made my skin crawl.

He looked up, his gaze faltering as he finally locked eyes with me, and I let my mouth curl sweetly into a smile.

I bowed my head forward, my body feeling stiff and jolted. With a sheepish gaze and mouth gaping open, his pen hovered mid-air. He must have known I was still here, unless all we were to the sponsors were numbers—not humans.

He quickly cast his eyes down, tapping his pen against the clipboard.

A soft beep emanated from a tablet, causing the Spokeswoman to jump up, smoothing her black jumpsuit down at the front and sides as she moved.

A smile crept onto her face, tugging at the corner of her lips.

"Welcome," the Spokeswoman said, her voice still loud and booming, despite the microphone being gone, "to the final eight." She ran her eyes across the room, going up and down the line twice before settling on a spot close to the centre. "In a few seconds, the head Organiser will arrive and this panel will kick off. The Sponsors will ask questions." She waved her hand to the men sitting on each side of her.

All but Mr. Venter looked up at the final eight women with intrigue and interest. They were like salivating dogs.

"Please answer them with your truth." She looked at each of us for a few seconds. "Now, let's welcome *the Organiser*."

Women had no names here, only titles.

The Spokeswoman turned her back and descended the stage. Her high heels clicked against the floor as she walked back towards the middle door, eyes on her watch. She waited a few seconds, moving from foot-to-foot and fidgeting with her ponytail before swinging open the door in one swift movement.

The Organiser glided into the room flanked by two large men—their muscled arms bulged against their black suit jackets, the buttons down their chest pulling the fabric taut.

She dashed forward on her tiptoes, her mass of red hair a mess of tight curls that bounced when she moved. She tugged at her red suit jacket, fidgeting with the hem and sleeves simultaneously.

Her bodyguards peeled off as she ascended the first step, their muscle still hovering behind her. She walked up and promptly plonked herself down in the high chair. She spun in a full circle before stopping to face us.

The two men retreated, walking backwards a few paces and

turning in a full three-hundred and sixty degree circle with wide eyes before planting themselves in front of the entrance.

The Spokeswoman returned to the stage, squeezing awkwardly past two sponsors to take her seat below. She only sat for a few seconds before bouncing back up, her chair spinning behind her with the quick movement.

"Ladies and gentlemen," she said, her voice puffed and breathless as if she'd forgotten her lines. "Please give a *warm* welcome to the Organiser and hostess of this year's *lottery*." Her sharp eyes looked through the crowd, her hands clapping as if to prompt us to follow.

The older lady beside me clapped without hesitation, her hands gently coming together. The rest of the women followed in quick succession.

With a frown, I stared at the red-haired woman; she had her head raised to the roof, her eyes looking straight up.

I left my hands in my lap and clasped them together, unable to force myself to applaud my own misery. It was strange. It felt so easy to get caught up in the competition, in the next challenge. I almost forgot that I was playing the part of a *willing participant*.

A lump pulsed in my throat, and I tried to swallow it down. I would have to grapple with that reality later. For now, I had to admit I did want to hear what the Organiser had to say.

With a loud sigh, the Organiser pulled herself up and out of her chair, patting the Spokeswoman on the arm. It was clear she had decided she was ready to speak to us now.

"Women," she said, her voice rough and scratchy. "Listen to the questions asked by the sponsors." Her head snapped left to right, running across us. "Sponsors," she said with a *click* of her fingers, "be clear, succinct." A loud sigh emanated from her throat and filled up the stage. "This is a strong final eight." She gave a single nod before sinking back into her chair and unbuttoning her jacket. That last line seemed like a strange inner thought that slipped out into the real world.

I forced myself not to make a sound. My brain whirled and I felt sick as I sat here in silence; waiting. I swallowed down my bubbling, mingled rage and curiosity. How had I gotten *this far*? It felt like a nightmare I couldn't wake up from.

Instead of letting my thoughts spill out of my mouth, I stared at the Organiser as she planted a cigarette in her mouth and struck at her lighter more than once to get it lit.

With a deep draw, her face melted, a genuine smile floating across it. It was the same way I felt when I took my first sip of beer on a Friday afternoon.The Spokeswoman spoke again, this time remaining seated. "Each woman will give a brief introduction to ensure we have the correct information about you," she said matter-of-factly. "Please state your full name, occupation, and marital status." A sharp nod was the only sign that she was finished speaking.

Each of the men turned to the front of the line, landing on the woman who had entered and been seated first.

She stood, her body stiff.

"Alison Lock, party planner, married to *Alistair Lock* of Lock and Gamble Casino," Alison said, her voice fast and squeaky until she reached her husband's name, which she took time to emphasise.

I tuned out and looked up into the roof rafters. I had no interest in listening to a line of women spruik their husbands' importance. Mrs. Astley roughly smacked my arm when she stood, which was my cue that it was almost my turn to speak.

I rolled my eyes as she clasped her hands in front of her in a strange, praying position.

"Astrid Astley." She paused for a few seconds, her voice sickly sweet, her demeanour careful to not be too loud or too soft. "Devoted Christian wife," she went on, pausing again—forcing me to resist the urge to roll my eyes for the second time in ten seconds, this time in a much more obvious way. "Married to pastor Francis Astley." She bent into a deep bow, followed by a curtsey before returning to her seat.

I pressed my lips together. Unlike the others, I stayed seated. "Alice Avery," I said, my voice ringing in my ears. "Biologist with a Master's." The sponsors shifted in their seats, and a small smirk danced across my face. I hoped I made them a little uncomfortable.

I paused, looking across the room until my eyes landed on the

Organiser. Her cigarette was now almost down to the end, two butts already on the floor in front of her.

"Single." I said. The word caused hushed whispers to break out around me. It was as if we had travelled back in time, and being single and pregnant was *scandalous*.

"Quiet, quiet," she quipped, waving her hand at the sponsors, who had all leaned in together, except for Mr. Venter, who kept his head down, eyes glued to his notes. He already knew *plenty* about me.

I smiled sweetly at the panel, who stared back at me in a strange, wary way. Their eyes never left my face as the next woman stood up.

The last woman gave her details, projecting more than the other candidates. She slid towards my chair as she spoke.

It was shallow, but to me she was another woman with a rich husband speaking to a crowd of paid sponsors.

The Organiser sucked in a long draw of her cigarette before clapping her hands loudly.

"Basic introductions complete." She clicked her fingers, blowing another stream of smoke straight up into the sky. Her consistent smoking created a haze above her head. "Timer. Ten minutes." She waved at the sponsors, her voice bored as she took in another draw of smoke. Somehow, despite the circumstances, I liked her.

The questions then flew thick and fast, with often more than one sponsor talking to a woman at the same time. They talked over each other and the incessant chatter made my eyes twitch. I sat in silence.

Questions flew about husbands' professions, connections, and wealth. The sponsors tried to zero in on who would be the best candidate to align with for future political and business gains; while I sat in silence, wondering if the sponsors considered me in the same league as the husbands or in a league of my very own.

The blood boiled under my skin; the injustice of the world sank into my bones. I forced myself to lean back in my chair, focusing on the way the wood poked into my back while the woman beside me was asked, with a straight face, if her husband was intelligent.

Her answer sent my head shooting up to look at the roof to hide my long, exasperated eye roll. The Organiser had said ten minutes, but clearly didn't intend to stick to it.

"Miss Avery," called a voice over the chatter. The noise died down with each question wrapping up. No more started after my name was called.

With what I was sure was a blotchy, red face, I pulled my head forward, searching for the source of the voice.

Mr. Venter sat in the corner, his clipboard poised and ready, his pen inches from the paper held there. His forehead twitched, the eye contact unbroken while I waited.

"Yes?" I said, my voice sounding a touch more sarcastic than I originally intended.

"Can you tell me a little about *your* academic background?" Mr. Venter spoke slowly, choosing his words carefully. I both cursed and appreciated his question - for once a question was addressed to an actual candidate.

The Organiser clicked her tongue, but said nothing. A hint of a smile crept onto her face and pulled at her cheeks. She would have known our connection, even if no-one else did.

"I can," I said matter-of-factly, feeling a strange prickling sensation on the back of my neck. The women on either side of me shifted in their chairs, each pair of arms crossing with narrowed eyes. I might be the only one to talk about myself during this question and answer session. "I graduated with my undergraduate degree at twenty-two. Top of my class." I tried to speak succinctly, aware that each sponsor was listening to my words now. "The same year, I enrolled in a master's program, studying biology. I graduated with a 4.0 GPA—not quite top of my class, but close." I smiled, the memory of another woman taking the top spot filling me with joy. "Now, I work at a top research lab. My current project is based on genetics—sir," I said, after a few seconds' pause. I smiled as Mrs. Astley's frown grew deeper and more obvious in my peripheral vision. I hadn't done it to piss her off, but I was glad it had that effect.

I watched the sponsors flip pages on their clipboards, their eyes darting up to me and down to their notes more than a few times. Silence hung in the air.

Eventually, the chatter returned. Each of the sponsors asked a few more questions of the women around me. This time, some of them even bothered to speak to the women as people and not vessels.

My name didn't come up again. The sponsors simply shot wary glances my way, their eyes curious. I wondered what was written on their paperwork labelled 'Alice Avery.'

I sat back in my chair, a small, unassuming smile forming on my face. I watched Mr. Venter interview three other women, asking them questions that were in some ways about them, rather than their husbands. My anger with him dissipated an inch with each inquiry. It was clear I was an underdog, and I wondered why no one had asked me about Mason. He wasn't a magnate or inextricably rich, but he was a man of science like I was a woman of science. I couldn't figure out *what* exactly the Sponsors were fishing for.

The Organiser stubbed out another cigarette on the side of her chair before clapping her hands. "I've been *very* generous with question time," she said. "It's time." The first drag of a new cigarette made her voice croak. "Sponsors, put forward your rankings."

CHAPTER TWENTY-TWO

THE COMMANDER OF EVERY ROOM

"Flip to the back page." The Organiser fiddled with her lighter, waiting impatiently to light up another cigarette. "Top candidate..." She twirled the lighter through her bony fingers. "...then one to eight." Her fingers fumbled to strike the lighter, then paused before sucking in a smoky breath.

I looked at the four sponsors, each of them leaning back in their chair. They stared at us with focused eyes and pursed lips, evaluating our worth.

I refused to blink or break eye contact, making my eyes burn. Each of the men held my gaze for a few seconds before averting their eyes and moving on.

I sat up straight. My legs crossed over each other, my bare feet intertwining and then sweeping underneath me. I felt like I was on display—for sale to the highest bidder.

One-by-one, the men pushed their pens to paper. They ripped off their score sheets and passed them to the Spokeswoman. Her hands shook as she collated them, her fingers fidgeting with the staples in the corners of each piece.

Mr. Venter was the final sponsor to hand in his sheet of paper; his was folded in two, unlike the others.

The Organiser patted the Spokeswoman on the arm. A gentle, *do what we discussed earlier* pat that caused her to jump up out of her seat and scurry to the right, where a small podium waited. She tapped on a black box, pushing a few buttons and moving a light over onto the space. With a flicker, a bright light shone behind us. My head immediately snapped back to take a peek.

"Miss Avery." The Organiser's voice rang out, stopping my head mid-turn.

As I turned back, I caught a glimpse of the seven women seated beside me. Each of their hands were pressed in their lap, clasped and poised, their ankles together and dresses laid out in a perfect, unwrinkled line. Each waiting to be told what to do. It seemed as though I was the one out of the information chain here.

"Curiosity is a virtue, but please, *humour me*," she said, a wry smile on her face as she sucked in the last of her fourth shrinking cigarette. "The rankings behind you are from a snippet of conversation. Remember that." Her eyes scanned down the line, lingering on a few of the women longer than others. My eye twitched, torn between appreciation at the reminder that we were more than the men here could ever know, and the fact that women like her were tangled up in this.

She passed over me with a tug at the corner of her lips. It was both flattering and infuriating that she seemed to notice that I was different from the rest.

"These rankings determine who each sponsor believes to be the top candidate, and whom their companies are willing to financially support—*for a price*." Her voice rang out in the large room. "Their rankings also determine who you will compete against in the next test." She almost immediately lit another cigarette as the one she was smoking flickered down to the butt.

"Compete against?" I said out loud. As soon as the words escaped, I grimaced; I'm sure it would have been more polite to raise my hand delicately; but what did that matter in a game like this.

"For those few who haven't been involved in *the lottery* before..." the Spokeswoman continued. The reverence given to those two words was almost unbearable. The Organiser let her take over, eying her thankfully as she fidgeted with her lighter. "...the next step is mother-and-baby versus mother-and-baby."

"Mother-and-baby-versus..." I murmured, my voice trailing off. I gnawed at the inside of my lip. It was like a gut-punch, and my stomach ached at the pure thought.

"A series of tests and questions in which you compete against another pair, and in the end, we will only have *two women left.*" She spoke too matter-of-factly about something so sinister, and it sent a wild tingle down my spine.

"Knock-out rounds?" I raised my hand this time, my arm shaking as I struggled to bite back my words.

"Another question, Miss Avery?" the Organiser asked, her voice croaky but almost excited. I was grateful she was humouring me, rather than telling me to be quiet and fall in line.

I nodded, lowering my hand and biting my lip. "What happens to the foetuses of the women who don't make it?" I made sure my words were clear and tried not to put any emotion behind the question. It was the one thing that I kept coming back to, and I felt like there was more to it than I understood. I had never thought about this before, and I realised what a horrid, earth shattering oversight that was on my part.

"Termination," the Organiser answered, her smile faltering with a single word. "For those who are unsuccessful, the outcome is *always* termination." She spoke plainly, but also with a sad, knowing smile. I nodded in reply, but she hadn't answered my true question. I was more interested in the *women,* not what was growing in their uterus. I wanted to ask more inappropriate questions, but not wanting to upset the other women with my curiosity I fell silent. Her words, I was sure, were truthful, but didn't allow me to reckon with the *whole* truth. I would have to file this away to my growing list of concerns.

"Sponsors will become allies," the Spokeswoman said, changing the topic without a second thought. "If you are chosen, you will meet with them after this to discuss their intentions."

I rolled my eyes, aware I wasn't the woman sponsors would want to back, privately or publicly.

"Spin, spin," the Organiser sputtered, coughing into her elbow. The hacking sounds overrode everything else in the room.

As I turned, my name flashed back at me in large black writing. 'Alice Avery' was written in the top left-hand and bottom right-hand corners.

I blinked, my forehead crinkling.

Realising everyone was already back facing the other way, I let myself stare at my name for another second. My eyes quickly darted around and found myself on the 'pair list,' across from a woman named Penelope James.

My eyes flashed back up to my twice written name at the top of the screen. The twitch in my eye set off, and I wasn't sure if it was the stress of seeing my name twice or *at all*. The thought of these men *choosing* me was far from flattering; and I wondered what they would want from me as my sponsor.

"Note the numbers where your name appears. The sponsors are from one—" She pointed to her left, where a middle-aged man raised his hand, his suit crinkled underneath. "—two, three, and four." Each of the men raised their hands with their assigned numbers.

"Four," I griped under my breath, making uncomfortable eye contact again with Mr. Venter. I should have *known* he would force me to converse with him here. Or maybe he was the one being forced.

"If the sponsors did not select you, please stand," the Organiser said, gesturing that the woman should move.

Five women stood, their faces painfully blank. A pang of guilt swept through me. I was not naive enough to think that these men had no power.

"You will continue to compete unsponsored. Go, go." She tapped the Spokeswoman on the arm, making her jump up out of her seat and hurry down the stairs two at a time.

The women filed off the stage, the only sound in the room their heavy footsteps.

A solemn Spokeswoman held open a door to the side, and the

women walked out in single file, heads bowed. They looked defeated, and I realised how much I didn't know as a first-timer.

"Three," the Organiser said, with raised eyebrows. "It's been a while since it was only three." She was matter-of-fact, and I couldn't help the raging guilt that sprang up in my chest at being chosen by two sponsors.

As she sucked in another breath from her cigarette, I stole a glance to my right and left. Mrs. Astley sat silently beside me, her lips pursed so tightly they had disappeared from view.

I smiled sweetly, looking past her to make eye contact with the third woman. Dressed in ruby red, her eyebrows raised as our eyes met. She was young and blonde, the engagement ring sparkling on her finger the size of a ten-cent piece.

She sat with her ankles crossed and a sweet smile planted on her soft face.

I pulled back, returning to the harsh wood as I stared at the Organiser. I didn't understand this underground world of councilmen, spokeswomen, organisers and sponsors—but now that I was here I would try and learn *everything.* I *had* to learn everything if I had any chance of taking down this corporation after I was released from my own prison.

"Will you both wait?" the Organiser asked, only bothering to turn her head after she had already spoken. "I'd like a brief moment with *Miss Avery* first."

"Yes ma'am," rang out the answer from two of the four men, known only as One and Four here. They were both falling over themselves to be accommodating, and it made me cringe. The other two stood there mute, waiting for the Organiser to turn her glare on them.

"Two, Three," she said, pointing to them one after the other. "Take your women, you are *excused.*" A snap of her fingers had them moving to their feet in a matter of seconds. Each of them scrambled for their briefcase before descending the stairs in a scrambled hurry.

A smirk crossed my face. The command she had over the sponsors was obvious. I loved seeing that at least one woman still had some power here. The thought both uplifted and crushed me. She spoke to almost everyone with that awful tone; I had to remind myself she wasn't our ally.

"Go, go," she said, not turning her head, but instead clicking her fingers at the hovering men.

The two men hurried around the back, ascending the stairs that bridged the gap between our stage and the sponsors.

A loud creak made my head snap up. The Spokeswoman appeared at the left side door. "The interview rooms are ready."

"Speak your truths." the Organiser said again, her little smirk returning as she rose to lead the way. One and Four stayed behind.

Keeping my face blank, I walked forward, falling a few paces behind the Organiser, as if I was the perfect follower. In reality, I was watching her, trying to get a read—trying to understand this mysterious woman and her mysterious power.

We filed out of the room in silence. The other women were close behind me with their new sponsors, their shoes clicking on the floor as my bare feet felt the sting of the cold.

She ushered us into the hallway, where three red doors were ajar.

Thick black numbers were painted onto each of the doors, labelling them from one to four. Hovering, I stood in the hallway as the Organiser entered the room.

I stole a glance at each side. The other women were also waiting outside of their doors, their hands clasped neatly in front of them with a strange, off-putting smile on their faces. I thought about running *again*, but it was useless. The underground lab was a cavernous maze. In truth, I had little desire to get lost, and I was undeniably curious.

Instead, I watched the Organiser quickly sweep the room, a cloud of smoke billowing above her head, clouding the glass.

She dawdled before sitting gracefully and beckoning me inside. The room was small and almost bare. The metal table and two chairs the only furniture, a backdrop of plain white walls only marred by the door we had walked in through.

She had curled her hands together against the table top. Her face was wrinkled and drawn, a tinge of yellow shining from her teeth.

"You are the only contestant with two interviews today," she said, her face crinkling.

I nodded, unsure whether a simple "yes" would suffice, or if she wanted to continue talking.

"Why do you think that is?" she let the silence stretch on for a beat too long.

"I'm an unlucky woman," I retorted. I wondered if I should have said something snappier after the words left my mouth.

"Educated, scientist, intelligent," she said, as if checking off the list of traits that made up a tiny part of who I was. "Normally, women *like you* don't end up here *accidentally*." She didn't chastise me; instead her tone was matter-of-fact, her dark eyes unblinking and piercing into mine. She wasn't being rude. To another curious soul, it seemed as if she was puzzled by me.

"We all make mistakes, ma'am." I shrugged my shoulders, my face flushing.

"Well…" she said with a slow drawl, "this mistake has landed you in the right place at the right time." She fumbled around inside her loose jacket pocket, withdrawing her trademark rolled cigarettes and a sparkly red lighter. She put a cigarette in her mouth and spoke in a strange tone. "Depending on the outcome of the lottery, you could be the sweetheart of the world. With a bouncing baby to boot." She fidgeted with the lighter but didn't make a move to light her cigarette. "Or," she eyed me more seriously now, "you'll be cast aside. Another clever girl atop the heap of failed contestants." Her words were too harsh. Even her raspy voice didn't match their dark connotations.

My eyebrows indented further into my forehead with each passing word. What was it she was searching for in my reaction, or was she just baiting me, looking for a fiery snap? I fought the urge to snap back. I didn't want a *bouncing baby,* and anyone who knew me at all would know I would overcome this. In a few months, this would be but a memory. I would walk away from this and find a way to change *all of this*.

"And?" I said, biting hard on the tip of my tongue, forcing myself to swallow my rage for now. A great feat in this moment of peculiarity.

"*And*, Miss Avery, we are *all* wondering what comes next for you." She lit her cigarette and stood up, her wooden chair scraping against the black-and-white tiles. "For now," she said, as she took a long drag of her cigarette, holding the smoke in her mouth until she reached the door, "your first interviewer awaits."

I watched her walk away—her petite frame atop platform shoes, her wad of red hair swaying from side-to-side, the billow of smoke encompassing her every few seconds.

It might have been a normal conversation for her, but I felt rattled as One took her place and stared at me with a different kind of intensity.

CHAPTER TWENTY-THREE

THE MAN KNOWN AS FOUR

I BREATHED DEEPLY, STEADYING MY QUIVERING BODY. ONE'S INTERVIEW had been as short as it was confusing. It had gone so far off track even I couldn't make sense of it.

I hoped One wouldn't write a striking opinion piece full of my unfounded thoughts on why more women should opt to remain childless; the last thing I needed whilst trying to rebuild this country after *the lottery* was dismantled was an article from Panacea Press—one of the best science magazines in the country—lording my own words over my head. My head spun, as I tried desperately to hold that end goal in my mind. I could cope with this if I could truly envision that future.

As Mr. Venter—*Four*—entered the room, his face turned a brilliant shade of pink. He didn't meet my eyes as he pretended to stifle a cough. I thrust aside my worries about my last interview, and turned my undivided attention towards him.

He sat with slumped shoulders, his face depicting a sad, solemn frown. If I hadn't known better, I would have thought *he* was the one competing in a foetus death game.

"*Four*, was it?" I asked sweetly. I curled my hands together, leaning forward to close the gap between us by a few short inches.

"Miss Avery," Mr. Venter said, his voice quiet.

A long, silent pause stretched out between us, and I kept my eyes locked on the top of his head as he continued to look down. He would look at me here; he would *see* me here.

"To what do I owe this pleasure?" I asked, frustrated at this lack of explanation. I would have preferred the Organiser stay—at least her words held riddles and information. Hell, at least my interview with One had included eye-contact and *talking*.

Mr. Venter clasped his hands together atop the table, the strain on his fingers sending them a pale shade of white.

I stared at him expectantly, trying to contort my face into one of calm determination.

"W-women like you have always been paramount to Rosalind Institute." He tripped over the words, and I knew I was going to enjoy making him squirm.

"Women like me?" I added a bit of confusion into my voice, as if I didn't know what he was implying. His face flushed as his eyes finally locked onto mine, his bottom lip quivering. It was pathetic, but I relished his discomfort. A small pleasure in this prison.

"Intelligent women." He swallowed. "Women of science." He nodded as if to confirm the script to himself.

I raised my eyebrows at him. I wanted him to keep talking, to keep rambling and offering fake words of praise. Even lies sounded good when they were about you.

"Rosalind Institute is thrilled with your performance so far." He fumbled with the locks on his briefcase, hands shaking. He tried the lock combination three times before it clicked open.

He slid a piece of paper across the table towards me. His fingernails were stubby and bitten down the core.

"A cheque?" I stared at it, making no move to grab it from him. It was only a symbol—we hadn't used cheques in years, but I knew what it represented. Rosalind Institute was here to *buy me*.

"We have covered all your living expenses. Your salary has continued to be deposited." He was speaking, but my eyes were fixated on the blank space on the cheque.

"The cheque—" I interrupted the string of nonsense words that he was repeating as if rehearsing for a spelling bee."Why is it blank?" I snatched it from the table, waving the cheque towards him.

My full name was neatly printed at the top. The cheque might have been fake, but what it represented was real, and I wanted him to say it, to tell me *I was right* and he was here to buy my allegiance on behalf of Rosalind Institute.

"Miss Avery," Mr. Venter said, sucking in a deep breath.

"Stop." I put my hand up. "Don't give me the contrived, practiced speech that Rosalind Institute has rehearsed with you."

He nodded, and his shoulders hunched. If I wasn't so angry, I would have felt bad for the man stuck in the middle.

"Alice," he pleaded, and my skin crawled. "The cheque is blank because you have always been difficult in the best way. Rosalind Institute knows that slapping a few thousand dollars onto a cheque won't buy them anything but disappointment." A hint of fire returned to his eyes. "You may lead." He waved his hand at both me and the cheque.

I stared between him and the cheque, my eyes flitting across both. I wondered how much they would spend to buy me—a girl they had never cared about that much before.

"Alice," Mr. Venter said, mouthing something at me and pointing surreptitiously at a small black camera attached to his lapel. His eyes were wide, and he had a sad look on his face.

"Sir," I said, wincing at the old force of habit from my previous life. "I *appreciate the offer*." I didn't, and I eyed the little camera pinned to his chest as I slid the blank cheque back towards him. "Unfortunately," the words formed in my mind just seconds before they tumbled out of my mouth, "we'll be parting ways here. I resign." I rested my hand on my stomach. The strange feel of the bump took me a few seconds to adjust to.

Mr. Venter smiled, both hands reaching out across the table. He didn't try to change my mind; he obviously remembered that once I made a decision, there was no going back. Thankfully, he dropped some of the formality.

"You were always one of our best." He squeezed my hands for a few dragging seconds. "That was all that I needed to discuss with you." He cleared his throat and got to his feet. I had expected him to push and ask again, to beg, to plead, but he busied himself with packing up his briefcase, the blank cheque tucked back within its walls. Rosalind must have known this would be my answer, but I was sure they didn't know the truth behind my refusal, not even Mr. Venter. I rose as well, ready to leave.

"Best of luck, Alice," he said, navigating his way around the table and closing the gap between us.

I took a few stumbling steps back, but was too slow. Two arms wrapped around me, the briefcase knocking into my back as Mr. Venter hugged me. The flood of warmth felt nice, but I froze just the same.

"Be careful," he whispered into my ear, his words rushing out low and soft. "The world is watching." He was talking so fast. "They'll send others. They want the publicity from this. *There will be others.*" It looked like a lingering hug from teacher to student, but his words stung and seeped into my body, freezing me in place.

Mr. Venter broke away, keeping his left arm on my shoulder.

He looked at me strangely, opening his mouth to say something else before shutting it and shaking his head.

I smiled at him, all the anger gone. He was just the first. That explained why he could walk away so casually. He was just as much a pharmaceutical pawn as I was.

"Whatever is next for you…" He crossed the room, pulling open the door and choosing not to finish his sentence except with a smiling nod. He wished me luck in his own silent way.

The door clicked shut behind him, and the room was left cold. The fluorescent lights flickered above me as I walked backwards. I slid down, my body contorting into a strange, misshapen ball. My legs splayed apart to make way for my protruding belly. They hit the ground like jelly, sprawling out in front of me.

A loud sigh escaped from within me, my body aching from the awkward position I had landed in. Everything felt too much—this place, this system, these tests, these dresses.

My fingers gripped the side of my face. I gripped tighter and tighter, my nails digging into my skin.

"This is your five minute warning," the automated system rang out, interrupting my wallowing. "Five-minute warning." The strange voice was a cross between robotic and someone uncomfortable with making announcements.

With difficulty, I pulled myself to my feet, my toes moaning against the cold tiles.

I wandered around the room, my fingers trailing against the stark white walls as I talked to myself. I must have looked wild or crazy, maybe paranoid or psychotic, and honestly, that's how I felt. A strange mix of curious and confused.

"This system favours wealth…" My eyes had glazed, and even inside I felt semi-vacant, like I was there and also not. "Every inch of the facility is recorded…each person is thoroughly invested in. All equipment is top-of-the-line."

I frowned, the tips of my fingers itching against the smooth, white paint.

The only real question repeated over and over. *Why*. I couldn't come up with a coherent answer.

A soft rap at the door made me jump; my hand dropped off the wall, and I turned to face the Organiser. Her arms were crossed across her chest, an off look painted onto her otherwise tough face.

"Come, Miss Avery," she said, her raspy voice shaking. She turned away.

I didn't move, but just stood staring at her.

She turned back, her wrinkled face appearing tired. She raised a single eyebrow at me.

"The final two contestants…" I said, a burning question propelling out of my mouth. "The public…" My words jammed in my throat.

"Yes, Miss Avery," she said, cutting me off mid-rambling sentence, "Selective public officials do vote. And so do we."

I bit my lip harder. I knew this in my gut, but hearing it confirmed still sent me reeling. Would Australia's Prime Minister be voting for or against me?

I could have sworn she winked, but the more I stared at her, the more unsure I became.

"Come." She turned her back on me. "Let's walk and talk," she said, muffled, as she lit up another cigarette. This time, a faint scent of strawberry infiltrated my nostrils. I appreciated the attempt on her behalf.

I hesitated for a few seconds, my legs feeling wobbly. She hung in the doorway, puffing on her strawberry scented cigarette with her eyes cast ahead.

Finally, my legs stumbled forward. Her thick platform shoes clonked against the floor.

I towered over her but still struggled to keep up with her swift pace, trotting forward as if we were in a hurry. And maybe she was—I on the other hand, had *nowhere* to be.

We rounded the corner, and she led me down a wide corridor. I opened my mouth, a little squeak coming out instead of words.

"The top eight are all having these discussions," she informed me, her head still facing straight ahead, as if she had read my mind. I wanted to know everything, but I bit my tongue and nodded. Like in slow motion, I opened my mouth again, the curiosity I had stuffed down about to crack and spill out. It was one of my worst traits, the inability to shut the hell up.

The Organiser shook her head, as if able to tell I was on the verge of talking. "Questions will be answered at the end if they remain." The rasp in her voice was low as her cigarette fell to the floor behind her, her thick platform sole crushing it into oblivion without a missed step.

Then we walked in silence. We wound through wide hallways and narrow side-alleys, until she stopped in front of a wide, yellow door. The hinges were painted vivid red—the same vibrant colour as the door handle and her hair.

With a flick of her wrist, the double doors swung open, their hinges squeaking. I wondered if the Epitome Lab had similar clearance chips to Rosalind Institute. They had become a wonder technology a few years ago; everyone above a certain level was granted the ability to have one implanted for ease of access and proof of importance.

The room behind the yellow doors was wide but small. I blinked a few times, letting my eyes adjust to the array of mismatched colours and patterns within.

The Organiser strutted forward, flopping into a large red chair. Its thick fabric swirled in different shades of red, with large fabric buttons sewed on every few centimetres.

The red of the chair differed from the red of the wallpaper, giving the room a strange glow.

"Sit, sit." She tugged at the arm of her chair, pulling it up to reveal a stash of cigarettes, lighters, and mints.

I looked to where she pointed. Another chair sat in the centre of the room, boxed in by thick wooden bookcases crammed with books.

Perched in front of it was a small coffee table littered with empty cigarette packets, accompanied by worn magazines, printed papers, and bits of ash.

I shimmied my way across to the chair, weaving around the stacks on the floor and trying not to bump anything that may dislodge and come crashing down around me. I hoped the hardest part of this was over.

"My apologies," she said as I took a seat and looked across at her, trying to keep my face neutral. "I wasn't expecting to brief any of the final eight personally." She followed her words with a handful of breath mints. The smell wafted across the room, and I was grateful to smell something that wasn't smoke.

I gave her a brief, weak smile. The strangeness of sitting here was finally sinking in.

"Miss Avery," she said matter-of-factly, "it's time you understand your unlikely position here." A frown tugged at her, but her face seemed bright. A tinge of happiness and excitement lingered in her eyes.

"My position?" My eyebrows tugged downwards. I repeated the two words, but my mind was stuck on another—*unlikely*. With a pang in my chest, I forced my body to sit still and listen.

"When *the lottery* was introduced all those years ago, it aided in slowing population growth and ensured we considered only the most viable foetuses for full-term births."

I knew at least this much about the history of the elusive *lottery*. When it was first introduced, it was somewhat of a secret. Women across Australia were asked to sacrifice for a little while for the *greater good*, but as it grew, so did its secrecy, reach, and power.

"However." She paused and let out a long sigh. "As with everything in life, men, money, and fame interfered in the process."

My eyebrows had knitted together, pressing so tightly that I thought it may never release. I may have been mumbling these exact words to myself fifteen minutes ago, but to hear them aloud here was shocking.

"Your frown is correct, Miss Avery. Now, the final eight contains five women who have the means to *buy* a spot." Her words hung densely in the air, wrapping their meaning around my heart.

"Only three of us are legitimate candidates?" My mouth gaped open. I had known something was wrong, but not to this extent.

She answered with a curt nod, her smile fading. She seemed remorseful, and I couldn't help but wonder how much of this was solely her fault.

"Money really can buy you anything." I scratched the back of my head, the hairs on the back of my neck prickling.

"*Almost* anything," she said, staring pointedly at me. "That is the way the lottery now operates." She slumped, summing up her talking points with a shrug of her shoulders. "Now," she continued, sweeping her hand across the room in front of her, "for the reason we are here. The briefing about the next test."

I nodded, trying to focus, my mind still processing the last batch of information. Could I really be one of only three legitimate candidates?

"From the final eight forward, each candidate must compete based on their own wit and skill."

My frown bounced into raised eyebrows, inverting to surprise.

"Yes." She nodded, sensing my disbelief. It was hard to believe she was telling me the truth. "The hard intelligence testing is complete, and that is both good news and bad news," she said. "The next test is unpredictable, and you aren't able to prepare for the outcome." A sad smile lingered on her face while she groped within her pockets, another handful of mints finding their way into her mouth.

I cocked my eyebrow. "I'm not scared of hard work," I said, and she shook her head. It felt strange—to sit here and talk calmly and candidly to one of your captors. I *almost* forgot that fact a little too often.

"The outcome has already been determined, we just don't know it yet," she said cryptically. The multiple mints in her mouth clinked together as she talked.

I opened my mouth to speak, but realised I had no words or theories popping to the tip of my tongue. Her words had thrown me.

"This year's lottery needs a female foetus," she said after a long, drawn-out pause. The words clicked into place. I understood them in theory, but in practice I was dumbstruck.

"A female…" I half-repeated. No question, *that* outcome was already decided, and no amount of hard work or determination could change it. "To make it this far…"

"Yes, Miss Avery," she said. "It is almost cruel. No woman can determine the sex of their baby…many try, but it is *at best* an inaccurate science." I lingered on the word *almost*, as if I was shocked they didn't outright call it torture.

"When?" I asked, the question popping out of me as she opened her mouth to continue. I needed to know when this would happen—when this next step would be decided. How much longer I may have to carry a foetus that had been doomed from the very beginning.

"The gender testing is conducted at twenty weeks."

I crossed my arms, feeling a strange tingle shoot down the back of my spine and into the tops of my shoulders.

"The sex is pre-determined each year. Ultimately, the balance of male-female is kept in line, although not in *exact* order," she said, caving and grabbing a cigarette, the end burning to ash in seconds.

She looked up as her breath seeped out, the smoke billowing into a cloud above her head. Her whole body visibly relaxed and loosened. I missed the ability to chug a beer and feel both a little sick and immediately calm.

"How many full-term babies are born each year?" I asked, trying to sneak my most pressing question in right as the nicotine hit her system.

She frowned, eyeing me as she took another drag. I didn't think she would answer, but she gave me a tiny crumb.

"The world is complicated, Miss Avery. You would do well to remember that." She wasn't mad, but her tone signalled the end of that conversation. She didn't leave a gap for anything else. "We are at the half-way point for this round of the lottery," she pushed on, as if my previous question had never existed. "Logic, mathematics, and chance tell us that on average, four women will be eliminated here. We will have our final four." A sad smile formed on her lips as they wrapped around the butt of her cigarette.

"And then, there were four," I said. "Wh—" I opened my mouth to speak before closing it again and chewing on my bottom lip.

"You may ask," she said, raising an eyebrow at me. Her face was a strange combination of old and gnarled, soft and kind. "But I may not answer."

"Are the foetuses aborted on site here through the different stages of the lottery?" I asked. I chose my first question carefully, not wanting to stop her answers immediately. I had so many questions around this part of the lottery, and I desperately wanted answers.

"Yes, Miss Avery." Her eyes narrowed and the corners of her mouth twitched. She was cautious, but it seemed she would tell me what she could.

I let my hands fall into my lap and repositioned myself on the uncomfortable chair. The air turned stale and uncomfortable as the silence grew between us.

"And are the foetuses *utilised?*" I whispered, straightening up and leaning forward.

"This is the most innovative, forward-thinking, *experimental* lab in the country," she said, her body folding forward towards mine. "No opportunity is wasted."

Her words rang in the air like a lit cannon, the wick burning down my chest and setting to explode in my stomach. She was giving me the answer I was searching for, *telling* me in no uncertain terms what was happening, all without actually saying it aloud.

I swallowed the growing lump in my throat. I didn't know whether to laugh or cry, to thank her or fight with her.

"The truth isn't always pretty, Miss Avery." Her eyes narrowed as if she could read my mind.

She was right. "Thank you for being candid." I cleared my throat, the acid in my stomach spreading and dissipating. I appreciated her honesty, but hated the answers.

"If I am permitted to answer your questions, I will, Miss Avery." She sighed and rubbed her eyes. "But, for now…" She took the last drawn out drag of her cigarette. The ash reached the very end and crumbled off as smoke escaped from the edges of her mouth. "We must return you to your living quarters." She pushed herself out of her red chair, her outline sunken into its soft fabric.

"Will I remain in my room until the gender scan?" I didn't make a move; my mind counted another fourteen long days between eighteen and twenty weeks' gestation.

"Yes, but…" A little smile danced across her lips, and she said nothing more.

I pulled myself out of the chair, raising my eyebrow at her. Everything about my body felt heavy. As I tried to squeeze myself out, my stomach knocked straight into the pointed edge of the bookcase. I had to admit I still wasn't used to the growing belly.

I managed to catch one book as the bookcase shook and four more books hit the floor.

"Sorry," I whispered, crouching and picking up the books, trying to re-arrange them on the shelf with little success. She watched me struggle for a few seconds before waving me off.

"There is no magic place for them," she said with a smile. I haphazardly shoved the last book up against another, both of them pointed at a strange angle.

She waved her wrist, and the heavy, yellow doors connected to their runners and swung open.

"After you," she huffed, her voice raspier than a few seconds ago. It seemed the slightest physical exertion took its toll on her throat; her feet, on the other hand, were far quicker.

She walked through after me, letting the doors close with a loud *thump* behind us.

I hesitated a few steps ahead, not knowing where we were.

She strode past me, teetering on her platform shoes, and took the lead.

I watched her back. Her red hair swayed in rhythm with her body. She paused for a second, her stride not missing a beat before twisting to the left, down a corridor. "For this two-week stint in isolation, we will provide you with your phone." Her tone was soft and pleasant, as if she had just told me it was going to be sunny tomorrow.

I jogged a few paces, so that we were walking side-by-side and opened my mouth.

"*A phone*," she said, eying me. The distinction was clear. I wanted to argue, but then they would just yank it away entirely.

"It is a rule in this facility that if you make it this far, you should be allowed a small connection to the outside world," she explained. "There are rules, of course." Her pace picked up again. My legs hustled to keep up and remain by her side. I found myself puffed in only a few steps.

"Of cour—" I half-puffed before she was rattling off the list of banned activities. They mostly revolved around not speaking to the media and not telling the whole truth.

I nodded, smiling. "So no talking to the media?" I confirmed sweetly after her rant. It was fun to pretend I hadn't really gotten it.

A stark look shot out from her side glance, but when she saw my face she let out an exasperated sigh. It felt good to still be the joker for a split second.

"You are free to talk to friends and family. However, do not be too specific. Keep conversations to personal thoughts and feelings, minimise information sharing about the facility." Her platform shoes swivelled from under her as she turned right, pirouetting at the last second, to send us down a new corridor.

We walked forward at breakneck speed, my legs having to jog every few steps to keep up. She might be small, but she was fast.

"The camera will be disabled, but the speaker will work. You are allowed three phone calls a day, each timed at thirty minutes." The rules just kept coming, and all I could think of was the excitement in Kit and Darcy's squeals and the sound of Mason's voice.

We halted. The Organiser looked back and forth down the corridor, at the rows of identical plain, white doors . We spun around, walking back the way we came.

I smiled silently as we wandered the halls, twisting ourselves around and turning back in on our pathways. This is why I didn't bother to run; even the Organiser had no idea which way to go. We were lost in the labyrinth.

She began to mutter to herself as she turned around again and again, twisting her body back to look once more at the way we had come. If *she* was confused, I would be hopelessly lost.

"Is that all the rules?" I finally asked when we turned down yet another corridor, this one containing all red doors.

"Yes," she snapped, stopping in the middle of the corridor and slamming her arms across her chest in a huff. She muttered to herself under her breath. I forced myself to walk a few paces away while she fiddled with something in her pocket.

I parked myself in front of one of the red doors, sneaking a few side glances back at her. She pressed a black hand-held remote with a large red button on it.

I stifled a giggle, and her head snapped towards me. I turned away, suddenly very interested in the embellished gold door knob affixed to the red door.

I stared at it, my eyes actually unfocused while I tried not to meet my guide's eyes.

She was scowling. The deep carved lines on her forehead were obvious even from a few paces away.

I chuckled, pacing a few steps down, towards another identical, red door. Everything felt surreal and funny for a moment; we were lost in the labyrinth of the facility, and my host was clearly known for getting lost—even with her own beacon button.

A loud shriek pierced my ears. The sound reverberated inside my ear drums.

I swivelled around on my heel; a second loud shriek pierced through the air behind me. My eyes darted around, looking for the source.

I turned on my heel again, going around in a full three-hundred and sixty degrees when I realised that the Organiser and I were the only ones in the hallway.

I spun around. An array of sharp screeches bounced along the walls of the narrow corridor. I ran door-to-door, pulling on door knobs.

"Miss Avery," she said, her scowl turning into a frown. She was commanding me to stop with just a look.

"That noise—" I choked out before another, deeper scream pierced my ears. I grabbed another locked door. My breathing jumped, and my chest tightened.

"Miss Avery," she said, more firmly this time. "This is the termination wing of the facility." The words felt like she had slapped me across the face.

I opened my mouth to say something, and then shut it again as another whimpering, sob-laden scream pierced the corridor. Now it was my turn to choke down a sob.

"As you can appreciate, the women here are mostly very upset." Her shoulders twitched, and the noises continued to come, intermingling as they seeped through the cracks and spilled under the red doors. I thought she would pull me away, but she didn't. She let me stand in the termination wing—*listening*.

I placed my hand on the nearest door, my fingers twitching against it. I tried to send a few words of comfort to the women behind the doors.

"Madame Organiser?" A deep voice broke through my thoughts. "Madame Organiser," the thick voice hollered again. This time, I turned away from the door, my hand dropping to my side limply. Those screams had shattered something inside me.

"Miss Avery," the Organiser called to me, clicking her fingers and turning away in a matter of seconds. It felt strange to both feel intense pity for the women here, and jealous that their journey was over. Pain today for peace tomorrow. I wondered if I would make that bargain here and now.

I trailed behind the two of them. They kept up a spritely conversation, chatting casually about good meals the cafeteria had served in the past week. Part of me was surprised at the normalcy; the other part had become so numb to the chaos of this place that I felt nothing.

I watched my feet, not wanting to see any more doors—red, green, yellow, or otherwise. I focused on the rhythmic sound of the footsteps that three people, out-of-sync, made against marble.

"Thank you, Minister," she said when we came to a halt.

I stopped a few feet away, head down, waiting. I had hoped the Organiser had simply gotten lost, but it felt like she had wanted me to see that, to *hear* those screams as a warning. I hoped I was wrong.

The minister cleared his throat and swiftly passed me, not saying another word as he rounded the corner.

"Miss Avery," the Organiser said, now rounding her body to face me.

We stood in-front of an ornate, green door. Three different shades of green swirled throughout the carved pattern, intertwining and lacing together.

"This will be your personal headquarters until the gender scan in fourteen days," she said, running her finger down the crease of the door until a small, black box popped out.

With a thumb and fingerprint and scan of her wrist, the door sprang open, revealing the room within.

"Please." She waved me in..

I shook my head, biting my lip. There were so many things I wanted to say, so many words and obscenities I wanted to scream at her.

"What was wrong with the other room?" I asked, lifting my head to stare at her. Tears prickled in my eyes, and I suddenly, desperately wanted to be alone.

"Other room?" she asked, almost confused, until she clicked her fingers and smiled at me. "We have different wings for each stage." She shooed me inside, her bony fingers poking into the fleshy part of my shoulders.

"Each sta—" I half-said before she pushed me all the way inside the new room. My jaw dropped open. The room was enormous, easily twice as big as the previous room.

I spun on the spot with wide eyes. It felt like a strange paradox between privilege and pain.

A giant four-poster bed took up a third of the room, its sleek, black frame shining under the warm lights.

I wandered forward, ignoring the bed and making a beeline for something the other room didn't have.

"Are these?" I asked, running my finger along the edge of the shiny black bookcase.

"Yes, Miss Avery," she said with a smile. "We consider your presented interests and stock the rooms accordingly." Stocked perfectly for my fortnight's *prison stay*, I wanted to say.

She didn't move from the doorway. She simply hovered, observing while I wandered around. In some ways, I was sure even this was a test, that even in these little moments I was being watched, scored, drawn, and quartered.

I ran my fingers down a few of the book spines. A haphazard combination of classic literature, medical textbooks, and trashy romances were piled onto the shelves, with no rhyme or reason to their sorting.

Next to the bookcase was a sleek, odd-shaped black desk, with an old model phone on its reflective, black surface. My hands grasped at it, turning it over in my fingers. It felt foreign, like I was really breaking their rules.

"Remember the rules, Miss Avery," the Organiser chided with a nod.

I clasped the phone tight to my chest, and she turned her back on me.

“Breakfast at seven, lunch at one, dinner at six,” she said, walking away. She moved her hand up in the air in a half-wave; the other hand madly dug in her pockets. I could just make out her pulling out a cigarette packet as the door creaked shut behind her.

“I guess this is it,” I said with a shrug. I clutched the phone to my chest. The small, glass screen was cold through my clothes.

I fell into bed, toppled into a heap, and closed my eyes. I took a few deep breaths, my pulse finally slowing, my body turning heavy. I finally let the tears come and lost myself in a long-held wave of sadness.

CHAPTER TWENTY-FOUR

THE ROOM

SOS, I TYPED INTO A NEW GROUP CHAT WITH DARCY AND KIT. THE BIG, bold letters looked foreign to me as I waited, almost holding my breath. I wondered if they would know, or if I would have to explain who was randomly messaging them at 11 p.m. on a Tuesday.

Kit's three little dots popped up first. The swing of their movement captivated me.

Who dis? Darcy fired back before Kit had even finished typing.

I snort-laughed, my eyes immediately tearing up.

Avery???? Are you okay? Where are you? What's happening? Are you okay??? Kit finally replied, the question marks in her text far outweighing any actual words. She had given me so many questions to answer. They were like chalk and cheese; Darcy, the brawn, Kit the brains, and then me—not exactly sure who she was anymore.

I'll explain everything, I fired back. The three little dots popped up from Kit again as I thought about how to answer her questions without breaking the rules.

Made it through to the next phase, I wrote. This was true without telling them any *real* information.

Physically, getting big!!!! I added, with a few sad face emojis and crying, laughing face emojis so they would know I was *mostly* joking.

Kit's dots disappeared for a few seconds before re-joining the chat again. She'd clearly changed her mind with what she wanted to write. I knew the feeling.

I gripped the phone, lying in bed and staring up at the ceiling. It was late, and my eyes burned, but I couldn't look away. I needed something to connect me to the real world.

"Maybe I should have called," I whispered to myself as both Darcy and Kit's dots flittered in and out of the messages, my head sinking further into the soft squishy pillows.

A soft *ping* rang out, followed in quick succession by another two. I held the phone above my head to squint at the bright screen.

When are you coming home, girl? flashed Darcy's message.

We miss you, followed Kit's, a photo attached to the text.

I clicked it open and it loaded in small segments, until it reached the half-way point and turned black, an error message displayed there instead.

Photos were banned from the outside, too—good to know. I sighed, sat up, and crossed my legs. My silk long-sleeved PJs kept getting stuck under the bottoms of my feet, far too long for my short legs.

Hope that's a happy photo of you two, I tapped back. *But alas, no photos allowed within these walls*. A pang tugged at my heart. I wished I could see their faces. It would feel so comforting to see Kit's frizzy hair and nightgown and Darcy's oversized smile and horrible tan.

Six sad face emojis shot back from Kit. *So tell us what's going on?*

Let's see, I wrote, trying to buy myself a few seconds to think what to say. *I'll find out in less than two weeks if the foetus is a boy or a girl.* My finger hovered over the send button for a few seconds longer than usual, until I backspaced and replaced the word foetus with baby. It felt like a big change, a milestone almost—like I was finally admitting something to myself. Scientific me knew that wasn't *completely* accurate, but in my heart it felt right.

They tell you that??? Kit fired back. I could hear the confusion in her voice.

The testers like to know, I wrote, wondering if that part would get flagged.

And do you want to know??? Darcy wrote, popping up again and disappearing just as quickly.

Kinda, I wrote, adding in the thinking face emoji. *It's late.* As much as I wanted to talk to them, I felt on edge, like my body was somehow screaming to call them and to end the conversation simultaneously.

Three-way call tomorrow? I typed, trying to get all my words out before either of them asked another question.

I'm in, Darcy fired back in a matter of seconds.

1pm? Kit wrote. She would forever be the keeper of time, even when we were separated.

Locked in, I wrote. I threw the phone down when I saw they had both seen the messages.

I stood and paced back and forth across the length of the room, which felt like it was shrinking. I ran my fingers across my bed frame, desk, and the spines of the books on my bookcase, muttering to myself. I couldn't find anything here that fully consumed me.

"Half-truths?" I mumbled. "Not the test specifically. Talk about how I feel?"

I struggled to workshop the questions I knew Kit and Darcy would want answers to tomorrow. But I had no answers, and even with two brains in one body, I felt sluggish and silly.

The soft leather swallowed up my butt and legs as I plonked myself down at the desk. I propped my feet up and leaned back as far as it would let me, bouncing on the spot.

"Not the facility," I murmured to myself, bouncing the chair back and forth. "Thoughts and feelings." I groaned and dropped my head into my hands. I scratched at my eyes, my fingers poking too hard, causing them to water. I had never been good at talking about my feelings.

I flung myself forward, pulling the computer closer to me. It felt strange to have access to information, and I knew what my heart wanted to search for.

With a few clicks, I opened a search bar and typed in *how do you feel about your pregnancy?*

With a frown, and an uncomfortable pit in the bottom of my stomach, I hit enter, and a never-ending list of results popped up before my eyes.

I scrolled down, trying to find an article title that didn't include *elated, miracle,* or *best-day-of-my-life* in the headline.

I scrolled meaninglessly through a few pages worth of cringe headlines, many with questions about how to hide pregnancy from doctors versus it being the best news ever with no factual information.

With a sigh, I leaned back, clicking onto a new page for the eighth time.

AI Babies: Way of the future? The headline caught my eye. Every adult in the sciences had heard the whispers of AI babies, but I hadn't given it much thought. It wasn't in the realm of my research, and it certainly wasn't a personal endeavour.

I clicked the link with a frown sinking deeper into my forehead. Curiosity peaked as the page loaded in dribs and drabs, and I tapped my fingers against the desk, impatient as always. The first few lines had short quotes about *designer babies* and *blonde hair, blue eyes*—nothing ground-breaking. The page was outdated; half the links were broken and the rest configured weirdly.

I was half-irritated, half-surprised that I had clicked on the link to begin with. These online conspiracy theories usually just gave me something to laugh about with other science nerds.

With a sigh, I shook my head, my fingers scrolling one last time.

I was about to close out when a single line appeared as a tagline at the bottom of the page.

It read *Manufacture Everything; Even your Babies Gender*.

I cringed at the incorrect use of the word 'babies' as I read the line over again. The frown deepened on my forehead, the lines pressing into my skull.

I just stared at the six words written on this very outdated, defunct website.

I shut the screen. The pixels that echoed in my mind went black one-by-one as my eyes glazed over. I had so many questions—about designer babies, the information shared with those in power, the fact money could now buy you *almost* anything.

I leaned back in my soft leather chair, my body sinking further into the fabric.

It seemed surreal to think a pregnancy journey hinged on this. I knew they could test gender earlier with the new blood tests, so why wait until now?

I rocked back and forth and roamed my new space. The room was foreign—the white walls, the coloured spines in the bookcase, the hint of gold that sprang from the bedsheets. It all melded together to create a strange tapestry of shades within my unfocused eyes.

Buzz, buzz.

I jumped and looked around. The loud ringtone blasted out of the phone as it vibrated against the desk, the screen lighting up every few seconds.

I paused, losing focus for a few seconds before the phone buzzed again, making me jump a second time before answering.

"H-hello?" I croaked out, awkwardly clearing my throat.

"Alice? Alice?" a huffing male voice shot through the line, soft and panicked.

"This is she?" I frowned and pulled the phone away from my ear.

No caller ID, I thought, rolling my eyes and wondering if my first call since getting a phone back might be a telemarketer.

Well, being a contestant in the lottery is a pretty good excuse to not buy whatever they're selling, I thought, chuckling to myself as the silence between us stretched out.

"Ah, hello?" I said again, my tone changing to snippy.

"S-sorry," the voice stuttered, the words getting stuck in their throat and coming out squeaky. "I-it's Mason," he said, after another long, awkward pause. "Kit messaged me you had a phone, a-and..." He took a long, shaky breath.

I looked up at the sky and cursed Kit for a few seconds before Mason began speaking again.

"I-is—" He started and stopped. "A-are—"

"Mason," I said firmly. He needed to stop rambling; it was making me more nervous by the second. The other end of the line fell silent except for the obvious tones of laboured breathing. "We already slept together. You don't have to be so nervous," I said, half-laughing, half-rolling my eyes. I was best at diffusing tension with a joke; I just hoped it would break the ice.

I heard a small chuckle from the other side, followed by a deep sigh. "I just wanted to see how you were," he said, his words finally coming out in a coherent sentence, which further cemented the smile that had been left on my face from before. His nerves were sweet, and I reminded myself that it showed he cared.

"Well," I said, wondering how honest to be, "physically, me and baby are fine. Healthy and growing according to schedule." I tried to give him a virtual thumbs up through the phone. My voice sounded weird, and I hoped he didn't know me well enough to notice.

"Good, good," he said hurriedly. "But..." He dived straight past my pathetic half-answer. "How are *you*?" he asked, a big emphasis on the *you*. *He knew*, and now it was my turn to be awkward and have trouble forming cohesive sentences.

My heart hammered against my rib cage, pounding in my ears. I forced myself to pull the phone away from my ear and took a deep breath. It was time to tell someone the truth, and Mason happened to be in the hot seat, happened to be the one who asked.

"I'm lonely," I said, taking a breath before I continued. "And I'm scared. Of what is going to happen, of what tests are yet to come, of the fact the *entire nation* might soon know my face...of winning, of losing." The words poured out of me like an upside-down funnel, trickling at first and then gushing out. This would be a good test of Mason's ability to calm me down. "And the next test is completely out of my control. I can't prepare, and I am *so tired*." My voice cracked at the very last word, my breath rattling. I felt the tears burning the backs of my eyes, stinging as I fought to keep them there. I didn't want to turn into an incoherent sobbing mess—that could wait until later.

"Alice," Mason said softly. But I wasn't done.

"And in all of this, *I am alone*." A choked sniffle escaped, and I tried to mask it with a cough. I cringed and fell silent. Mason's silence stretched on, and I wished I had just stayed quiet, said I was fine, pretended this wasn't wearing me down.

"Alice," Mason said again after a few seconds' pause. I imagined him making an excuse to hang up, to say 'chin up' or some sort of pathetic empty words. "I can't possibly understand what you're going through." He paused and I realised he was really in this; he was hearing me. "I called because I didn't *want* you to feel alone." His words were clunky, but the meaning behind them was genuine. He might not know what to say to the woman he slept with once, who was now locked up because of their love child, but he was still trying, and that counted for something.

"Thank you," I whispered. "I know I'm not alone." I let the tears fall; they crashed down my cheeks, cascading towards my chin and neck. "I-I have K-Kit and D-Darcy." My chest heaved. "A-and I-I have…" I trailed off, not wanting to add the *you* that hung on the tip of my tongue. The horrible snot that comes with crying filled my nose. "B-but this isn't w-what y-you w-want," I heaved out as the tears continued. I was mortified, trying desperately to stem the flow, searching internally for the cool-chick he met in the club.

"I slept with Alice Avery," Mason said matter-of-factly. "You are what I want." He was the calm one now. He was so earnest, his voice soothing as I continued to sob, my snot-filled voice rattly and broken. It was the perfect opportunity to say something back, to acknowledge the *something* between us, but I couldn't bring myself to speak any words that mattered. Instead I opted to return to my default and change the subject.

"C-can I ask you s-something?" I asked, the tears still falling, but their ferocity calming.

"Anything," Mason shot back.

I sucked in a deep breath, not used to the sincere offer of honesty. The more I got to know Mason, the more I genuinely liked the man he was.

"H-have you seen K-Kit or D-Darcy since..." I trailed off,, both of us understanding what I meant.

"Seen? No," Mason answered. "But I have spoken to them both. Relatively regularly, actually." The hint of a proud smile shot through the phone, making my eyebrow raise. He chuckled at my obvious lack of response. "I wanted to do the right thing after our last, er, meeting." He stumbled over what to call the awkward encounter we had shared, shackled to a table and forced to share intimate details with an almost-stranger.

"The fated test, b-bringing people together," I laughed, my tears slowly drying up.

I tried to wipe my nose on my shirt, blowing it as Mason continued on.

"So I called Kit, and Kit dialled in Darcy." I could visualise him shrugging as he said the last sentence. "And we chatted." He sounded a little too nonchalant, as if he was trying to be casual. Mason was *anything* but casual; it didn't suit him.

"Oh, you chatted?" I asked, half-amused, half-curious. I looked down at the phone, noting we had already been talking for 17 minutes and 23 seconds, the seconds ticking by as we spoke. Time really did fly when you were baring your soul and having fun.

"And was anything of interest discussed?" Now I was the one trying to sound casual and doing a terrible job.

"We spoke of many interesting things." The grin on his face was visible to me through his words. "Politics, the state of the world, our opinions on global warming," he rattled off. "And," he said, pausing, "the life and times of Alice Avery." The grin changed to a smirk in my head as I groaned, mortified. I gritted my teeth. Those two were in *big* trouble.

"Those two should not be allowed to describe the history of Alice Avery to *anyone*." I tried to sound light, but inside I was mentally calculating what this man now knew about me.

"They are marvellous historians," Mason retorted. "Quite the record keepers actually, *and* they provided photographic evidence to back up their historic claims." A loud chuckle shot through the phone now as I groaned, louder and longer than before.

I took a dramatic, quivering breath. "The first thing I'm going to do after getting out of here and hugging both of them, is kill them." I laughed. My shoulders shook and my chest felt a little lighter. They were lucky Mason still seemed so kind and interested, but I guessed they shared things with him because they *knew* he was.

"It's nice to hear you laugh," Mason said, a hint of sadness mixed with his cheery voice.

"It's nice to feel it," I said, sure my voice sounded the same as his. "So, any big news from the outside?" I tried to change the subject before I cast any more of a downer on the conversation that Mason had worked so hard to turn fun and light.

Mason paused for a few seconds for dramatic effect. "*A lot* of celebrities have gotten married…and then divorced." He chuckled, and I imagined Kit telling him some of these details and Mason being too polite to tell her he didn't care. "Actually, you're probably the only other person who would find this tidbit interesting." His tone changed to excitement.

"Tidbit," I mouthed to myself, shaking my head. "What are you, *ninety*?" I laughed.

He chuckled and sighed, not acknowledging my words. "My company has just announced something big."

I was sure Mason was talking slowly on purpose. He loved the slow build, but right now was *not* the time for it—calls cut out at midnight and the minutes were ticking by.

"They have been hinting at it for weeks," Mason droned on, talking in circles. "And then yesterday—bombshell." He made a weird exploding noise. He was such a *dork*. Why was he also *so* endearing?

"And *what* would that *bombshell* be?" I said through gritted teeth, trying to sound patient and calm, but knowing my voice was thick with irritation.

"Glad you asked." He clicked his tongue a few times and cleared his throat three times.

I looked down at my phone screen.

"Mason, I don't mean to rush you," I said, "but calls stop at midnight."

"And it's 11:57," he said, clearly having checked the time. "I got the grant," he strangled out, and I knew ruined his big, building moment with my impatience.

"You got the grant?" I whispered, heart beating with both pure joy and pure jealousy.

Mason's words were flowing now, coming in over the top of mine. The excitement in his voice was giddying. I wanted to let him have his moment, so I stayed mostly quiet with only the appropriate sound effects until he ran out of words.

I knew the phone was about to cut out any second. It was like being catapulted back in time, and waking up with regrets. I wished I could open up more to Mason, but my heart ached with everything I was missing out on and everything I was experiencing alone.

"Hey," Mason said, realising the same. "You can always get me on this number. Rain, hail, shine…midnight, midday, three o'clock slump. Happiness, sadness, vent," he said. "I'll be he—"

The phone went silent; the phone call was over. They had warned me that there would be no calls between midnight and eight in the morning, and like everything else, their timing was impeccable.

I put the phone face-down and rested my forehead on the cool, black surface of the desk. I sat still for a second cycling between grateful, embarrassed, and nervous-excitement. Talking to Mason had lifted a tiny bit of weight off my chest, but even as his offer to call again still hung in the air, I knew I was unlikely to take him up on it. The vulnerable side of me that came alive with him filled me with dread.

The white carpet was soft under my toes as I got to my feet and stalked back-and-forth, my hands moving from my belly, to the back of my head, to my hips in quick succession.

"*The lottery*," I mumbled, churning over the thoughts in my head. "A platform." I thought, scratching the back of my head. I didn't want to be here, but now that I was, maybe I could do something meaningful.

"They might listen..." I trailed off. I rubbed my hands against my face, trying desperately to work through the radical idea that was forming in my head. I remembered all the autobiographies in every book store, and the idea finally clicked. This might be a chance to speak *and* be heard. "It's decided. It's *showtime*."

CHAPTER TWENTY-FIVE

GOSSIP

BUZZ, BUZZ.

I jumped, my body laid out against the soft sheets of my four-poster bed, the quilt half covering my face. I'd been whiling away time somewhere between dreaming and day-dreaming.

Buzz, Buzz.

The sound shook underneath my pillow. My face vibrated as I struggled to move, limbs heavy. Groping around, I groaned as I groped around, my eyes only half-open.

"H-hello?" I said. A loud yawn escaped my lips.

A chorus of "Alice!", "Avery!", "Hello!" came screeching down the phone. The two voices were so intermingled and loud that I had to pull the phone away from my ear. I pulled myself up to a seated position, immediately awake.

"Hi, hi," I said, cutting off the racket. I stifled another yawn and stretched out my body.

"Hi? That's all we get?" Darcy asked, her fake-irritated voice a grand impression of her real-irritated voice.

"Did you just wake up?" Kit jumped in, waving off Darcy's fake annoyance with an air of concern. I wasn't sure which made my tears prickle more.

"Sort of." I pulled my legs out of the blanket and sat up. "Growing a human is exhausting, you know." I smirked as I pulled myself out of bed. My feet hit the soft carpet, and I started pacing. I didn't say it, but there was nothing else to do here, except stalk the time and make plans I couldn't share.

"How's *that* going?" Darcy butted in.

I frowned to myself as I tried to focus on the conversation, "It's going," I said, trying to add a little chuckle onto the end. I wanted to keep things light, but I seemed to have the opposite effect at the moment— weeks in segregation with tests spliced in between will do that to you.

An awkward silence fell, none of us knowing what to say. I knew I should say more, like I had with Mason, but I couldn't bring myself to be that vulnerable twice in the space of a few hours, and the only other information I had, I couldn't share. I struggled to come up with something, *anything* to break the silence.

"I made it to the final eight," I offered. I knew I should have thought more about this chat—mapped out my statements and questions for the girls.

"Top eight?" Kit asked.

"They've already culled down to the top eight?" Darcy said. They both sounded surprised.

"At only eighteen weeks?" Kit jumped in again. "Have I got those dates right?" I imagined her counting pathetically on her fingers.

I nodded a silent sigh of relief as their normal curiosity returned.

"Those eight women will make it to twenty weeks," I said. "That's the date of the next challenge." I paced back-and-forth, rubbing and dragging my feet against the soft carpet. I pushed my toes in, and the ligaments pulled, the soft carpet leaving tiny, red marks up and down the tops of my feet.

"Come on," I said, "tell me about the outside!" I knew I sounded a little too peppy and excited. They would know it was fake, but I hoped they would indulge me.

It was Kit's turn to waffle on for a few minutes. Her voice was an octave higher than normal as she spoke of celebrities, restaurants she had been to, and about a colleague that got fired for stealing office supplies. All tame, but I laughed at her explanations.

By the end, I was laughing so hard my stomach was shaking. It all felt *so* normal, too normal.

"And then," Kit continued, finishing her story, "they searched everyone...and I had condoms in my desk drawer!" Her voice was incredulous and animated, rising and then getting softer before she groaned into the phone.

"You should have seen her," Darcy said, still laughing. "By night her cheeks were *still* bright red."

Kit groaned again. This time it felt like it came from within, the low, loud sound rumbling out of her.

I laughed, leaning my body up against the wall. The cool surface pressed against my back and neck, and the cold seeped in through my shirt. It kept me grounded.

My face pulled taut as I smiled, my cheeks aching. It felt good to really laugh about something so small and silly.

With a sigh, I tuned back in. Kit and Darcy were still discussing the redness of her face.

"Wait—" I said, putting my hand up as if they could see me. "Why did you have condoms at work?" The words came out barely audible and like wisps of smoke seeping out of my body. They were holding out on me.

"Yes, Kit," Darcy quipped, "why *did* you have condoms in your work drawer?"

Kit immediately started stammering. "W-well, w-what it is," she said, starting again and then pausing before saying anything. "The thing..." She started again, before sighing.

I laughed alongside Darcy as we listened to Kit stammer and struggle, the corners of my eyes prickling. I missed sitting across from them, talking about work, boys, and sharing silly stories between us. I missed feeling like I could tell them anything, but being monitored constantly really put a dampener on my ability to share.

Kit sucked in a deep breath.

"Harry, lunch at work," she said, the entire sentence not quite making it out of her mouth.

I laughed as a single tear dribbled out of my eye, snaking down my cheek and settling on my upper lip. I felt both happy to be here, having this conversation, and sad to be here having this conversation. It was a strange and awful paradox.

I sunk back into the bed. My body pressed into the soft fabric of my sheets and sank into the mattress.

Kit stumbled on for a good few minutes, giving half words and gushing half details about Harry—her latest squeeze. I listened in silence, her joy and embarrassment almost my own.

My mouth couldn't decide whether to smile or frown. My eyes prickled every few seconds as any new piece of information came up about my two best friends. I missed them fiercely.

"I'm incredibly surprised you've gotten this far without giving it away," Darcy laughed, her voice so airy. My stomach churned.

"And what secrets do you have to share, Darcy?" I piped up, my voice sounding foreign inside my head. I knew I had to keep talking, keep trying to be present.

I pulled the phone back, looking down at the clock on the call that read 17:54 and continued to rise. Her words weaved in and out of my consciousness as I stared at the ticking seconds.

Closing my eyes, I lay back, placing the phone in the middle of my forehead. It balanced there for a few seconds, the eerie, distorted sounds of Darcy's voice coming out, soft then loud. In that moment, I almost broke, almost spilled the dangerous and chaotic plan I was forming.

"S-sorry guys," I cut over Darcy's last sentence. In typical Avery fashion, I wanted to cut and run. "Timer is running out." I cleared my throat, the corners of my eyes stinging as I fought to keep my words clear.

"A, come on." Kit's sweet, kind voice broke over my half-hearted attempt to jump off the phone before the tears started. I felt so ashamed and disconnected, and I just wanted to get away.

"We have no idea what you're going through," Darcy said, her voice sounding sweet. She wasn't usually one for mushy kindness.

My eyes filled up, tears jiggling on the brim. I knew I wouldn't be able to hide them if I spoke again.

"Talk to us," Kit said, talking over my now near-constant sniffling.

"Be real," Darcy added, her voice sterner than before, although it wavered towards the end.

"R-real?" I said, the tears finally spilling over, my cheeks flushing red as I tried to suck in a breath unsuccessfully, the air catching in my throat. "All I wanted was an orgasm," I said, through the tears. "I got *way* more than I b-bargained for."

Kit and Darcy's laughter shot down the phone, loud and honest.

"And now…" I laughed and cried at the same time. "I think I want to win. To have a platform. To speak. To fight. And I have these weird, bubbly, awkward feelings for Mason…And I have to compete against other want-to-be-mothers." I let out a weird, shaky sigh. "They want their babies *so* desperately. And this place—" I sucked in a deep, wavering breath and bit back the words I wanted to say. I didn't want to risk our call being cut short. "And, worst of all," I said, changing the subject as my tears dried and my heart beat faster, "this growing-a-human thing is *exhausting*, and emotional, and uncomfortable, and my belly is getting huge." It was all true, but it felt strange to say any of it aloud.

"Circle all the way back…" Kit said.

"You have feelings?" Darcy said, cutting her off.

"*For Mason*!" They both said in unison, sending a shiver down my spine.

"Yes?" I said, although it came across as a question, not an answer. "Maybe? I-I…" now it was my turn to stutter, realising I shouldn't have said anything to these two women knowing they were talking to him on the outside.

"Since *when*?" Kit said, her voice strangled and quiet. I could imagine her startled face, her mouth gaping open, eyes wide. She always had the best shocked face.

"Probably since the beginning," I said, sighing and hating to admit it. "But I only realised it *for real*," I added, throwing up air quotes to the empty room, "when I spoke to him last night." My voice sounded calm and collected while my heart hammered inside my chest, drumming against my ribcage and thumping in my ears. "This is *your* fault," I said laughing.

"A–" And then the voice cut out and dead silence rang from the other end of the phone.

"H-hello?" I stuttered, pulling the phone away from my ear and staring down at the screen. It was blank; the call disconnected. Thirty minutes went fast when you had been separated for weeks on end.

"Fuck," I whispered, knowing I was only talking to myself.

Well, now everyone important knows. A tiny groan escaped my lips as my cheeks flushed. "Except Mason," I whispered. I dropped the phone on the bed, losing it in the mess of soft, white sheets.

As I turned over onto my side, my eyes blurred.

My phone buzzed again from somewhere within the sheets, its screen light flashing through every few seconds, a little buzz accompanying every message.

I groped around in the sheets, finally finding the cool metal and reading the string of messages flying through from Kit and Darcy.

I smiled and scrolled down. Kit's first messages were full of questions, with twenty question marks following each one, and Darcy talked in GIFs to express her feelings.

I didn't reply. I couldn't reply—not now. It was too much for one twenty-four hour period.

I rolled onto my back and stared up at the ceiling, unsure of what came next.

With a loud, irritated sigh, my body sunk in on itself with my legs curling up to my chest as far as they could. It was becoming more and more obvious that my stomach was growing day-by-day.

Head shoved into my pillow, I let out a stifled scream. The frustration bubbled over and pulled my body up and out of the bed as I threw the pillow across the room. My feet hit the soft carpeted floor and propelled me forwards, pacing back-and-forth across the length of the space. There were too many things to think about. Too many jumbled thoughts racing through my brain.

As the light above me flickered, my thoughts crashed into each other. I stopped for a second, staring up at it, its brightness causing flashes across my vision.

I waved my hand at it, as if staring at the lightbulb would give me a lightbulb moment. It didn't.

Body still quivering, I jumped as two loud knocks at the door interrupted my spiral.

Rooted to the spot, I turned to see the door swing open, another knock coming through as a silhouette stepped into the light.

"Dr. Hidalgo?" I said, the surprise coming through in my tone.

Her small silhouette stepped forward, the light just reaching her. Her warm smile was contagious. My eyes swelled with tears, and I took another few steps forward, stopping just short of throwing my arms around a familiar face.

"Good evening, Miss Avery," she said with a coy smile dancing on her lips.

CHAPTER TWENTY-SIX

NINETEEN WEEKS AND SIX DAYS

I walked into the stark white room, and my eyes fixated on the man in the centre. He stood straight, his arms by his side, expression harsh.

"Miss Avery?" the tester spoke, his drawl bored and flat. He fidgeted with the buttons on his suit jacket as I walked the final few steps. His eyes didn't move when our feet stopped toe-to-toe.

"Yes," I said, trying to project a calm, sweet voice that I wasn't sure I was capable of at that moment. His eyes swept over me, followed by a barely concealed grimace before he turned away, stalking toward the left.

With a wave of his wrist, a small, black box popped out of the plain, white wall.

With a frown, I watched him enter a series of numbers before placing his fingerprint on the screen. The black box retracted as quickly as it had appeared, the lines in the wall now invisible. To our right, the wall began sliding open to reveal a brightly lit corridor concealed behind it.

Without a word, he brushed past me. The starchy fabric of his coat sleeves rubbed against my bare arm and sent a shiver up my spine.

Silently, he marched off, leaving me behind. The lights in the room flickered off.

I scurried forward, assuming I was expected to follow. I stayed a few paces behind him through the labyrinth of underground corridors and rooms.

With sharp right twists and snaking left turns, the only sound I could hear was the *thump* of our footsteps. After we took another right, I almost gasped. Instead, I coughed and lowered my head…but not my eyes.

Ahead of us, another male tester in a grey suit and a very-clearly-pregnant female walked towards us, their strides in sync. The woman smiled, patting the top of her protruding belly. She looked serenely happy from afar.

"Idiot," my tester muttered, low and guttural. He stalked past with me in tow. The other tester averted his eyes, but my head followed them until after we passed each other. I realised the other woman wasn't happy but barely present. Her eyes gave her away, downcast and far away. As they turned the corner, the tester wrapped his arm around the woman's shoulder as her feet wobbled underneath her and they disappeared out of sight.

I opened my mouth, but the words stuck on the tip of my tongue. I knew the lottery was done in stages, but it was clear she was no normal contestant. I started to ask, but the tester stifled my words with his own.

"The interim testing to determine your eligibility to compete is about to commence," he cut over me, his blunt statement hanging in the air like thick, black fog. "From your brief, I was led to believe you understand what this entails." His words were not a question, and left no room for one to be asked.

I nodded, and we stopped in front of a plain, black door. The tester nodded twice as if his explanation was finished, and the silence returned. I wanted to ask, but I had promised Dr. Hidalgo I would stick to somewhat of a script. Everything I was about to do was dangerous.

"I've always found ultrasounds interesting," I said, after the silence had stretched on a beat too long. I had to play this just right; I could ask Dr. Hidalgo about the strange woman later.

The Tester gave me a side-ways glance as he swiped his wrist then a key card. As if you were more likely to steal his arm before his plastic badge.

The door swung open, and a large medical lab sprung up before my eyes.

We stepped in, my feet slow and dragging. My eyes were glued to the tiny details of my scientist dreams coming to life.

"Welcome to the Accelerator Lab," he said, his pitch and tone adding a dash of excitement for the first time. "*Here,* we map the future of science."

We walked through the lab, winding our way through rows of top-of-the-range microscopes, countless computers, and pristine books open to specific pages. Half-full beakers and lit burners flickered as we snaked our way to the back of the room.

My mouth hung open. I believed him. This lab had everything I had ever *dreamed* of at your fingertips.

I reached out to touch one of the microscopes and the Tester snapped. "Follow me." It was both a warning and command.

In the back corner, past an array of noisy clinks, bangs, and dings of working machinery, a small red door sat closed.

The Tester flung the door open, ushering me inside. I dawdled, trying to figure out what each machine was working on—trying to cling to the few futile seconds to take it all in.

As I crossed into the room behind the red door, I chewed on the inside of my lip.

With a wave of his hand, the Tester gestured for me to sit down. The only space available was atop a silver flat bed that sat in the centre of the room. This room felt cold and clinical, nothing like the vibrant lab just outside.

I pulled myself up onto the cool metal, my thighs breaking out in goosebumps.

He was silent as he bustled around the room. With his back to me, he laid out multiple implements, each an odd shape and covered in a thin film of plastic.

He peeled off the plastic with shaky hands, his fingers awkward and fumbling with each tiny movement. He was nervous, and that made *me* nervous.

A frown sank into my forehead as I tried to form the words that I had practiced with Dr. Hidalgo.

"The technology here is incredible," I blurted, my words feeling wobbly. I said the right ones, but they somehow felt wrong here.

He didn't turn around—he only nodded, acknowledging that he had heard me. I had to keep going, even as my stomach twisted in knots.

"I-It's similar to the ultrasound technology on the outside." This time I took a break for a moment before continuing. "I'm glad I had the opportunity to be trained in reading the results—so *fortunate*." I was unable to keep the stinging sarcasm from interlacing with my lines. I'd found my sweet spot—sarcasm covered nerves.

The Tester's back visibly stiffened. His hands stopped mid-air momentarily.

With an audible sigh, he turned to face me. His lip changed between a quiver and a snarl as he looked me up-and-down. He was measuring me, and I forced myself not to shrink. If he was going to look for a sign of weakness, he wouldn't find it written on my face.

"Unfortunately, Miss Avery," he said, his voice flat, "this technology isn't *quite* the same." His eyebrow twitched.

I had him; and we both knew it, I just had to keep pushing.

"I'm sure it has some scientific principles rooted in the past," I retorted, smiling at him. His face turned a vibrant shade of pink. We both knew I was right—but instead of answering me, he turned his back to me again without another word. His shoulders hunched up around his ears, and he peeled the last few pieces of plastic off the new equipment.

Stomping and muttering, he stalked over to the opposite side of the room, pressing his wrist against the wall three times before a soft *click* opened up a small square hatch.

With his back to me, he pressed a sequence of buttons, and the wall behind us folded back. The creased wood zigzagging closed, each layer imprinting into the one before. Even the walls had better technology than I had ever seen.

Within seconds, the entire back wall of the office disappeared, leaving a gaping hole and two large black and white machines.

A loud rap at the door made me jump, but I couldn't tear my eyes away from the machine.

The Tester started muttering. His shoulder twitched as he rubbed his hands together and stalked across the room, already barking in annoyance when he flung the door open. "This is a private tes—" he almost shouted, his voice high-pitched and strangled. Then he took a few steps back, his shoulders sinking down.

"Thank you for the appraisal," the Organiser's curt voice rang out. My head snapped towards her as she entered the room. Her mop of curly, red hair was slicked back today, an unlit cigarette hanging from her lips. She was clearly prepared to light up as soon as she was finished here.

"Organiser," I murmured, a smile seeping up from my chest and spreading onto my face. Dr. Hidalgo had told me this was all done in secrecy, and I was thrilled to find out this part might have changed—or maybe she was simply feeling nosy.

"Miss Avery," she said, swivelling around to face me. Her small body teetering on the top of her high, wedged shoes. "Obligatory check-ins with all the patients," she explained with a wink.

I beamed back at her. Maybe she had felt something sinister as well.

"Show me your preparations." Her voice changed to commanding, and she threw me a raised eyebrow before turning around and closing the gap between her and the Tester.

"Y-yes m-ma'am," he stuttered, his hands now shaking more violently.

"Has the machine been calibrated?" she pressed, her unlit cigarette still hanging between her lips. Her hands groped in her pockets for a lighter and came up empty. It must become a habit, that searching.

With a quick, irritated sigh, she flitted around the room, striking a small fire on an unused bunsen burner. She clearly couldn't wait. The first drag of her cigarette made her shut her eyes.

I giggled, covering my mouth with my hand.

"The machine is in perfect working order," the Tester said, his teeth grinding together. He produced the doppler; a long, white cord stretched out.

With a nod, the Organiser flitted back to my side, her hair wafting a strange mix of peppermint and cigarette smoke in my direction. I crinkled my nose and immediately felt a mix of justified and rude.

"Questions, Miss Avery?" She spoke so casually standing at my side, one hand on her hip, the other keeping the stream of cigarette smoke from clouding around me.

"No," I croaked, trying not to breathe in too deep. "I understand basic ultrasound technology." I glanced towards the now-busy tester who kept his back to us. This was the first time I hadn't had a million questions to ask. But right now, this bad feeling that had been seeping into my bones was just a gut feel, and a secret hunch of Dr. Hidalgo's.

"Good." Her loud voice crackled and boomed in this small space. "*Any* concerns, you can call an attendant." She placed a small, red buzzer in my hand and eyed me with a raised eyebrow and a sharp, crooked smile. "This year, the higher-ups are checking every viable pregnancy *closely*." She backed away from me with a little flick of her wrist and a wave of her hand over her head.

As the door shut behind her, I waved my hands around my face, clearing the last remnants of smoke. Even if I wasn't pregnant, the smell was one of my least favourites.

The Tester didn't speak. His nostrils flared and his eyes narrowed as he crossed the distance between us. He smacked a small black button on the side of the metal table. The table shifted, and I shuffled my body to lie comfortably. I scooted down, my head and feet now raised, my mid-section exposed and flat.

A loud zip startled me and stiff hands pressed against my skin. The Tester ripped open the fabric of the hospital gown, shoving it out the way.

His silence was unnerving. His dark, pinprick eyes fixated on anything but my face as his hands went through the motions.

He swivelled on his heel and turned his back to me. The loud *clicks* of his thick, black, leather shoes echoing in my ears. The room felt smaller than it had thirty seconds before.

Turning onto my side, I laid my head down, observing. He flipped a few switches and dials before jamming his hand onto a large, green button at the side of the huge machine.

With a slow but immediate response, the machine creeped forward, the Tester controlling its movement with a small, black joystick attached to the side. Seconds later, the machine clanged against the top of the metal bed and clicked loudly into place.

I scooted down. The machine clicked into the small indents in the bed and slid into place with a loud and reverberating *click.*

The Tester dropped his hands and circled back around me, returning to my left side. His eyes were dull and lifeless, his face blank except for his top lip that continued to quiver. I felt almost sorry for him; he was clearly in a tough spot.

He pushed away the fabric that had folded over my stomach. His hands were still icy, but his touch was a bit softer.

Pressing another button above my head, a large, silver arm clicked out, hovering inches above my body. The thick cord was twisted into tight curls.

With a quick tug, he gripped the mini-machine tightly, his fingers turning vivid shades of purple and white as he worked.

His eyes were transfixed on the screen above me.

"Three, two, one," he murmured, as if a countdown clock had been provided for him. "Cold pressure." Again, he cut through the silence with the least possible amount of words.

The doppler pressed down on my bladder and squished my internal organs, and I swallowed down a gasp. Only male doctors pushed this hard during scans; it was as if they didn't understand female anatomy at all—that, or they really did hate us.

A few sharp pushes, quick wrist movements, and then he nodded to himself. His face almost transformed as he looked at the small screen which now held a clear view of a head, a body, two arms, two legs, *and the gender of my unborn child.*

"Is that?" I whispered, contorting my head backwards to make out the screen that hung above my head. The black, white, and grey movement was overtaken by a loud *thump, thump, thump* that didn't stop. The whooshing beats filled the whole room with so much life it stopped me in my tracks.

"That is the foetus's heartbeat," he said matter-of-factly. "To ease your mind, the foetus is in perfect health." The twitch of his lip was clear, showing off his teeth every few seconds. I knew he was telling the truth; I could see it with my own eyes.

"A-and what ab—" I mumbled, not wanting to push, but also desperate to know. Was he going to tell me boy or girl? Truth or lie? The Organiser's words rang in my mind – this year, the foetus needed to be a girl.

He cleared his throat, his eyebrows knotting together. He stared at the screen, unblinking, unmoving, jaw clenched together.

Silence filled the room, only broken by the loud thumps somehow echoing from within my body. I shifted in my seat, peeling my eyes away from him and the screen and staring down at my exposed bump. My alien body, puffy and protruding. A body that felt like someone else's and also never more *mine.*

"This foetus is a boy," he said, sighing. His voice was defeated as it tumbled out. Dr. Hidalgo had warned me he might lie, but it still shook me.

"And could you show me?" I hardly let him finish speaking, *just like we practiced.* His forehead beaded with sweat, his twitchy eyes giving him away. I *hated* him for it. How many women had the testers done this too? And *why*?

He sighed again, louder this time. "No, Miss Avery," he said, his voice low. "I cannot." His eyes were closed, his lip trembling.

"Can I ask you a question?" I wasn't sure why I had shifted from my initial retort.

He gave me a curt nod, his eyes still downcast and twitching.

"Why don't they use harmony testing—blood testing—which is *far better* than human technology for this part?" I surprised myself with my curiosity. It was true though; anything with human interference was open to bias, manipulation, and pure mistakes.

He smiled weakly, an understanding taking over his face.

"A true scientist," he said with a soft, lifeless chuckle. "The answer isn't all that complicated. Human verification is what the Epitome Lab is known for. We don't let simple tests provide all the answers. Our human scientists *always* investigate." He gave a shrug.

I nodded in understanding. Even when tests proved me conclusively right, I would look for ways to test the test results.

"And you?" I said, my voice lower and firmer. I wanted to know the why, the how, the history.

"The *why* of the human condition is complicated, Miss Avery," he said wearily. "You are having a girl." His voice had dropped low, his eyes darting towards the door over and over. "I will r-report as such." A lump had clearly sprung up in his throat as his words came out crushed and breathless. "Use that knowledge wisely." He turned away from me and hit the large, green button on the sidewall with a shaking fist.

Above my head, a green light flickered on, shining and bathing everything in a soft hue.

"The ultimate test awaits," he finished.

CHAPTER TWENTY-SEVEN

THE BEGINNING OF THE END

I PACED BACK-AND-FORTH, THE SMALL, WINDOWLESS ROOM SHRINKING and caving in on me. An hour ago, a stranger had arrived at my door and pulled me from my comfortable room to stand here. Alone and wondering, my feet padded against the carpeted floor, wearing the thread thinner with each lap. There was nothing at all in the room. The only sound was the black buckles on my shoes jingling with every step.

I tugged at the weird, form-fitting dress. The high neck pinched my skin, and the zipper rubbed and burned the back of my neck. This time I wore black. The long, sheer sleeves shimmered under the pale, yellow light.

"What's taking so long?" I asked no-one, half-hoping the automated voice would return. I placed my hands up against the plain, concrete walls. The rough texture rubbed against my hands.

A faint thumping sound filled my ears.

Thump, thump, thump.

The sound grew louder.

With a frown, I pressed my ear against the wall. The reverberations grew and bounced underneath my fingers. It sounded like a group of people converging in on me.

With a loud creak, the sound stopped, replaced by one muffled voice. Sharp words were thrown, but even straining against the wall I couldn't make them out.

I held my breath, pressing harder against the wall, and a second later, a louder creak echoed.

A loud voice coughed and pierced through my eavesdropping, and the heat drained from my face as I swivelled around on the spot. The Organiser stood in front of me, hands-on-her-hips, her mane of curly, red hair drowning out the rest of her face. I'd been caught, and I had no intention of apologising.

"Miss Avery," she said in a raspy voice, her eyebrows raised so high they were almost invisible.

I tried my best to smile sweetly.

"Forever curious," she said with a wink. She stepped further into the room, followed by a man in a tailored navy suit. The man's red tie gleamed under the bright lights, and his slicked back hair and trimmed beard shimmered against his pale skin.

"Miss Avery, this is Mr. Dunn," the Organiser stated, her hand waving to the new arrival. I gritted my teeth and forced my smile to remain in place.

"We've had the pleasure," I said, my hands now gripped together behind my back. My chewed fingernails dug into my skin as I stared back at the two visitors. One semi-welcome, the other not at all.

Without missing a beat, Mr. Dunn stepped forward, his tall, gangly frame outstretching a hand towards me.

"Miss Avery," he said, his voice as velvety as I remembered. "I wasn't sure you would remember me." His outstretched hand was only a few inches away from my protruding stomach. We both knew that wasn't true. Men like Mr. Dunn always expected you to fawn over who they were, who they had become.

One-by-one, I let my fingers go and stepped back before shaking his hand. His skin was soft, his handshake tight.

"Most unusual," the Organiser said, side-eyeing Mr. Dunn. Even she could sense the tension. "How are you acquainted?" she asked, almost too casually.

"He's my boss's boss's boss." I crossed my arms against my chest, my eyes bouncing rapidly between them. I wanted to know why he was *really* here.

A nod was all that was returned; her face remained unreadable.

"Come." She twisted on her heel and retreated out the door. "We have a lot of explaining to do." Her voice was high-pitched and sing-song as she exited, her mop of red hair bouncing and disappearing around the corner.

"Av—" I cut Mr. Dunn off and scooted around him, the gap between him and the door just big enough for me to shimmy through. I sighed as my stomach brushed against the wall. I had no intention of making small-talk with him.

The Organiser stood at the end of the hallway, her head flicking right and left while she waited for us to catch up with her. Without a word, we turned right, following the winding hallway down and around, up two flights of stairs, and then down another. We criss-crossed back on ourselves, never saying a word. The more time I spent here, the more I understood how we got lost; this place was more confusing than an actual maze.

As we turned down yet another corridor, a loud exhalation escaped from our leader's mouth.

Back on track, she turned her attention to grappling with her coat pockets. Both walls held framed pictures of past lottery winners, their beaming smiles blazing. They all looked happy, but their eyes looked dead—it was a new detail that made me shiver.

With one more left turn, the Organiser lit up a cigarette. The smoke wafted back and filled the small corridor behind her.

Clamping my hand over my mouth and nose, I scooted to the side, brushing up against Mr. Dunn, who had stepped out of the smoke line as well. Our shoulders bumped together, and I stumbled, pulling myself back.

I opened my mouth to say something, but the Organiser beat me to it.

"This year's lottery is a little different." She turned to face us. The cigarette hung out of her mouth, clinging to the corner of her lip, the tip now red with lipstick. "We're about to explain *why*." She shook her head sadly, as the doors she had pressed up against opened wide.

The florescent light that shone from within made my eyes water. I stumbled forward to follow her bright yellow pumps—three of her steps to one of mine.

We flew up a flight of stairs, with Mr. Dunn staying by my side. Our shoulders rustled against each other—he was too close for comfort, and I scooted behind him on the last flight of stairs.

At the top, four women sat on a small stage, each in a styled black dress, each with a person standing behind them.

"Please sit," the Organiser said, her hand flourishing towards one of the vacant chairs. She peeled off to her place with the other event coordinators.

Watching my feet, I joined the four seated contestants, lowering myself down into the soft, red-velvet chair. My body sunk deep—another reminder that I was slowly getting bigger and my body was not my own.

Mr. Dunn's rigid frame slinked into the space behind my comfortable chair.

Intrigued, I stared down the line of women, their pristine hair and make-up similar to my own. Their dresses were tailored to fit their bodies like gloves. I had never seen so many pregnant bellies. I felt my breath catch as I stared a few moments too long. I *really* had never seen a pregnant belly. It both filled me with dread and unnerved me at this new reality.

This would have been a nice moment if not for the games to come.

I wanted to rest, but I couldn't keep my eyes off the women, half of them whispering to the person who stood beside them; the other half stared straight ahead with almost vacant expressions. I wondered why some seemed happy and others seemed heartbroken.

My frown deepened when the next contestant waltzed up the stage, her high heels clicking against the wood.

Mrs. Astley wore a beautiful sequined black dress draped across her shoulders. The sheer sleeves tailored down her arms; her bump was small and cradled by her hands as she strutted elegantly across the stage.

I noticed she was holding hands with the gentleman beside her. The squat, chubby man's face was plastered with a pleasant smile, his pastor's outfit on full display.

My lip quivered as she sat beside me. Her eyes ran over me, her beaming smile pointed in my direction. The way she looked at me with a combination of disgust and disbelief was unparalleled. I opened my mouth and closed it again. I would've loved to tell her to *fuck off*, but this wasn't the moment.

My stomach bubbled as the seventh woman made her way onto the stage, chaperoned by a thin, suited man who kept his distance.

She took the last seat, and I spun my head back around. Seven women remained. This had to be more than usual, more than all the collaborators expected.

The collaborators stood huddled in a small semi-circle, facing each other. Their hushed voices were muffled as they gestured towards each other. With seven women remaining, they must have been scrambling to reassess their plans.

The Organiser wore a deep scowl on her face. The lines on her forehead were so deep they looked like they may crack apart. She was talking fast, her lips moving in a tight, pursed way. Her fists were balled as one of the other women talked back, her arms crossed against her chest.

With a final flick of her hand, the woman arguing with the Organiser waved her off and side-stepped her, making her way to the front of the stage. I raised my eyebrows; we were about to find out who was really in charge.

"Welcome, contestants." Her voice was sweet and high-pitched, loud enough to carry through the large hall and onto the stage. "Congratulations for making it this far," she continued, eyeing the line-up. Her eyes lingered on certain women, with brief nods bouncing back-and-forth. I rolled my eyes. Even here, in these final moments, money talked. "I…" She paused, running her hands down her tailored, black suit. "...am the Executor of the final tests. You will address me as such."

Her shrill voice reverberated from wall-to-wall. She was so exaggerated in the way she walked and moved; it was *almost* comical.

"I will now explain recent changes from *previous* years." She paused again, this time descending the few steps that separated their raised stage and coming to stand in front of the row of contestants. "Previously," she said, quieter now, "women have competed against each other in the final rounds, intellect-versus-intellect, mother-vs-mother, forcing women to rely only on themselves." She finished with a small sigh, as if this had been a grave error.

I kept my eyes forward, tuning out for a few seconds while the Executor waffled on about women, intelligence, and disadvantage. Instead, I watched the Organiser walk down the stage, her steps small, her movements silent. I half-hoped she would tackle the Executor and I would get to see a fist fight.

"This year," the Executor called, once again forcing me to tune in. My eyes still half-glazed as I watched the Organiser hover a few steps behind her, "we have introduced a new rule. One man from your circle can assist you in your quest for victory." A vibrant smile wiped across her face. "That man is standing behind you."

The blood drained from my face. My cheeks drooped, my mouth flung open. I tilted my head, making eye contact with Mr. Dunn as he stared down at me, his eyes shining under the lights. His smirk covered the entire bottom half of his face.

Wide-eyed, I turned back around. My hands gripped the sides of the red velvet chair, my knuckles turning white.

"Now," she said, clapping her hands together, "Madam Organiser has a few words about how things will *run*." She stung an obvious emphasis on the last word, accompanied by a hard stare as she stepped forward with a curt nod. Two women battling for power would have been more amusing if my fate didn't rest in Mr. Dunn's hands.

"Contestants," she said with a sigh, her voice flat. "Before competing, we will give you a sixty-minute session with your ally. Strategise, discuss, decide how you will compete together." Her voice drawled, and she exhaled loudly again. "You will compete as a team against another team. The winners will move on until there are just two teams remaining. That is where this test will conclude." Her eyes travelled down the line of men that stood behind us, an abject sadness painted below the surface. "Men." Her shoulders sank. "Support your contestants to the best of your ability." She sucked in a deep breath. "As the highest bidders, we hope—" With a loud growl, the Executor stepped forward, and threw her hand in front of her face, cutting her off.

"Thank you, Madame Organiser, that will be *all*," she said curtly. Her eyes narrowed and her nostrils flared wide as she shooed her off the stage, clicking her fingers. The Organiser didn't look sad or chastised at all; instead she glowed. She had told us on purpose.

Highest bidders—the thought ran through my head over-and-over. My fingers ached from the tightness of my fists.

I sat still, eyes following the Organiser being escorted off stage, three large men flanking her. They exited the room, the bounce of her red curls the only parts visible. The doors thumped shut behind her.

The Executor stood with her back to us, her thrown back shoulders high, waiting until the door closed behind her. She lingered for a few moments before turning back to face us.

"There is only one other piece of information to share," she said, her fake sweet voice returning. "As there are seven contestants remaining, the most senior competitor will sit out in the first round. She will join in for round two and compete against the winner."

I bit the inside of my lip, knowing what was about to slide out of her mouth. I braced, but her words still had bite.

"Mrs. Astley." She tipped her head, and Mrs. Astley replied with a gracious bow of her head and clapping her hands together in prayer.

I resisted the urge to both roll my eyes and throw up my hands in an act of sheer willpower.

"As was explained," the Executor continued, a sneer appearing along her mouth, "you will compete together with your appointed partner. You become a team for this test, and both of you will be eligible to answer all questions. You will also be able to discuss answers throughout the game. However, this test is designed for the first correct answer to win the point. Speed is as important as accuracy."

Her words all ran together. It was as if she was explaining the rules of a game-show, not a battle for babies. Her chirpy voice and sweet words made me sick.

"We will provide full rules in the room where you and your assigned partner will meet after this session is adjourned. Please read them carefully." A little sigh escaped her lips. How exhausting it must be to come up with new ways to torture women.

With arms crossed against her chest, she fell silent, her face painted with a deep frown, followed by a forced smile.

"Are there questions *about the upcoming test*?" she asked, her voice sharp towards the end. She was clearly warning us not to ask questions she wouldn't be willing to answer.

I dared a flick of the eye down the row. Most of the women were sitting up straight with thin, polite smiles painted on their faces.

But the woman at the very end of the row twitched. Her shoulders rose to her ears and then pulled away every few seconds. Her eyes were wide—almost wild.

The gentleman that stood behind her wore a smirk, his dark features eying her suspiciously before placing a large hand on her shoulder. His fingers wrapped themselves across the muscles and bone underneath.

With a whimper, she fell back into her chair.

I swallowed, venturing a behind glance.

Mr. Dunn stood with a muted expression, his eyes cast down on me. His mouth was pinched into a thin, white line. I smiled sweetly at him before turning away, my arm thrusting up into the air before my head had snapped back to the front.

"Yes, Miss Avery," the Executor said with a loud, obvious sigh. I was glad she had been briefed about my "curiosity."

"Thank you, Ma'am," I said, bowing my head. I put on my best innocent smile before rising out of my chair. "We are competing *with* our partners, correct?" I asked, waving at the line of men that stood behind each chair.

"Correct, Miss Avery." The curt snap of her voice irritated me. Her eyes narrowed and she stared at me. I could tell she was calculating, trying to figure out ahead of time where I was going.

"Can I ask whose answer will be final?" I got straight to the point.

"Final?" She looked at me quizzically.

"Let me pose an example." I smiled sweetly, speaking up for all the women trapped by the lottery's rules. "Say Mr. Dunn and I are posed a question. Let's make it easy," I said, gesturing to him. "What is five plus five, Mr. Dunn?" I looked at him.

"Ten," Mr. Dunn answered through pursed lips, his mouth twitching. He was clearly unhappy, and that made this whole scenario a little sweeter.

"Perfect," I said with a nod, sarcastically thanking him for his participation. "But say *I think* the answer is nine. *Who* gets the final word?" I forced my hands to stay at my side, my fake smile still in place.

The Executor stared at me, her mouth open. The pleasure of seeing her brain tick over made me wild with joy.

"We've made it this far," I said, adding another layer to make it sound like a plea, "on strength of will or *wallet*. Should *we* not get the final word?" My eyes lingered on the woman seated at the end of the row. The man behind her glowered in my direction, his eyes reduced to pin-prick slits, skin flushed red-raw. He was here to fuck with her, and I was here to fuck with them all.

"Contestants," the Executor said, waving at me to take a seat. "The final word is yours. Use it wisely."

CHAPTER TWENTY-EIGHT

MR. DUNN

MR. DUNN'S ELBOWS RESTED ON THE TABLE, AND HIS BODY LEANED forward on his clasped hands.

The silence in the room was palpable. The lack of noise other than the inhale-exhale of breathing made me increasingly uncomfortable. I sat perfectly still, controlling every inch of my physical body; my sweet smile stayed in place as my insides raged. A deep fire was burning through my entire body, setting alight every nerve and sinew.

I cleared my throat, then let out an irritated sigh. "To what do I owe the pleasure?" My voice was flat with just a hint of curiosity that I couldn't hide. I hadn't wanted to talk first, but I did want answers.

"The pleasure is *all mine,* Miss Avery," he said after a pause, a little smirk dancing across his lips. "Rosalind Institute asked me to check in on one of our *star* employees," he said, his voice fake-excited. The mention of Rosalind Institute was enough to crack my pretend pleasantries.

"Unfortunately, it seems you've been misinformed," I said. "As I told Mr. Venter when he tried the spiel," I took a second to force down an eye roll, "I quit."

The smirk slipped off Mr. Dunn's face and reappeared on mine. I might just enjoy this little game for a few minutes.

"So that wasn't a farce," Mr. Dunn said, dropping the excited act. His voice was now grave and serious, his eyes narrowing.

"Let's cut the pleasantries." I raised an eyebrow at him. "Why is someone at your level here?" I leaned back in the uncomfortable steel chair, the hard slats digging into my back. I folded my arms across my chest.

"Rosalind Institute would like you to reconsider your resignation. While I appreciate your *moral* stance," he continued, without letting me interject, "there must be a price." He smiled, more genuinely at this, as if he had said something clever.

"Everyone has a price, Mr. Dunn," I said with a shrug. "Rosalind Institute simply won't be willing to pay mine."

Mr. Dunn waved his hand behind his head, his unblinking eyes boring into mine.

A soft click reverberated through the room. The lights flickered once before returning to normal; a loud humming sound that had been radiating behind me slowed and then cut out.

"We both know," Mr. Dunn said, unbuttoning the top button on his shirt, with a quiet sigh, "this place is borderline unconstitutional," he finished. "Borderline abuse of government power. Borderline abuse of women's rights." His eyes widened and his nostrils flared.

"Borderline?" I whispered, my eyes flicking around the room. Something had changed. Mr. Dunn had changed.

"The recording has been paused," Mr. Dunn replied casually.

I raised an eyebrow at him, a little surprised and more than a little impressed.

"Everyone has a price, Miss Avery." His smirk returned. "Do you want to institute change? Do you want women's rights to jump forward into this century? Do you want reproductive rights to be redefined?"

My heart thumped in my chest as Mr. Dunn rattled off a perfect check-list of the things I wanted.

"Yes," I said matter-of-factly. "Yes, to all-of-the-above. Yes, to women being able to choose. Yes to change…Yes." I found myself leaning forward, my voice now haughty and breathless. He had hooked me, and we both knew it.

"Rosalind Institute will back you," Mr. Dunn said. The words hung in the air. "Win —" He paused and his sudden intensity scared me. "— and Rosalind Institute will *publicly* back you when the time comes. Win," he said again, "and you will have a platform." I tried to take in the severity of what he was saying.

"Win," I said finally, feeling breathless, "and I could change *everything*." My eyes went wide. I leaned back, letting the breath seep out from between my lips, my fingers intertwining together. I wanted to say more, wanted to let myself imagine what my life *could* look like. But if I was honest, there was no world in which I could see myself as someone's mother. The mere thought of it sent a shiver of ice through my veins.

"As much as I would like to change regulations and amend world views on women's rights," I continued, forcing myself to come back to reality and take a deep breath. "What makes you think that between us we would have the power?" I wanted to pretend we could change the world, but I needed more than empty promises from a man I barely knew.

I shuffled in my chair, twisting to the side to get comfortable. The metal bars dug into my back no matter which way I sat, leaving me to heave and sigh.

Mr. Dunn knew this as he stared at me; his eyes softened.

"We have money, Miss Avery," he said simply, with a shrug of his shoulders. "And if you win, you will inherit fame. That combination has..." he trailed off for a few seconds and raised his eyebrows, his dark brown, brooding eyes wide and flaring.

"Understood," I said with a sharp nod.

I sat silently, calculating the cost of working with Rosalind Institute; it made me sweat and feel nauseated at once.

"What will it cost me?" I asked, unable to allow the silence to stretch out for another second. Everything worthwhile came with a price.

"Time, Miss Avery," Mr. Dunn said, his face sombre now. He knew I would ask—I must have been more easily readable than I thought.

"Time?" I frowned, chewing on my lip. I wanted him to spell this one out.

"Miss Avery." Mr. Dunn sighed, understanding and exasperated in the same breath. "While you may not believe this, Rosalind Institute has been investigating the lottery runners for years. There is more than meets the eye at play here. Power breeds corruption. Greed breeds exploitation." A small twitch flickered through his left eye. He was passionate about this—something I hadn't expected. "The lottery started with reasonable intentions, albeit with a flawed premise."

I nodded with each word Mr. Dunn uttered, finding myself agreeing with him. He was right, but I still felt like a pawn in a game far bigger than I was.

Mr. Dunn smiled at me, his face more relaxed and open than I had ever seen.

"Mr. Dunn." I didn't want to cut off our open, honest conversation. "There was a time here..." I bit my lip and worried mid-sentence that this was a bad idea. There was a risk in telling him the only shred of information I had, but as his eyes softened, I found myself desperately wanting to trust him.

"You are the first contestant on the inside I have personally known, Miss Avery. That experience alone counts for more than you understand, so please..." He nodded. The way he spoke made me think he would believe me. That he *already* believed me.

"I saw a woman," I said, not quite knowing how to explain it. "She was heavily pregnant, and she wasn't competing." The tester's curse rang in my ears. "We passed her in the hallway. Probably by accident because my tester cursed." I shrugged as I added that final, mundane detail. It seemed both vital and silly.

Mr. Dunn smiled and nodded, like I had just clicked another piece into place.

"I told you," he said, "power breeds corruption. And that is why we *need you*." His eyes were blazing as I tried to fully grasp the situation. It was as if Rosalind had been waiting for me.

I dropped my eyes down to my lap, where I stared at my clasped hands. My fingers turned red, then white as I squeezed them tighter. Mr. Venter's warning rang in my ears, and I hoped I wasn't stepping into a blazing fire.

"How rich do you have to be?" I whispered. "To *not* compete."

Mr. Dunn shook his head and shrugged his shoulders. The question burned like acid along my teeth and tongue. "Our research only tells us a fraction of the story."

"Can I do anything to change that?"

Mr. Dunn looked at me with a smile.

"You *already have,* Alice Avery," he said, a little smile pulling at the corners of his mouth.

He went on, "With your insider knowledge and access, by the time you win—" He winked, which didn't suit his serious face, but made me smirk just the same. "—you will know far more than any other woman. But don't forget," he added with an ominous pause. "Knowledge is power, but knowledge can also be dangerous."

I nodded sharply as I stared Mr. Dunn in the eye. I was about to do something that scared me, and I hoped I was making the right decision. "I'm in."

CHAPTER TWENTY-NINE

THE SET-UP

"CONTESTANTS, PLACES, PLACES" THE EXECUTOR BOOMED AND CLAPPED from her high, glass podium. Her eyes sparkled under the bright yellow-tinted light. Her floor-length, gold dress shimmered as she turned to wave her arm fluidly towards us.

We stood in silence. A forced smile was painted onto each woman's face. Our shoulders rubbed together; the breath of the men who stood behind us was hot on our necks—their bodies were so close that you could feel their outline.

My eyebrows kept trying to fold down into a scowl. My head hurt from the forced plainness my face was displaying. I wouldn't smile sweetly and play that game. The Executor watched us before carefully fixing her hair and readying herself to present.

"Join me," she boomed, her voice upbeat, the sound reverberating off each wall in the large room, "in welcoming the women in this round of the lottery."

With a small push, we were shepherded up onto the large glass stage. The glass was hard but crackled under my feet. Little glass rocks were strewn across the floor, and I picked my way across gently. I wasn't used to wearing such high heels and I worried I would fall.

As I found my place amongst the other women in the line-up, I watched some of them plant on bigger, fake smiles, turning sideways to tuck their dress over their now-visible, pregnant bellies. They looked like a strange mix of runway and fitness models by the way they stood—except for the giant, protruding lump in the middle of their torsos.

I stood still, looking straight at the Executor. The women on either side of me bristled with anticipation while I felt a sea of dread.

"In no particular order," she continued, her face now tilted upwards, her enormous smile somehow gaining ground. She was introducing us, but it felt forced and staged.

I scanned the room as the Executor boomed out multiple loud names. I didn't catch any of the details, only the strange feeling that we were being watched.

"Mrs. Astrid Astley." The name broke through my quiet introspection. I scanned the large, almost-empty room, turning back to see Mrs. Astley waving at nothing, straight ahead of the stage. Her face displayed a sweet, sombre gratitude. She rested her hand against her stomach where her large, diamond wedding ring sparkled under the bright lights.

My eyebrows caved in, and a deep frown painted itself on my face. I stared, unblinking, at the spot where all eyes were focused.

I squinted, trying to make out any tiny detail between the large wooden doors. Even staring, I could see nothing.

I took a long deep breath, my eyes still unable to move on from the spot at the end of the room as my name was announced.

"Alice Avery," she thundered, her head snapping towards me. I spotted the little black microphone attached to her cheek and nodded to myself. Something was happening here, and I had a nagging feeling I wasn't going to like it. With my name hanging in the air, I opted to wink towards the spot the other two had looked at—just in case my bad feeling was right.

The woman on my other side, the last woman in the line-up, shook feverishly as her name was called.

"Genie Goodall." The voice sounded quieter, and the woman beside me shook more vigorously.

Her body didn't move as we all waited for her, her eyes cast down, her lips a strange pink and blue tinge.

"Genie," I whispered after the Executor turned around, blaring more words that drowned out my own. "You okay?" My eyes darted from her to the front of the stage.

Genie gave me a quick shake of the head, her face turning more pale, the blue tint seeping from her outer lips to the middle. She coughed a few times before sucking in a deep, rattling breath.

"Wait," I said, louder this time, trying to catch someone's attention. I ran forward out of my spot in line, and just managed to catch Genie as she fell backwards. She was out cold, her limp body heavy as stone. The man behind her stepped back, shooting us both a disgusted glare.

"Executor!" I yelled, barely making an impact over her loud gabbing. Her words rambled on as she twisted and turned, wandering back and forth across the stage. She was completely oblivious.

"Executor!" I screamed, louder this time, right as she took a quick breath.

I was now crumpled on the floor, the limp body of the woman who had been standing beside me in a heap on my lap. No one else had come to help; it was as if the line had been frozen in place.

The Executor finally spun around. Her eyes narrowed in my direction. She was upset at the interruption until she saw the scene.

"Oh my," she said into her microphone. The other women beside her took a few steps back.

"Her pulse is steady," I blurted, having had my hand on her wrist and pressed against her chest since she collapsed. "But look." Her blue lips now quivered uncontrollably, and her eyes leaked tears as she lay there, unconscious. "She needs a medic," I said, now irritated. The Executor was unmoving and slack jawed. "Medical attention," I repeated, louder this time, clicking my fingers like an irritated mother with a toddler who wasn't listening.

I brushed the hair out of the woman's eyes. Her forehead was sweating profusely; the hair morphed from stuck to her forehead to slicked back against her skull.

"Alert, alert," I heard the Executor call. "Medical emergency." Her words were flat and dull, almost bored.

I shuffled my body out from under the woman. Her eyes fluttered as I leaned in closer.

"You're okay," I murmured, "medics have been summoned." I grabbed her icy hand and gave it a tight squeeze. I tried not to think about the ache in my back as I leaned over her; her stiff hand squeezed mine, the rest of her body still.

With two loud *thumps*, two male nurses arrived, loading the woman onto a stretcher without checking her vitals.

They nodded to me before lifting her up, jogging off the stage. The woman jostled from side-to-side as they bounded down the stairs. My eyes were glued to her. They flew down the second flight of stairs and through the large, red wooden doors that we had come through.

I blinked rapidly for a few seconds after the doors clicked shut, still kneeling.

"Come on, dear," Mrs. Astley said, her taloned nails digging into my arm. She pulled me up from the floor, her lips gnarled with her back to the rest of the room.

"Thank you." I smiled at her sweetly. Anger flared through her eyes and nostrils for a split second before being overwritten by her fake, kind demeanour.

She moved us side-on, brushing me down and fixing my dress and hair with a gentle smile. Her lip only twitched once more before she stepped away from me, retaking her position in line.

I looked back at the closed door a few times as the showrunner fluffed around, talking to a man in a suit that had bounded up on the stage at the same time as the woman who had fainted was carted off.

Returning to my still stance, I strained my ears, willing myself to catch anything said between them.

They were now engaged in hushed whispers with the fallen woman's sponsor. I had never seen a face so red and angry with words spoken so softly. With a push, both gentlemen departed, a look of irritation on both faces. They both were fuming at the situation and I couldn't help but wonder if the woman's highest bidder would be seeking a refund.

"Moving on," the Executor sighed, patting her hair back into place against her skull. She smoothed down her pristine, gold dress before turning again to face the front of the stage. "A little drama makes the contest *more fun*," she said, as if the microphone had returned, closer to her mouth than before. "Let the games begin," she finished with a grin. She wasn't planning to address what just happened—a typical response.

The *thump* of hard-soled shoes behind us drew my attention. The loud steps echoed in unison as a row of suited men and women entered the large room. They came to a halt behind us, standing as far back on the glass stage as possible.

"We will now split you into pairs for phase one," the Executor explained. "Women along with your chosen pair." She clicked and twirled her hands to tell us to turn around.

My eyes darted to the side. None of the women moved; they were all frozen in place. I assumed I would be the first to move *a lot* today.

I spun on my heel, turning to face Mr. Dunn. Our eyes locked for a few seconds before his gaze returned to the front of the stage. He had his part to play, and I had mine.

"Suits," the Executor clicked, her voice echoing behind my back. The men and women who were standing at the edge of the stage now bounded forward.

We were joined by one man and one woman, their hands full of what looked like black wiring and electrical tape.

"Excuse me," the woman said to me, almost shyly as she approached. "It's time to be fitted with the technology for the final round." Her face flushed a dark, brilliant shade of pink, her eyes darting from my face to her feet. She looked as nervous and uncomfortable as I felt.

With the most genuine smile I could muster, I stepped back a few paces, giving her space to scoot in behind me, her counterpart already threading and looping the black cording around Mr. Dunn's body.

"Are you allowed to explain what you're doing?" I asked, keeping my voice low and gentle. I didn't want to get anyone in trouble, but, as usual, my curiosity was piqued.

"Somewhat," she said with a flushed smile. She unspooled the black wiring that had been clenched in her hand. The wiring glowed as it unravelled. "The cording—" she said, unravelling the last few inches, her eyes flicking up to meet mine again before darting away—"includes thousands of tiny sensors." She tapped my arms, gently tugging them out far enough so that she could wrap the black cording around my stomach. She twisted it from the bottom of my protruding belly, up the centre, and then ran the final length across the top, sticking a small, black circular sticker against the side of my chest that my heart was on.

She went on, "This will measure the ba—foetus's brainwaves throughout the next test." She took a step back and peeled off the small, stickered dots on each of the tiny sensors. They ran every three centimetres, making it a painstaking and tedious process.

"And who will be monitoring the brainwaves?" I dropped my voice as low as I could while still being understood.

The suit looked up at me for a few seconds, her hands trembling as she finished attaching the final few sensors.

She didn't speak, but her eyes darted from me to the Executor.

I gave her a quick nod and smiled. I didn't want to get her in any trouble.

"The last part involves *y-your* head," she stammered. "Or more accurately, your brain."

I nodded, kneeling down. I was getting slower the bigger I got, and it was painfully obvious that I wasn't agile on my feet at that moment. I watched the final wrap of black cording go around Mr. Dunn's head.

With a groan, I tilted my head forward, perched and waiting. My knees were already aching against the cold, glass floor.

I held myself still as the Suit walked around me, fixing the black cording against my skull. I counted to three as she circled my head, her sweaty hands and fingers pressing against the skin on my forehead, and intertwining with my hair.

"And this one?" I asked quizzically, imagining that they would watch my own brainwaves as well.

"Two fold," she said, coming to a halt in front of me. Her fingers pressed against each of the sensors that were now stuck to my skin, checking and re-checking each was secure. "Brainwaves and mi—" She stopped mid-sentence. The Suit beside her cleared his throat and gave her a stern look.

She said nothing else as she stepped back. With a nod, she pulled out two small, black screens and attached each of them to the end of the cording with a soft *click*.

The small screen lit up, a slow bar darting forward and backwards a few times before moving up permanently. My eyes drifted between the slow, loading screen, the Suit, and the other contestants.

I suppressed a huge eye roll as I noticed Mrs. Astley tucking two single flowers into her wired headpiece—a little pop of yellow. It would have been cute, if she wasn't so fake and nauseating. Why was it that those that preached acceptance were always the least tolerant?

"Can you tell me what the tech is called?" I whispered to the Suit while she tapped a few buttons on the screen. It was loaded and displayed different charts and graphs.

"This is the Oculus Awakening." A hint of a smile danced across her mouth, her eyes still transfixed on the ever-changing screens.

"Oculus Awakening," I repeated under my breath, a smile finding its way onto my face. If I hadn't been trapped in a death game, I was sure the technology here would be fascinating.

She looked up and nodded at me, her eyes wide.

"You're all set, *Alice Avery*." Her use of my full name sent a shiver down my spine before she pivoted and joined the line of Suits leaving the stage.

Six women now stood side-by-side on the stage in their beautiful black formal dresses, their hair and make-up flawless. The black wiring looked like gothic flower crowns weaved across their heads and stomachs.

Their faces held wide eyes, tight jaws, pursed lips, and plucked eyebrows. It was a strange sight.

"Each of you," the Executor boomed, making me jolt, "has passed your own set of challenges to be standing here today." She stared down at our small line-up, a sleek smile on her face. "And now, you have almost reached the end." She paused for a few seconds, still staring at the same spot in the dark hallway. "Six women," she continued, "six *extraordinary* babies...Pregnancy is complicated in a world of plagues, overpopulation, and politics, and yet, here we stand. On the verge of something great." Her voice sounded almost teary as she neared the end of a speech that made me want to vomit. Instead, I settled for an uncontrollable eye-twitch and a growing, gnawing pit in my stomach.

"The lottery!" she boomed, the noise reverberating through the entire hall and dinging in my ears. "A privilege, a societal movement, a sacrifice, a new beginning—officially reopens today."

Her words stopped, but her echo faded slowly, still bouncing off the walls of the large hall, and between my ears. I felt stuck on the word *reopens*.

"Let the games begin," she finished, the microphone now held in her hand. She paused for a few seconds, holding her exact pose in place. I half expected the word *cut* to come screaming down from above. Instead, after a few beats she dropped the act and a blank, lifeless expression spread across her face. Without a word, she brushed past us, leading the exit procession.

CHAPTER THIRTY

A DYNAMIC DUO

Two Suits moved around my body, their cool fingers intertwining with my hair, skin, and clothing. They checked and rechecked my wiring, connecting it to another, larger screen. Sweaty hands and hot fingers slithered against my skin. I had never felt less human and more experiment than in that moment.

The TV screen hung above us, suspended in the centre of the room. It was clear that it was the centre piece to the next game.

I tried to make out the room beyond, but the raised black platform was obscured by the fluorescent lights. Even squinting, I could barely see.

Beside me, Mr. Dunn was getting the same treatment. The Suits combed over every inch of the technology attached to his body. I fidgeted, wiggling my fingers and toes as the woman who sat directly across from me—and her sponsor—stared me down. Their unblinking eyes unnerved me. I stared back. I might have been out of my depth, but they sure as hell wouldn't know it.

I was spun in a full circle as the Suits vetted their equipment, and with a final nod, I heard the magic words.

"Confirmed," one Suit spoke into a radio headpiece before she stepped away from us. Her eyes ran over us again, and then she backed away. She seemed sure but unsure, and I had never resonated with that feeling more than I did then. "Test phase one. Start," she said down the radio.

The TV that hung in the centre flickered to life, turning from solid black to four split squares.

I blinked a few times. The TV flickered to display patterns and graphs on three of the four split screens. I scanned them, noticing that two of the squares had two heartbeats displayed.

"Which one..." I murmured to myself. The Suit now bustled around beside me, touching the sensors across Mr. Dunn's head until something flickered on the screen.

I was trying to piece the information together as I looked at Mr. Dunn's screen. His heartbeat and brainwaves had flickered to life. The screen then shrunk to add the third, small, currently black square.

The Suit approached me, touching the sensors against my head. Her eyes moved to the top left of the screen, beside Mr. Dunn's screen.

She fiddled with the sensors against my stomach, tugging at the soft fabric of my dress, and peeled and re-stuck the final few. With a nod of her head and a flicker of my screen, she walked away. She didn't speak or make eye contact, and I couldn't fault her. This was a strange moment.

She gave the same treatment to the pregnant woman sitting opposite me. The other woman's body recoiled when she touched her forehead. It didn't make me superior to have resisted the urge, but I did feel a little better the longer I watched.

The woman quivered as the Suit stepped back. Three of the four squares inside the big screen now held the same blank black box, along with the rest of our vital signs.

As the woman caught sight of the screen and entwined her hands together, her eyes dropped. Her mouth moved, as though she was speaking, but no sound rang out. Everything that happened here made you a strange kind of speechless.

The final black square came to life on the screen, and the Suit gave a sharp nod.

"Commence testing phase two," she said into her radio matter-of-factly.

With a loud crackle, a voice came out of the TV, shooting into the room like a bullet and making all four of us wired contestants jump.

"Test question one," the voice said robotically. "What is two-plus-three?" The crackle only got louder as silence grew.

Immediately, the number five flashed in my thoughts, but I kept my mouth shut, unsure whether I was expected to answer out loud.

The number five materialised on each screen, one-by-one. The four contestants' eyebrows raised in unison.

"Calibration successful," the Suit said through her radio. It felt strange to piece together what was happening through screens and cryptic words.

"What you say and what you think," a crackly voice echoed from the screen, "are often different." A long pause stretched out, and it finally clicked. "In this sequence of questioning, there will be simple quizzes, intelligence testing." She paused again for dramatic affect. "All the while giving us the ability to understand your inner mind." In other words, we couldn't hide our thoughts, even if we put on the sweet good-girl act.

The sound warped at the end, and a loud sputter spit out from within the TV. I broke out into a wide grin.

"*Think* wisely," the voice said, before a loud *thump* echoed from the back of the stage.

I tried to twist my head, but the black wiring caught me and entangled me in its grasp. I was like a mummy all wrapped up in wires.

As I spun, the Executor ascended a set of long stairs. Her body bobbed in and out of the light. She had changed; her hair was now pulled back into a slicked ponytail, her forehead dragged back with it.

Clearing the last step, she paused and smoothed down her flowing red tulle dress. My eyes narrowed as I watched her be primed and preened by two Suits, their hands tugging and tucking across her body. She looked great. But in this context, it felt wrong—like she had dressed up in colour for a funeral.

With a sharp nod, the Suits stepped back, and the Executor stepped forward. She glided into the centre of the room and planted herself directly under the TV screen.

The Suits fiddled with the lighting, flicking the fluorescents off and changing the glow to a soft, warm yellow. With a quick nod, the Suits then silently exited the stage.

The Executor stood still with small, black cards held in her hand, her eyes closed.

With a sudden jolt, her eyes burst open, and she threw her hands up in the air in exaggerated theatrics.

"Welcome to *the Lottery*," she beamed. A wide, energetic smile plastered on her face. "The fifty-second, quarterly competition where everyday women battle it out. Wits, cunning, brainwaves, and babies…it all comes down to this."

Her smile faltered, and a loud sigh escaped from her lips before she shook her head, glancing at the black cards she clutched in her balled fist. All I could think about were all the women who had come before me in fifty-two rounds of this shitshow.

The Executor rolled her shoulders, moving her mouth before recomposing her body and contorting it back into the professional spokeswoman she wanted to be. I could feel my jaw clenching as I bit back a laugh.

"Welcome to *the Lottery*," she repeated, the focus squarely on the second word this time. The fake, wide smile reappeared on her face, tugging at the sides of her mouth. "We've reached the fifty-second instalment, but this year, we've added a t—" She cut herself off, a louder sigh escaping her lips as she stepped back, scanning the cards again. Her nostrils bulged and flared.

She stepped forward again as I bit my lip. I had to stifle a giggle while she announced the lottery for the third time. This whole situation was beyond ridiculous, and listening to the scripted lines read imperfectly was just the icing on the cake.

"Welcome to the Lottery…" She pinched her nose. "Just use the first one," she huffed, talking to someone I couldn't see. She fluffed and fussed with her hair. The lighting was dim away from the stage, but as my eyes scanned the space, little red dots danced across my vision.

"Cameras..." I shook my head, horrified. My mouth pulled into a tight circle. "*Everywhere.*" I should have known, but this was more sinister than I expected.

Without a word, the Executor clasped her hands together. She looked down between the two sets of contestants for the first time. She dropped the fake excitement, which was a plus.

"As you have gathered," she continued, fidgeting with the nail on her left index finger, "this experience is going to be televised. *Sensational new reality TV*, fall in love with real people—blah, blah, boring." She rolled her eyes and tore them away from her own finger. "This portion is *unscripted*," she said, looking at the other contestants. "*However*, I suggest sticking to answering the questions asked, *not* going off on a tangent, or spruiking some idyllic rant." Her eyes lingered on me for a few seconds longer than anyone else. I raised my eyebrows but said nothing. If I was unscripted, I would say whatever I damn well pleased—what did I have to lose?

"Filming is constant," she said, waving her hand around the room and above our heads. The small, red dots flickered in the distance. There were so many more than I originally thought, and their sheer numbers were overwhelming.

"I will make brief introductions, then the questions will come fast and furious," she said with a nod. "Answer, don't answer. Freeze, don't freeze." She shrugged, barely taking a breath before she started to continue.

"Pause," I said, inserting my word into her brief break between breaths. "Do we need a buzzer? A codeword?" My frown pressed into my forehead. If this was a gameshow, wouldn't we need something more?

She laughed, loud and fake, and shook her head. The way she looked at me curdled my stomach. "Your *brain* is your *buzzer*, Miss Avery."

I looked up at the screen. The number five still danced against the black background. They shimmered and spiked as I raised my hand, speaking before I was granted permission. "Can this machine output complex sequences?" My eyes lingered on the TV screen.

"You will still need to articulate your answer *aloud*, Miss Avery," she said, exasperated. "The TV will simply pull a few keywords and answers to display above your head."

I nodded, noting the brain-buzzer was for show. A strange chasm opened in my chest. The screen would display the key to your thoughts, enough to ensure everyone knew what you were *really* thinking.

"*If* there are no more questions," she said, "let's begin."

The Executor turned to the side, her back now to me, her body twisted to speak with the other contestants.

"Welcome to the Lottery," she said, this time her words directed at another woman. The woman smiled, her pristine, white teeth shining under the fluorescent lights. I watched the Executor check her notes. "Mrs. Goodall."

"It's an honour to be here," she said, her lips quivering. "Genie is fine," Her voice squeaked and the Executor brushed past her answer.

"Very few women make it this far. What makes *you* extraordinary? Tell us your story."

Silence fell across the stage, as if no one was breathing except for my direct competitor, who was almost hyperventilating.

"M-my husband and I have always longed for a child," Genie stammered. "T-this is our fourth attempt to enter *the lottery*."

"Three unsuccessful pregnancies?" the Executor chimed in, her face pouting in sadness while her voice was a bit too cheery. "Well, number four might be the charm." Her upbeat voice was in odd contrast to the rest of the room.

Losing interest, she spun on her heel, and I realised no names or information had been shared. She crossed the stage, irritation visible on her face.

"Let's see if this side of the room is more *entertaining*." The words snapped out of her mouth viciously. Under all the glitz and glam, she was really just a nasty woman drunk on power.

My fake smile rivaled her own as she touched herself up and planted herself on my side of the stage.

"Welcome to the fifty-second quarterly Lottery," the Executor started, trying to dress up her words a little more with each take, striving to add some new spin.

"Alice Avery," I said with a wink. "*Thrilled* to be here."

Her pupils shrunk and narrowed, while the rest of her face was still cemented in a kind, open, wholesome way.

"*Miss* Avery," she said, the enunciation on the *miss* too obvious not to note. "A surprise if I ever did meet one."

I smiled widely at her. The banter came easy, if I pretended I didn't dislike her so fervently.

"Surprises always have the best stories, and the most *astonishing* wins," I said, another wink cascading out before I could rein it back in. I was going overboard, but this had just gotten a little more fun.

"Why don't you tell us your story?" The tiny twitch of her mouth was the only indication of her annoyance. I could see it was killing her, but I must have been doing something right.

"My story? Maybe just the highlight reel," I said, chuckling. I knew that whatever I said would be edited and cut down if this did air on television. "For the record," I went on, looking at the Executor, whose eyes flashed, "I'm every woman who has had a one-night stand and found themselves in this situation. *Except* that my baby turned out to be a genius." I finished with an almost-real laugh.

"Were you surprised when you found out your baby might be something special?" she interjected. Her voice was high-pitched and interested, even though I knew it wasn't real. I couldn't match her fake enthusiasm, but I could match her fake surprise—even if mine was real.

"It surprised me to find out I was pregnant." I gave a half-laugh. "The baby-genius part was an additional surprise."

"Alice Avery, *full* of surprises," she quipped, raising her eyebrows before mouthing *cut*.

I frowned at the use of my full name; it still didn't feel quite right coming from her lips. My knees jiggled and knocked together out of nervous energy. I wasn't camera shy, but I was 'broadcasting to all of Australia' shy.

The Executor stood still in the centre of the stage as a crew of people rushed in. They patted her face with powder and touched up her lipstick, tucking her hair back into pristine place, pulling at her dress.

She stood like a statue, poised in position, only holding out her right hand which was grasped around a phone. Her fingers moved furiously, the screen emanating so many small taps the sounds blurred together.

I tried and failed to make out anything on the tiny screen, but it was too far away.

"Are you really single?" came Genie's mousy voice from across the stage. I barely heard her amongst the din of the bustling, working party.

My eyes flicked to the woman who sat across from me. Her big, fake smile had disappeared, and what remained was a hollow, pale, and sweaty face.

"Yes?" I said, happy it didn't sound too much like a question.

"Interesting angle," she mumbled, dropping her eyes. She was very clearly nervous, but her words still stung.

I frowned. "Angle?"

"You know, something to make you interesting. The public loves weird," Genie retorted. She was louder and more confident now that she wasn't meeting my eyes.

"I'm sorry you've been unsuccessful three times," I offered, trying to choose my next words carefully. This system pitted women against each other, and I wanted no part in that game. "If it had been up to me, I would have had an abortion when I found out I was pregnant." I paused. "And you would be able to have the baby you long for."

I smiled at Genie as she slowly lifted her head. Her eyes were wide and brimming with tears.

"Miss Avery," the Executor's microphoned voice interjected into the conversation. "Did you consider abortion?" Her voice had turned haughty and breathless. Her team of puffers was gone the moment her voice rang out.

"I didn't consider it," I said matter-of-factly, "I asked for it. Requested it. Tried to *demand* it." A little prickle was forming in the back of my throat. "But the right to choose is not always ours." I rested my hands on my stomach. It felt passive-aggressive to place my hands so delicately on my growing stomach during these questions, and I hoped everyone watching could see it.

"No, Miss Avery. It is not," she said, her voice now soft. The microphone she had held so close to her mouth now hung against her side. It was strange to see the Executor miss a beat. She was usually all business, engrossed in the spectacle of *the lottery*. She looked deflated for a moment, and I had to wonder, was she realising for the first time the impact this had on women? The Executor shook her head slightly and swallowed, and in that split second her normal haughty smile was back. I sighed, any chance of her being who I needed in this moment vanishing. I looked back to the large scoreboard. The screen jumbled for a second, before the heart-rate in the top right faded to black.

My eyes shot to where Mr. Dunn had been standing a few moments before, inches from my side. Instead of his lined, serious face, another all-too-familiar face smiled back at me.

His golden hair was longer than last time. His toothy, goofy grin was imprinted across his face, his eyes focused on mine.

Mason reached out and squeezed my hand. His warm skin sent a string of fireworks up my arm. Just seeing him sent a jolt of hope and then dread through me. I stared at him for a beat too long, questions flooded through me - the *who, what, how* circling my brain. But as he squeezed my hand, the gratitude and relief of getting to do this test *with* Mason chorused through me. He was here, and I was thankful.

I barely opened my mouth before the Executor drowned me out; she had no intention of letting us catch up or explaining his sudden appearance.

"Time to begin." She threw her shoulders back, shaking her body. I looked around briefly for Mr. Dunn and saw two of the suits shepherding him away. His forehead was deeply lined and his mouth was pulled into a line so tight it almost disappeared.

I turned back and stared at the screen. The little brainwaves of each person flickered and danced.

"Welcome back to the Lottery. Let's jump right into the questions. Ladies, gentlemen, start thinking!" Her voice bellowed, now hyped and louder than ever. "I ask, you answer," she said, almost repeating herself. "I talk, you think." She paused for a second, picking up large, gold-rimmed cards from the small glass table behind her. She held a strange side-on pose. She clutched the cards to her chest, sucking in her stomach with all the strength she could muster.

I shook my head, wondering if she hoped this would be the image of her they used in advertising—her tiny waist flashed across billboards and ads.

"Contestants, let's go." She flipped the first card over, gripping it in her hands. Her eyes shimmering intensely between each of us. She stared at us all in turn, and when her eyes locked onto you, it was unnerving. I swallowed when she finally spoke.

"What age did you lose your virginity?" The booming question flew to the four people on stage.

I raised my eyebrows then sniggered, thinking back to my fifteen-year-old experience with a mouth full of braces, too-heavy breathing, and palpable silence. My eyes shot to the board. My *fifteen* was clearly displayed. Mason cleared his throat, mortified, as the number *nineteen* flashed up on the screen.

I shot a glance towards him. His head was covered in the infamous wires and his face was beet red. His arms crossed against his body as he glared at the board.

"Not quite the line of questioning we signed up for," I tried to speak just loud enough for Mason to hear. "But I have less to hide than—" I sniggered and my thought was cut off as my eyes flashed across to the couple who sat opposite me, a loud gasp having broken through the quiet stage.

Genie had her hands pressed against her chest as though she had seen a ghost.

Just as fast, my eyes flew to the display board. Written on the opposite side to my fifteen and Mason's nineteen were two *very* different numbers.

"Sixteen?" Genie kept repeating. Her voice was low but scratchy as she glared at her husband, her nostrils flaring.

He opened and closed his mouth. His face was a pale shade of grey.

He had started to stammer as the Executor swanned over to their side, sticking her face in between the argument that was about to erupt. She had no shame, and I watched on as the horror unfolded.

"A ten-year age gap," she said. Her face was smug; the little smile dancing on her lips pulled against the straight-face she was trying to keep. "Sixteen versus twenty-six," she added, swaying closer. She was pressing for an outburst, anything to make the views climb higher. They told us nothing behind the *why*, but I could speculate it cost a lot to run this kind of population management. That, or they had become so depraved they had forgotten how these games affected *real* women.

Genie cleared her throat and a shiver ran down my spine and I turned my attention outward, I would have time to think about this later; or to talk about it with a therapist. The glare Genie directed at her husband was wiped away as she faced the Executor and the cameras.

"A little misunderstanding," she said sweetly. "My *husband can explain*." Genie grabbed her husband's arm roughly and pulled him forward, his bald head shining under the bright lights. Little beads of sweat gathered across his forehead.

All he could do was stammer, his voice high-pitched before clearing his throat.

"I liked your story..." the Executor cut-in, cutting off his incoherent stuttering. "Met at twenty-three, married at twenty-six. *Saved yourself* for marriage and your one true love," she cooed, her voice turning gooey. "But..." She held herself still for dramatic effect. "Maybe not the fairy tale we envisioned." Her face inched closer and closer.

"The test must be calibrating falsely," the man spat out. "Maybe *their* results mixed with mine." He jerked a finger in our direction. It was always that way; when people didn't like the results, they blamed the tests or technology.

"Unfortunately for my comrade," I snapped, "our results are perfectly accurate." I side-eyed Mason, who cringed and lowered his head as he nodded along with me. "I think your wife's number was reflected accurately, too." I stared him down. I had no interest in snivelling, lying men getting away from the consequences of their own actions.

The Executor waved her hand up in my direction, cutting me off before I out-right called him a liar to the whole population. She was the judge and jury here and she would see to his public downfall. For once, we agreed on the next course of action.

"Miss Avery is correct," she said. "You lost your virginity at sixteen. Machines don't lie, only *guilty people* do." She raised her eyebrows at both of them, stepping away and retaking her place centre stage. "Well, well," she boomed, holding herself with poise in an odd position again. "The questions only get tougher." Her smile beamed more genuinely than before.

She flicked a card over in her hand. Excitement flashed across her eyes as she read the words, and her widening smile made me think something big was coming.

"Our sexual history makes us who we are," the Executor radiated, "so we must know your magic number." She clicked her fingers loudly as she almost yelled the question: "How many people have you slept with?" Her voice bounced around the large room, dinging off the walls and bouncing back to the stage.

I made sure not to shrink or bow my head as my number flashed on the screen. I wasn't ashamed, and I didn't want anyone to think I was.

"Not quite double digits," I whispered, flashing a small, brilliant smile towards Mason. The number *nine* was illuminated on the screen in my square.

Mason almost dropped his head into his hands, a loud sigh escaping his lips as the number *five* illuminated in his spot.

I raised my eyebrows at him.

"Not bad," I mouthed with a wink, realising this was as much a live television game as a get-to-know-you game couples play.

Mason and I had had one cup of coffee and one great night, and not in that order. It seemed only fitting for our strange, possible romance that our third date would be a televised game show where we talked about our sexual history for all to see.

I opened my mouth to whisper another question to Mason when a stifled shriek pierced the room.

Genie was now on her feet. Her hands were balled at her side. Her seated husband averted his gaze, his shoulders low, his back hunched.

My eyes darted to the screen again. Illuminated for all to see were the numbers *one*—clearly the faithful wife—and *seven* for the husband who refused to meet her flaring nostrils.

"Are you telling me—" Her breaths were short and shallow, the words getting stuck in her throat as she inched her way closer, "—that you have *fucked* seven *different* women?"

My eyes widened at her use of the word *fucked*. It felt strange coming from a woman who had sold herself as the perfect Christian housewife, but anger and betrayal made us into different people, and she clearly deserved to break character.

"And I've been *stuck* with your unsatisfying dick for the last *ten years?*"

It was a picture-perfect mic-drop line, and I was almost impressed. Genie's hands went limp and fell to her side as she pulled her shoulders back and took a few steps to the side.

"Executor," Genie said, twisting her spine.

The Executor glided forward. She was loving every second of the unfolding drama, her eyes glimmering with the ratings and numbers as she leaned forward.

"This is the end," Genie said, now swivelling to face her. "We withdraw."

Without another word, she stalked across the stage, descending the stairs in record time before marching towards the large double doors.

The Executor was stunned into silence for a few seconds, her eyes glazing over momentarily. I watched her closely, wondering whether a withdrawal was technically allowed. The Executor was whispering into her ear piece hushed and fast; her back to us, her hand pressed to her ear. She must have been given a direction to continue and she nodded and resumed her poised facade. She sauntered over to where the husband sat, head in his hands. "Do you have anything to say for yourself? Justification? Explanation?" she pressed, waiting only a few seconds before her tongue flashing out as she licked her lips. "No comment? *Standard* from the cheating husband."

My jaw almost hit the floor. She wasn't pulling any punches. I was more interested in the inner workings of the competition. Now that this was being televised, they must not want the whole public to note *women couldn't withdraw*.

I swallowed the lump rising in my throat. Whoever was calling the shots must have decided this woman *could* withdraw. It was both interesting and irritating. I ground my teeth together, the injustice of how differently we were treated still pounding through my head.

The Executor stepped a few paces back, almost returning to the centre of the stage, when the man stood up. He wiped his face. His hands left large, red welts against his cheeks and chin. Knees knocking, he made his way across the stage, stopping inches away from the edge.

"I have a few words," he mumbled, his eyes cast down.

The Executor paused for a second, her eyes travelling up and down. His suit was now more fit for a funeral than a celebration.

"Make them marvellous," she whispered, stepping aside with a graceful bow and shuffle.

The man hovered in the centre of the stage, his head down for a few seconds too long. His fingers picked at the threads on the end of his suit.

He cleared his throat a few times as he raised his head, searching the large auditorium. His eyes scanned through the stacks of chairs, dipping and raising, until he caught sight of his wife. She had been trapped in the back corner, the bodyguards of the room blocking her way out. She might be distraught, but her leaving quietly didn't make for good TV.

"Genie," he spoke softly at first, his voice escaping as a croak. "Genie," he called again, louder this time.

My eyes followed his, tracing through the stacks of chairs and finding Genie as she tried to climb over the last row of chairs. The door she had hoped to go through was now being swarmed by guards.

As he called her name, she paused for a second, legs straddling the back row of chairs. She didn't care that people were there. She was going to try and claw her way through.

"Genie, please listen!" the man shouted now, his cracked voice sending a jolt down my spine. I didn't feel sorry for him; he had made his choices, but everyone could see he loved his wife.

Genie stood still, flanked by guards who tried to slowly turn her around.

My eyes darted back to the husband, my heart thumping in my chest. It was hard to admit, but I was starting to understand why Kit got so invested in reality TV.

"When we met..." He stepped forward a few paces. Genie stood rooted in place, and tears had flooded her cheeks.

I spared a glance at the Executor. Her eyes were wide, darting eagerly between the man and Genie, her hands pressed together in a tight ball at her chest. I couldn't tell if she was acting or invested.

"I wanted to be a man you could fall in love with," he continued.

I was sure I had missed some of his words by watching the theatrics.

"So I lied."

A long, silent pause filled the auditorium. That wasn't exactly a ground-breaking revelation, but at least he was being honest.

The only echoing sound were the man's footsteps shuffling towards the edge of the stage.

"I lied about what and who came *before* you. Nothing else," he cried, his voice curdling.

Genie had turned away from him, her back was still to us all, but her shoulders hung a little lower.

"There has been no one since *you*. I've loved no one like I love *you*." His voice dropped, lowering to a barely audible muffle.

My body crept forward, teetering on the edge of my seat. The speed at which my eyes darted between them grew faster and faster with each passing second.

My eyes lingered on Genie's back. Her shoulders now shook violently as she reached for the door again, and this time the guards let her grab it.

Without a moment's notice, she ripped the door open, pulling it with such force that she stumbled back a few paces. Her shoulders shook as she walked out of the room. She didn't look back. She had heard his words and his begging and she still decided to walk away. There was power in that.

With a loud *thump*, the man fell to his knees. His sobs were real, but my sympathy for him was almost non-existent. He wasn't sorry; he was sorry he got caught.

The Executor jumped back to centre stage, crouching beside the man.

Her lips moved, pressed almost up against the man's ear, but even as I strained, I couldn't make out a single word.

"It's hard work being righteous," Mason whispered. His tall body leaned over towards mine, his eyes as wide as mine felt. I wondered what Mason thought of men like him.

I simply nodded, unable to take my eyes off the man. He was now a crumpled mess in the centre of the stage, the tears that streamed down his face now hitting the collar of his suit.

"What happens to them now?" I whispered out of the corner of my mouth, not looking at Mason as the man pulled himself to his feet with help.

With a flick of the Executor's fingers, four Suits bounded up on stage, flanking around the man and disassembling his mind-reader within a matter of seconds.

The first Suit laid all the equipment in a thick, black box, folding and tucking it away while the other Suits led the man off stage. His heavy footsteps clunked against the wood floor as he neglected to pick up his feet. They were supporting almost all of his weight. I'd never seen someone so heartbroken.

As they exited the stage, the Executor stood still in the centre. Her eyes followed them until they reached the bottom and were met by another two men in suits. Their slicked back hair and thick black clipboards were their only distinguishing features.

The men nodded to the Suits, dismissing them and crossing the auditorium with the man in the centre. Their hands were pressed firmly into his shoulders as the wide, double doors swung open. He would get to follow his wife, but in my gut, I knew their journey was over—both here and beyond.

I frowned and bit my lip as I stared at the now-closed double doors. Two lives, a marriage, and a baby all gone in a matter of minutes.

"What hap—" I went to whisper to Mason for a second-time as the Executor's loud voice boomed over mine again. My hand instinctively went to my stomach, as if somehow being jolted back to the game had pulled me back to reality.

"A tale as old as time. Fate is a fickle thing," she said, deepening her voice. Her tone dripped with fake sympathy. "Miss Avery." She turned her gaze towards me, eyes burning.

I raised my eyebrows, forcing myself to remain still.

"Yes, Ma'am?"

"I believe congratulations are in order," she said formally, nodding her head towards me. Her eyes were narrow, her cheeks drawn in, but she did smile. "With the *official* withdrawal of your opponents, you advance to the next round." Her eyes never left mine. They bored into my skull. She was searching for something.

My eyes drifted to the side where the other women waited off-camera. They looked as terrified at the technology and display as I felt.

I managed a nod, hopeful there would be no more questions about my sexual history displayed for all the world to see.

"Alas, we don't want to end the game this soon, do we?" The Executor phrased it as a question, but she wasn't asking for my opinion. Maybe this was part of the plan: parade around the woman who had a one-night-stand and let the world laugh.

"I have nothing to hide," I said, stifling the sigh that was sitting in my throat. I would play the game, and when the time came, I would become the queen. I placed my hands in my lap and smiled up at the Executor. I had to bide my time; my words wouldn't matter *yet*. But I hoped soon that would change.

"Shall we have a quick speed round?" she said, raising her eyebrows at me and flashing me a dazzling white smile.

I shot a side eye towards Mason. He was silent, but I could hear his internal groan.

The Executor waved a hand above her head.

"Look," she snapped, dropping her camera-ready smile and poised stance, "that drama was great, fabulous television, but two questions is *hardly* a game." She shrugged her shoulders, twisting and turning her body. "Participate and I'll make you a deal," she said with an irritated sigh, our silence clearly bothering her. "One hour, alone, in a room. Just the two of you. A moment to *catch up*." She raised her eyebrows as she looked between us.

"No cameras?" Mason said.

"And no chaperone?" I chimed in. My heart thumped against my chest. I didn't want Mason to know how much I *longed* to be alone with him again, just the two of us.

"Deal," she said, her smile returning. "*One hour*. But first, a few more questions."

CHAPTER THIRTY-ONE

A FEW MORE QUESTIONS

THE EXECUTOR PACED AROUND THE CENTRE OF THE STAGE, FLICKING through the cards and discarding another every few seconds.

She frowned, but then smiled. I tried to gauge what was coming for us.

"Hey," Mason whispered, his voice so low I barely heard him. My attention was still somewhat focused on centre stage.

I flicked my eyes towards him, raising my eyebrows. His big, wide smile beamed back at me, taking up his entire face. My stomach flipped and the harshness of the day cracked and melted slightly.

"I've got so much to tell you," he mouthed.

My cheeks pinched as I smiled back at him. I wanted to jump out of my seat and wrap my arms around him. Suddenly I knew that being close to him would feel like being home.

A barking cough told us it was time. The Executor crossed her arms. "There will be plenty of time for catch-ups and reunions later," she snapped. "For now, please at least *act* as though you want to be competing in the lottery on national television." She twisted on her heel and stalked back to the middle of the stage, her puffers on her heels. As they fiddled with her hair and pulled at her dress, I shot a glance at Mason. His goofy grin was still in place, immediately turning my way. He winked at me. My stomach tumbled; had he always been this cute?

"Sorry in advance," I mouthed, grimacing and nodding my head towards the answer screens. With the questions we had seen so far, I wasn't sure what was coming, but I was sure we were about to get to know each other *really* well.

The puffers exited the stage, leaving the Executor alone in the centre.

She took a few deep breaths, eyes closed, before signalling something behind her with the flick of her wrist.

Her dazzling, wide smile returned, spreading across her entire face.

"The untimely demise of one of our couples sees Miss Avery and the father of her baby advance to the next round," she beamed, looking in our direction. "But we aren't done getting to know this extraordinary couple *just yet*. We have a few more *tricky* questions to ask." She paused, flicking through the cards in her hand, the pile now looking thinner.

She shuffled until she reached a specific card, placing it on top, her eyes sparkling.

"Let's call this the speed round," she said, now looking to the left. A camera was clearly planted in that direction. "I ask, you answer."

"You say jump, we say how high," I muttered under my breath. A slicing side-eye shot my way.

I stifled a giggle into a cough. Her mismatched glare and huge grin were almost too much to bear.

"Some are fun, some are tough, and some are downright difficult, depending on your answers."

She paused dramatically again, holding her place for a few beats too long.

"Let the *games begin*!" Her voice rang in my ears as the screen flickered to life above us.

The two other scores and names had disappeared. The screen now split straight down the middle.

The screen still didn't display our names. The top now read 'Player

1' and 'Player 2,' like an outdated video game. It would have been fun in different circumstances.

The Executor cleared her throat, her dramatic announcements growing more prevalent and irritating.

"Literature is a good measure of the human psyche," she started. "It can explain our fears, hopes, dreams, and demons." She clutched the card before lowering it to her side.

"Tell us, what is your favourite novel of all-time?"

The question made me raise my eyebrows. My answer locked in before I had given it a second thought or replaced it with something more age-appropriate and less embarrassing; but even I had to admit it was better than the last two questions.

With an audible groan, I looked up at the board.

Harry Potter and the Goblet of Fire was listed under 'Player 1.'

"I guess I am Player 1," I murmured, my face flushing as a loud laugh barked out from Mason's seat.

"Good choice," he chuckled, forcing my eyes across to his half of the board.

Under 'Player 2' flashed the words *Harry Potter and the Half-Blood Prince.*

I giggled, realising that other than sex, we hadn't talked about much—certainly not our love of Harry Potter or anything in that realm.

"I guess we have more in common than we realised," I said, half-joking, half-wondering why we hadn't had a proper first date before remembering that it was one-hundred-percent my fault—Mason had tried, multiple times.

"Well, well—" She interrupted, her eyebrows raised. "More in common than you thought?" Her voice sounded almost sincere.

"So it appears," Mason retorted, quicker than I was to provide a snarky reply. The more he talked, or back-chatted, the more I liked him.

"Out of curiosity," he asked, turning to face me now, "where does *Half-Blood Prince* feature on your ranking?"

My eyes flicked towards the Executor, who gave me a curt nod, the corners of her smile twitching.

"Third," I replied with a smirk. "*Order* beats *Prince.*"

Mason fake gasped and grabbed his chest for dramatic effect. "*Prince, Goblet, Order,* in my so humble opinion," he said with a toothy smile.

"Fascinating," the Executor rolled her eyes, mouthing the word *cut* to someone in the distance. "Next," she barked, moving herself back into position. "Tell us," she started, her voice flip-flopping between irritation when we talked out-of-turn, and interest when the camera was pointed at her. "What is more important to you? Smarts? Kindness? Or straight-up sex appeal?"

The way she phrased the three options made me giggle. My cheeks burned at the phrase 'sex appeal.'

Without thinking, I knew what my answer was.

I looked up at the board. *Smart* printed on my side of the screen. I tried to keep my face blank, realising the politically correct answer was probably kindness. But I was nothing if not painfully honest.

Instead, my eyes flicked to Mason's screen. It was blank.

My eyes darted in his direction. He had his head bowed, and his eyes closed, as if this question was the most difficult one he would ever be asked. He was clearly having an internal crisis.

The Executor beamed, scooting herself forward and coming in close to Mason. She could sense his struggle, and of course she wanted to pounce.

"Your side of the board is blank," she said. "That is *very* unusual."

Suddenly, a word that wasn't proposed popped up on the screen, and Mason lifted his head.

"Finally," he sighed and I realised he hadn't been struggling; he'd been thinking with all this might until the computer system gave in. "None of those three words are as important to me."

"As 'curious?'" she cut him off.

"Curious," Mason repeated.

I wanted to squeal that it wasn't fair that he had picked a word outside of the three, as there were other things that were more important to me than smart or kind.

"I didn't know we could just choose any trait," I moaned, more joking and only a little irritated. He'd gotten me, and I was pissed.

"Technically," she said, "if you think hard enough..." She trailed off and I knew she didn't want to give us any more ammunition. "Although I would *appreciate*..." She paused for a few seconds. "If you followed the parameters set for you."

I smiled, realising that I could change my answer depending on how I thought.

Scrunching my eyes shut, I summoned and funnelled all my brain power into a single word—the word that I believed was my one, honest choice.

Through one eye, I peeked up. The screen flickered and the pixels distorted as the word on my side scrambled.

"Miss Avery," the Executor interrupted, "if you wish to share a diff —" The screen switched over.

The word *honest* was now displayed on my side, the O misshapen and wonky.

"Honesty, Miss Avery?"

"Honesty," I said. "Without honesty, what else do we have?" I could have said more, but what else was there to say? "Yes, Executor. My answer is honesty."

"You are an interesting woman, Miss Avery," she said curtly, stepping back to centre-stage and cutting off my monologue. "On to harder questions." She tugged at the cards in her hand and discarded another few. Their edges bounced off the floor as they dropped.

"Honesty is important," Mason said, tilting his head to look at me and whispering out of the corner of his mouth.

"Whatever honesty happens next..." I whispered, keeping a close eye on the front of the stage. The Executor's head was down, her eyebrows furrowed as she looked through the final few chosen cards. "Promise you'll stay afterwards," I squeaked out before the Executor straightened up.

Mason nodded at me with his signature goofy smile, not daring to whisper another word.

"You talk about honesty, Miss Avery," she said, her face glowing with pride, "so I wonder, do you follow your own rules?"

I frowned, trying to rack my brain in the few seconds between her last ambiguous statement and the next words that flowed from her mouth.

"Show us, have you ever cheated on a partner? Emotionally or physically? Engaged in behaviour you wouldn't want the other person to find out about?"

Her loaded questions came thick and fast, one-after-the-other. They almost ran together through her rapid fire. It was as if she was trying to cover every conceivable option of infidelity, just in case a minor transgression might trip us up.

The word *no* appeared on my side of the screen. I wasn't a cheater. Not when I was an immature sixteen-year-old in my first relationship, and not now, fourteen years later.

I stared at Mason's side of the screen, waiting for what I hoped was matching answers.

"Well, well," said the Executor, inching closer to us again. "A woman of your word, Miss Avery."

"Always practice what you preach." I shrugged, not wanting to sound cocky or remind everyone of the previous couple's untimely exit.

I stared at Mason's screen, curious why it was taking so long for him to confirm a simple yes or no question.

Finally, the word *no* flashed on the screen, and I released the breath I didn't realise I had been holding. We had both been wondering about the long, drawn-out pause.

"And you," she said, rounding on Mason, "why the *excruciating* pause?"

For once, she asked the same question I wanted answered.

She waved at someone at the bottom of the stairs, clicking her fingers and pointing at Mason.

"Y-your question covered so many facets," Mason stuttered. "I was racking my brain, searching through my memories." Two Suits bounded up onto the stage. Their swift movements were stiff and purposeful. They stood on either side of Mason, fiddling with his black headpiece, twisting the sides and moving the sensors.

Both of them frowned the entire time, their faces bent low over their work.

With a nod and a bow, they exited the stage as quickly as they had appeared.

"The recalibration *should* now compute your *immediate* answer," the Executor said with a snappy sigh. She returned to the centre for the fourth time.

My eye twitched as she lowered her head, once again reading through the final few cards she clutched in her hands.

The back of my neck prickled, and I felt hot and sweaty.

I lowered my head, focusing for a few beats on my breath, in and out, my hands clenched into fists. All of this felt so *trivial*, so *contrived* and I hated knowing they were going to edit whatever they deemed juiciest anyway.

"Hey," Mason whispered, "we've almost made it." It was as if he'd read my mind and jumped in at the perfect moment. I gave him a weak smile, grateful he had chosen those specific words, but choosing to remain silent. I didn't think I could speak without my voice wavering.

A warm hand squeezed my shoulder. The heat lingered for a few seconds after he had already let go, like a fleeting moment of calm within the eye of the storm.

The Executor cleared her throat. Her loud, throaty cough echoed in my ears, and I forced my eyes open.

As I looked up, the Executor looked down at me. Her eyes narrowed.

"Shall we continue?"

I gave her a small nod, wanting to shake my head. I was all for honesty, but answering question after question was exhausting. My nerves were shot, and I didn't even have any big secrets to hide.

"Two more," she said, quieter this time.

"I can answer two more," I whispered, pulling my head and shoulders back, trying to talk myself into participating; Mr. Dunn's words still swirled around in my mind.

"Welcome back." The Executor's smile radiated, her body facing a camera slightly off centre.

"We're down to the wire, the final two questions...the *hardest two questions* yet." She stared into the camera. "Let's get right into it." Her voice was filled with dramatised tones. Her acting was top-notch, even if her charade felt ridiculous.

"Love is all-encompassing. Deep," she said, starting her little monologue.

"Love," I groaned under my breath—the *last* thing I wanted to talk about with Mason present.

"It can be fleeting, or long-lasting. How many times have you been in love?" she asked.

My number was low, but there was no need to think too hard. I looked up at the big screen.

"Wha—" I garbled the word. It was unrecognisable as it slipped out of my mouth. The television screen flickered and illuminated the number *three* on my side of the board.

"You seem confused, Miss Avery." The Executor swanned down towards me. She was enjoying this far too much. She was the queen of picking on me in my weakest moments.

"No." I shook my head, my internal thoughts screaming *yes* as I struggled to keep my calm demeanour on show. Maybe the real actor here was me.

"Three great loves, Miss Avery?" she said again, her body closing in on mine, so close I could feel her radiating warmth. She was coming for me, and I wasn't ready.

"I-I..." Now it was my turn to stutter and stammer.

"You still seem *so* confused, my dear," she continued. "Are you having a revelation here on the stage? Realising something you may have shoved down?"

She kept talking; her voice filled up the room.

"I've only ever been in love *once*," Mason cut through all the chatter inside my head and gripped everyone's attention for a few seconds. He was being chivalrous and kind on my behalf—I didn't deserve it.

"Once, Mr. McConnell?" she asked, less interested, but entertaining him all the same.

"Once," he repeated. "Once is enough." He peered in my direction with his huge, goofy smile.

I smiled back at him, my facial muscles moving before I could think or react. My face burned with red-hot heat. What I had said to the girls in my sad, sobbing state was true.

I was in love with Mason.

Just as the revelation opened a pit in my stomach, pulling everything from my chest and below into it, reality smacked me in the face.

"Any final comments? Revelations to share?"

I hesitated for a few seconds. I wanted to say something that would tell Mason I felt the same way without announcing on television that I had just realised *we love each other*.

"Love takes you by surprise sometimes." My voice shook.

The little red dots around the room flashed and zeroed in on us, creeping closer, but I said nothing else. Instead, I glanced at Mason again, his cheeks shining as brilliantly red as mine felt, and I knew he knew—and that was enough.

"Well, well," the Executor said, shuffling back only a few steps, "and we have saved the hardest question for last."

She gripped a single card in her hand, and I doubted anything could be harder than the last question.

"Let's talk about all things pregnancy. The average woman won't have a child. With *the lottery* in place, only a select few women carry a child past ten weeks." I half tuned out as she babbled to the camera about how our country worked, how Australia had chosen to tackle this issue. Something that every woman here was living through and therefore aware of.

The Lottery had been taking place for years, and the temporary governance that surrounded it was air-tight, seeking to decrease the next generation's population.

I clenched my jaw and kept my mouth shut as she continued.

"Women vie for the few available slots, seeking the best mates to give them the best chance." Her impassioned pitch was winding down and I felt queasy.

"Or paying the most money to buy a spot," I said under my breath, but a little too loud.

"Yes, Miss Avery," she said, "or assisting our further research and development with monetary gain and skipping the first phase." She looked at me hard, and I knew they would cut that out. "Alas, regardless of money, the best foetus and woman *will win*. That is why you are still sitting here, and we are having this conversation." She spoke curtly, but her demeanour softened in acknowledgement of my irritation. "With all that said: was all this planned?" She eyed me now, as if she too was curious about this answer.

Without missing a beat, both sides of the board flashed *no*, almost as instantly, before the last word was out of the Executor's mouth.

"There was more to the question," she said, smirking now, "but clearly, this was a fortunate acc—surprise."

I smiled at the near slip-up.

"As I've said right from the beginning," I piped up, repeating myself one last time. "We had sex *once*. We hadn't, and haven't, ever been on a proper date."

"Not for lack of trying." Mason spoke over my last few words. I rolled my eyes but smiled.

"We met, we hit it off. We fucked. The. End." I paused after each segmented section. It sounded harsh, but it was true; that was our story.

The Executor paused for a few seconds, her mouth pursed. I wondered whether it was my candid explanation or my language that annoyed her.

"Maybe I can ask a different question?" she pondered out-loud.

I sighed, realising I would have to answer the additional question, television appropriate, if I wanted to be finished with this. They needed their editable, raw material.

"We're down to the wire." She started her speech at the beginning, and pretended my last answer didn't happen. Clearly, they hadn't gotten the response they were seeking.

"The final frontier," I mocked, clapping my hand over my mouth, embarrassed and annoyed with myself. I was running out of politeness for today.

The Executor sighed, winding herself back again. She didn't scold me, which was a surprising twist.

"The last question. The most difficult one of all," she said, her bouncy, brilliant demeanour unchanged whilst she was filming. "How did you feel when you found out you were pregnant?" Her eyes flicked to Mason. "When you found out *Alice* was pregnant?"

I bit the inside of my cheek. I hated the use of my first name almost as much as I hated being pregnant against my will.

The word *devastated* flashed up on my screen, which summed up my feelings about the whole situation pretty well—and clashed with Mason's *bittersweet.*

I braced for the multiple follow-up questions I knew were coming.

As the Executor opened her mouth, I forced myself to swallow my rage. The burning hot irritation wound tightly down my throat and landed in a pit in my stomach.

"Devastation?" the Executor said, almost licking her lips. She closed the gap between us, her slender body leaning over towards me.

"Yes," I said, trying to sound matter-of-fact and without wavering.

"Care to *elaborate?*" she pushed.

I sighed, my hands clamping together in my lap. Each of my intertwined fingers pressed against the other until they hurt.

"I didn't see children in my story," I said, trying to pick the right words. "I didn't think they were written into my fate after…" I trailed off. While the Lottery had sealed my fate, I had been on the fence about children long before.

The Executor raised her eyebrows at me.

"Not part of the plan, Miss Avery?" she cooed, almost baby-like. I couldn't tell if she was curious or goading, kind or cruel.

I shook my head, choosing not to answer her with words for a few seconds.

I forced in a few deep breaths. The rage swirled around in my stomach, seeping into my chest and legs as the silence between us grew longer.

"And Miss Avery," she pushed innocently enough, "once the initial shock wore off, were you happy? Sad? Excited? Annoyed? Walk *us through your emotions*." She smiled at me, a huge grin threatening to bloom on her face. Now she was taunting me. Now maybe my temper would win them views. This was what she wanted.

"I felt nothing but inconvenience…to begin with," I added.

"*And then what?*" the Executor whispered as if I was speaking about a great, universal secret that the world needed to hear.

"And then I found out I had missed the cut-off." The rage bubbled up in my chest, tiny bubbles finding their way into my throat "And I was…" I stopped. "Furious. The lack of choice for women in this country *astounds* me." I clamped my lips shut, puckering them together.

"Go on," she pushed.

I shook my head and sighed again. I didn't want to say the same things *again*, then lose my temper *again*, to be labelled a hysterical woman *again*.

"No more to say?" she goaded, her words swimming around inside my head. The temptation squirmed inside me, but I stayed silent. The outspoken woman never wins. I had to pick my moment.

"Very well. The Lottery's purpose is unlikely to be fully understood by the public anyway," she said snidely, her body swivelling towards Mason.

"The lottery is just another way those in power regulate our bodies," I lashed out as the Executor turned to look me in the eye. "Another way that we are devoid of choice. Another way the government extorts its power. Another way women are controlled. Another way our bodies are not our own." I rested my right hand atop my protruding bump. "I asked for an abortion," I said, this time speaking freely—fuck it. "*More than once.* I was denied."

Her mouth opened, but I cut her off.

"Denied an abortion on the grounds that the *foetus* growing within me *might* be extraordinary—*might*," I repeated, throwing my hands in the air for dramatic effect, irritated at my own theatrics.

My breath came in short, shallow bursts. The Executor's eyes were wide and vibrant, her nostrils flaring as she looked down her nose at me.

"The foetus growing within you *is* something extraordinary," she said, "or you wouldn't still *be here*." Her words shot out like slithering venom, wrapping their tendrils around my chest and fluttering against my heart.

"Regardless," I retorted, "women are being denied the right to choose."

"The end justifies the means," she snapped, talking directly to me now. She was off script and clearly wanted to debate openly with me.

"The end?" I snorted, shaking my head, my eyes linked to hers. "Forcing women into pregnancies they don't want? Forcing the termination of very wanted pregnancies?"

"Yes, Miss Avery. You may not understand this, but our Earth cannot survive our population."

"Don't flatter yourself," I snapped. "Don't forget, you're talking to a scientist." My teeth ground together, my jaw set. "I have a suggestion: allow women the right to sterilisation if they request it. *That* might help with population control." I knew I was speaking in a sarcastic tone. Goading her to ask follow-up questions, daring her to push *me* now.

"Sterilisation?" she scoffed, her eyebrows pushed together with such force that they almost looked like one solid line. "And who would request *that*?" She shook her head and I couldn't wait to voice my response.

"*I did*," I said, my words clear, "on four separate occasions. With four separate specialists. Long before I found myself locked away here."

I fell silent. I would have smirked if I wasn't so angry. The only sound that could be heard between us was that of my laboured breathing.

"This has *always* been about control," I whispered, the hairs on the back of my neck standing on end. The Executor raised her eyes to meet mine, her unblinking face drooping as I drove my point home. "All of it."

CHAPTER THIRTY-TWO

AFTERMATH

I SAT IN THE LARGE WAITING ROOM, MY BACK PRESSED INTO A PLUSH sofa, my eyes glued to the door. The room was big but barren, with stark white walls and an air of emptiness.

I kept my eyes on the door, hoping to catch a glimpse of Mason from somewhere within—but all they found were tiny cracks and imperfections in the paint.

A loud *beep* made me jump. My body tensed, as the wooden door in front of me swung open to reveal the Executor and Mason. They stood side-by-side, their shoulders so close they almost touched.

Without a word, she stepped forward, crossing the threshold of the room towards me. The door swung closed in Mason's face. His sad face and half-raised hand was shut out of sight.

"I won't take up much of your time," she said. Her voice was a little shakier than I was expecting. She must have used all her star-power on stage in the last few hours. "Out there, on the stage…" Her voice was strained and off-beat. "Something you said rattled me."

She pulled a file out from under her left arm. It was thick with pages and tatty edges. In big block letters, my full name and date of birth were scrawled across the top.

"Alice Avery," she said, flicking through several pages. My whole life in medical records was at the tip of her fingers; it felt strangely personal and certainly invasive.

"Sterilisation request; denied." Her finger ran down the length of the page before turning it over.

I swallowed hard, my eyes prickling as the Executor flipped through more-and-more of my medical history.

"Second sterilisation request; denied." Her finger stopped about halfway down the page. "Patient too young…" She didn't finish the rest of the sentence.

She flicked through the file, stopping a few times. I was silent; my words would change nothing and the pages she was reading would prove everything.

"Immaturity," she mumbled, "Too young…Big decision…" Her mouth pulled down as she snapped the file shut. "It appears I owe you an apology, Miss Avery." She pinched the bridge of her nose.

I stared at her, my eyebrows raising into my hairline. I had never expected an apology, and it felt strange from her lips.

"Executor," I sighed in return, "I'd *love* to blame you, but this isn't *entirely* your fault." I wanted to direct my years of anger at her, to yell and tell her she ruined my life, but even in my anger I knew that wasn't true. "Doctors failed me long before I landed myself in your facility." I shrugged, sinking into the thick, plush chair. "Besides, Mason and I also bear *some* of the blame." I flushed as she nodded. Her face was still taut. There was a lot more we could say to each other, but both of us stayed silent.

"As promised, Mason will enter as I exit. One hour," she said again with raised eyebrows.

I smiled weakly at her, and she turned on her heel. The door slid open as she approached to reveal Mason, his fidgety fingers snapping to his sides.

"And Miss Avery," the Executor said, looking back as she stepped aside. She waved Mason in, and his quick strides crossed the threshold and bounded towards me. "Good luck." She looked down at my file again as the door slid shut in her face.

"Why do I feel like she was going to say something else?" Mason said, flopping down on the couch beside me. His presence immediately made me smile.

"I do, too," I agreed, looking back at the door. I pulled my attention back and looked Mason up and down. I would have plenty of time alone later to contemplate everything that just happened.

Up-close, his face had a few more tiny wrinkles, their thin tendrils snaking into the lines in his smile and across his forehead.

"How?" I finally stuttered out. My mouth unable to force out more than this very simple question. I needed to know *how* Mason ended up taking the stage instead of Mr. Dunn, before I could comprehend the *why*. It was clear I couldn't *or wouldn't* have answered any of those questions with Mr Dunn. But I still couldn't figure out the motive for the bait and switch. I opted to believe they wanted this to unbalance me, to ensure I was caught off guard and would therefore tell the truth; but it felt more personal than that.

"It's a *really* long story," Mason said, cutting across my spiralling thoughts. The big, goofy smile I loved took over his face and I felt my stomach knot but my chest relax. "Although the highlight is that they pushed me out on stage without too much warning." He inched a little closer to me, the plush couch sinking further in as the distance between us shortened.

"You didn't know?" I shifted my body weight forward.

"Know I was going to be sharing *that* information? No." Mason shook his head, his face flushing. His hands crept forward, his body shimmying against the couch, closer to me. "They fitted me with that device, and all they told me was it was for further testing." He paused. "And then. There I was." His body was now only inches away from me. His skin radiated heat.

"Then, there you were," I said, biting my lip. "They told us it was more intelligence testing too." My eyes stayed locked on his. My fingers crawled across the soft fabric, stopping only a few inches from Mason's thigh. I wanted to say more, to unpack the clear misdirection of the way this televised stunt had been explained.

"Intelligence testing?" His eyebrows raised. His body shifted one last time so that my fingers rubbed against the fabric of his clothing.

"How many times do they have to test our intelligence?" He laughed as his hand reached for mine.

His skin was warm and soft in our intertwined fingers. He squeezed my hand.

"It doesn't matter," I said honestly, not wanting to think about their motives or schemes anymore. I squeezed Mason's hand back three times. He might not have known the signal, but it felt good to be in control for a fleeting moment.

He pulled my hand up and kissed the back of it, his warm breath sending a shiver down my spine.

I leaned forward and pressed my face into his shoulder. My body shuffled forward to close the last small gap between us. Relief washed over me as I laid my head against Mason's chest and he wrapped his arm around me, kissing me on the top of my head.

"You've been gone a long time," he whispered. "How are you holding up?"

I shrugged, my shoulder moving against his. "Still devastated. Still furious," I said in jest, my eyes dropping. There was something about the way he looked at me that pushed my honesty button. "I'm—" I said, more seriously now. "Tired of jumping through hoops. I just want this to be over. Let me win, or set me free."

Mason nodded, kissing my forehead this time as I looked up at him. "What are you going to do if you win?" he asked, a little too nonchalantly.

"You mean *when* I win." I lifted my head to wink at him.

"Alice," he said a little more seriously. I normally hated my first name, but when he said it, somehow it sounded good. Somehow it made me melt a little bit.

I shut my eyes and laid my head against his chest.

"I know," I whispered. It wasn't an answer; it wasn't anything. But for once, I didn't know what to say. I could play the games and be smart, but I was only now considering what winning *meant*.

We sat in silence for a while, my head rested against his chest. His fingers ran in circles against my shoulder, our breath in sync.

I listened to the thump of Mason's heart. The slow rhythmic beat lulled me into a calm alternate reality. In a different life, we could be snuggled up on my couch, talking about dinner plans, or laughing with Kit and Darcy at the bar. I closed my eyes, letting the moment stretch on, not wanting to move.

"I'll be beside you," Mason whispered, his lips so close to my ear that it sent a tingle across my neck. Snuggling into his shoulder a little more, I nodded.

My eyes prickled as he changed the subject. He always knew when to push and when to be kind. It was a peculiar talent.

"So you're pretty much in the final. What do you think the interview will be like?" His big, blue eyes glittered in the harsh light. How was a nerdy astrologist *so* good looking?

I groaned, leaning back. I exaggerated a little, but it felt good to think about something trivial. "All I can hope for is no more questions about my virginity," I said, half-laughing, half-mortified.

Mason laughed, his body shaking against me.

"Let's hope for more intelligent questions," I said. "About my job, about my field of study." I sunk further into the lounge. "About you," I said with a wink. As soon as I winked I felt my face flush—who *was I*?

Mason half-laughed, half-groaned. His face flushed a light shade of pink. "Make me sound cool," he said, his goofy smile returning.

The door flew open, the Executor planted in the centre.

"Has it been an hour already?" I blinked, my heart sinking into my stomach.

"No," she snapped. "We've had a breach."

She looked at me, her gaze unwavering for a few seconds, until it shifted to Mason. His body moved uncomfortably in our chair.

"Search them," she barked. Six Suits pushed past her and stormed into the room, splitting in the centre. Three stomped towards each of us.

Six hands ran across me roughly. They pulled and prodded at every inch of my body, pushing my dress up and snapping my underwear.

"Clear," my trio said in unison.

"Clear," the trio attached to Mason said, seconds later.

"Wha—" I stuttered as they pulled Mason out of the room, four Suits flanking him. "Wait!" I shouted.

They pushed Mason across the threshold out of the room. The two remaining Suits grabbed onto my arms, their fingers pressing into my skin; shooting pain emanated from each pressure point.

Mason looked back at me for a split second, our gaze holding as they dragged him away. The door snapped shut. My hands were still pinned at my side.

In a split second, they let me go, returning to stand at attention, blocking the door.

"What just happened?" I rounded on the Executor.

She paused, her posture relaxing. "Leave us," she waved at the hovering Suits.

"Yes, Madam." They bowed, and their hurried footsteps pattered out the door in a matter of seconds.

She sighed and flopped herself down onto the large green sofa. Her body almost crumpled in on itself. "There's been a leak. A breach." Her voice sounded shaky, but she'd already said this when she barged in. I wanted new information.

"Care to elaborate?" Anger swirled in the pit of my stomach, threatening to tear out my throat with each passing second. They had carted Mason away, and I wanted answers.

"*Someone*," she said, the venom in her voice returning for a split second, "filmed parts of that last Q&A session and has already leaked them to the press."

I frowned.

"And why is that a bad thing?" I snapped. "I thought the whole reason for that ridiculous charade was press attention?"

The Executor met my gaze for the first time since she sat down. "There are some things that are better to be heavily edited or edited out." She narrowed her eyes at me.

"So *my* words have been leaked to the press?" I said. My stomach swirled, a strange combination of mortified, flattered, and impressed.

She nodded curtly, holding her tablet out to me. "Take it," she said. "You may as well see what's happening."

With trembling hands, I grabbed the screen, scrolling down the length of the news website that was open.

My face was splashed everywhere. Both flattering photos and terrible ones. I was both a heathen and a spokeswoman. I was both a leader and a madwoman. Snippets of words like *whore, harlot, visionary* caught my eye; unable to see more than headline after headline.

"What *is this*?" My finger kept scrolling. My face popped up across the screen every few articles. "*Mason*," I gaped. A feature piece with photos of the two of us stood front-and-centre in the entertainment section. They must have photoshopped us together, because we had *never* taken a photo – or had we? Would I remember after a drunken night?

"You've gone viral," she grimaced. She took the tablet back from me. "Every major news outlet is running the story. *Your story.*"

"*Why?*" I chewed my lip. My heart hammered in my chest, sweat prickling against the hairs on the back of my neck.

"It appears, Miss Avery, that most women agree with your stance." A little smirk finally danced across her face.

"They do?" My voice rang in my ears. The uncertainty that had been bubbling in my stomach reared its head.

"They do, Miss Avery. It appears you have become somewhat of a *celebrity*." I thought she was going to snort or laugh, but her eyes narrowed and she pushed on. "And as we were planning to rely on a voting system after the final two, you may have an advantage." She said this matter-of-factly, but her lip quivered towards the end.

I shook my head, not quite able to collect my thoughts.

"As you were the subject of the leak, I wanted to keep you informed. You can imagine that I now have a lot of work to do." She stood, looking down at me, her frame seeming much smaller than before.

"The final two interviews are scheduled for three days from today."

"The final two?"

"Yes, Miss Avery, the final two. You have made it this far..." She smiled at me as she hesitated in the doorway. Her head turned back, her eyes locking with mine. "You might want to start considering what you will do *if you win.*"

CHAPTER THIRTY-THREE

THE FINAL COUNTDOWN

"YOUR PHONE AND LAPTOP HAVE BEEN REMOVED DUE TO THE BREACH OF private information." The robotic voice echoed as I entered a new, lavish room.

Two guards gave me a curt nod after they dropped me inside, the door snapping shut behind them without a word. A loud spin lock and deadbolt clicked shut outside my door.

I wrapped my arms around myself. The cool air blasted from the air conditioner, blowing against my skin and sprung goosebumps.

The new room was smaller than the last one, but just as beautiful. The ornate wooden bed in the centre took up most of the floor space, the dark blue covers inviting me towards them. Flopping down, I curled myself into a little ball. Half-tired, half-wired, my body alternating from back-breaking fatigue to a ball of energy, made me want to get up and pace the room.

I couldn't believe what the Executor had said. The word *viral* bounced around in my head. I rolled onto my back and stared up at the ceiling. Mr. Dunn's words rang in my mind again, and I groaned at the ease at which 'fame' had come—now I just needed to *win*.

My stomach balked at the thought as a loud knock boomed at the door, and I had to admit I am thankful for the interruption. I raced to stand, and a shooting pain shot across my stomach. It was still hard to believe I had been forced to get *this* pregnant, my body held hostage by endless tests and checks.

I had barely moved when the click and spin of the deadbolts outside announced my guests' impending entry.

"I guess pretending I'm not home doesn't work in a bunker," I grumbled, tugging my dress down haphazardly. Everything in my body felt wrong; too much, too big, too uncomfortable. I could feel myself twitching as the door swung open to reveal a thin figure. They were obscured by the light until they stepped forward into the glaring lights of my new room.

"Dr. Hid—" I barely got any words out before the tears started streaming down my face.

"Miss Avery," she said kindly, her signature tight ponytail pulled into place along with a large grin. The door snapped shut and the lock spun outside; they had locked us in together and I was still only grateful to see her.

"What are y—" I whispered as she stepped into the room.

"I have been tasked to talk to you," she said, the smile that had danced on her lips faltering. "Come, come." She waved me towards the pair of chairs. The sound of her high heels clicking against the floor was a kind of familiarity I had missed.

Dr. Hidalgo flopped herself down on one of the emerald green plush armchairs that made up the living-room portion of my room. The fabric squeaked as she shuffled her body, her thin frame sinking down into the cushion.

With a slight waddle and two raised eyebrows, I followed suit, lowering myself less gracefully down into the armchair opposite her. My body felt awkward as I twisted and turned, settling in a distorted position with my legs wrapped around each other.

"Tell me how you're feeling," Dr. Hidalgo said. I shifted my body again, my hip throbbing as I untwisted my lower body and sighed.

"Honestly?" I almost panted, trying to catch my breath from the torturous act of getting comfortable. "Uncomfortable." I leaned back with a long, loud stream of breath. Women might be built for this, but I certainly wasn't.

"Any pain?" Dr. Hidalgo leaned forward in her chair. "Any sharp pains, stabbing pains, aching pains?" She stared hard, giving me a few seconds to answer. Her eyes were focused on me, and she looked worried.

I shook my head, finding a comfortable position and meeting Dr. Hidalgo's eyes. "Just general discomfort from growing a human being," I said, half-jovial and half-groaning. Why did I always think I was diffusing the tension when I made jokes?

"Any bleeding? Spotting? Discharge?" she continued, ignoring my loud, uncomfortable groan. "Mucus?" Her smile told me she was enjoying my red-hot face and burning cheeks. It might all be normal, but it didn't feel normal to talk about so casually.

"No," I wanted this line of questioning to be over. I had answered enough invasive, personal questions for one day. But at least these ones were less likely to be leaked to the press, and more likely to be necessary information for my doctor.

"Do you have questions for me, Miss Avery?" Dr. Hidalgo asked, her posture relaxing now that she had confirmed my wellbeing.

"Why are you here?" I blurted. "*How* are you here?"

"I am here because the team recognised we have somewhat of a rapport," she said matter-of-factly, "and the higher-ups have recognised this may be their only chance for someone to speak with you candidly." The smile that danced on Dr. Hidalgo's lips let me know that she was enjoying this.

"What is happening out there?" I whispered, my eyes darting to the closed door. The silence was palpable.

"Your words created quite a stir, Miss Avery. And the fact they were leaked to the press, *pre-editing*." She paused, a brief twitch of her lips visible. It was hard to tell if she was impressed or irritated at what had happened.

"An entire generation of women has been dictated to…" I said with a shrug. "Thirteen years." I shook my head. "If you want to ban procreation outside of your own little games for that long…" Now the smile danced on my lips. "You better be able to stand up to one woman's opinion and scrutiny."

"That is the sentiment being picketed for in the streets," Dr. Hidalgo spoke succinctly. Not rushing or tripping over her words. Her lack of both excitement and sadness was unnerving. Something had changed—*she* had changed.

"Dr. Hidalgo?" I lowered my head, my eyes meeting hers for a few seconds. When I raised my head, she raised hers, her left eye blinking a few times out of sync with her right eye.

The off movement sent a shiver down my spine. She wasn't *my* Dr. Hidalgo anymore.

I stood up, my feet sinking into the soft, spindly carpet as I paced across the small space between the armchairs and knelt down in front of her. I took her hand in mine and saw her wrist chip blinking red. For some reason, that unsettled me more than anything.

"What kind of *woman* do they want me to be?" It was the first thing that popped into my brain; but the words sliced my throat on the way out. Dr. Hidalgo wouldn't answer, but the tiny flicker made me think they were watching through her eyes. What a terrifying thought that was. What if her suggestion I *keep fighting* had really come from someone else? What if she had told me to speak up so she could leak my words? My thoughts were spiralling when Dr. Hidalgo spoke again.

"There is a reason we only permit certain women past the initial stage," Dr. Hidalgo said, her head snapping towards me, jarring her face. "Pliable. Usable." Her head tilted, and shook again. She was fighting their override. "Puppets of—" Her sentence cut off half-way through, and her head flopped forward. Her breath grew shallow and laboured, her body still. She was desperately fighting whatever war was waging in her head, clawing at her wrist as her body vibrated. "Avery—" she whispered, her head still down, her body shaking. "—tell—truth," she said, her words coming out in a jumble. "*The* truth," she said again before she slumped back in the armchair. The door swung open with a loud thud. Six Suits poured into the large room, four carrying a thick, black stretcher. I backed away, staring as Dr.

Hidalgo was lowered onto it, her arms dangling off the edges as the Suits backed out of the room. The only thing I could see were the giant claw marks down her arm. The final two Suits walked backwards with their eyes pinned on me.

"What happ—" I said, my heart thumping in my chest before the door swung shut, the six sets of footsteps retreating. A sob bubbled in my throat. They had wanted her to break me, but instead they broke her. Dr. Hidalgo had been one of the few women I had felt *understood,* but as the door swung shut behind the Suits, I wondered what price she had paid for her kindness towards me.

"Miss Avery." A thick voice penetrated the room, swirling towards me.

I turned wildly towards the unfamiliar voice.

A tall, slender woman stood in front of me. Her knee-high boots cupped over the arches of her knees, and her thin, shimmering black stockings glinted against the bright lights.

I kept my eyes on her feet. Her pointed boots were a strange shade of brown-black. A tiny scuff mark was visible on the left side.

"Miss Avery," she said again. Thick, loud, and commanding, its deep, honey melody song-like as it played in my ears.

Our eyes finally connected. A curt nod and not a slither of a smile emanated from the woman's face. "As the Director of the Lottery, I am here to congratulate you for making it this far." She looked me up-and-down. I couldn't tell if it was in appraisal or disgust. "As there has been a significant amount of controversy for this quarter's Lottery..." She looked me in the eye now. Her harsh glare narrowed in on me, raising my heart-rate with every second she held my gaze. "The final filming location has been moved."

Her eyes snapped to the black tablet she clutched in her hands. I wanted to ask her what they had done to Dr. Hidalgo; but knew they would *never* tell me.

"You're still planning to hold the final interview round?" My eyebrows hit the roof of my hair. I hadn't expected that—why were they hellbent on seeing this through?

"Yes, Miss Avery," she sneered. "A little additional publicity will be good for ratings." It was then that I realised that the Director was a believer in 'no publicity is bad publicity.' "Tomorrow at 7 a.m. you will be escorted to a new location." Her eyes remained glued to her tablet. "For security reasons," she said, her stubby fingers tapping the same spot on the screen multiple times, "that is all the information we will provide."

She looked up from her tablet, her eyes narrowing.

I said nothing, instead deciding to return her gaze, unblinking, with only a slight nod of acknowledgement, my mind still racing.

With a loud click, she closed her tablet, crossing it over in her arms against her chest, her gaze unbroken.

"A lot of well-respected women have been taken by you." Her eyes flicked up and down across my body. "I am yet to see *why*." Her lips pursed before she shook her head. She turned on her heel, stalking away from me. I swallowed, my heart hammering at the thought that *she* had been the one behind Dr. Hidalgo's episode.

"Maybe they appreciate honesty," I squeaked to her back, my voice coming out like a thin, wiry line. I sounded pathetic, but I couldn't let the moment pass and say nothing.

"Perhaps, Miss Avery," she said, pausing for a few beats too long. "Perhaps they are looking for a leader. Perhaps they are looking for a speaker. Perhaps they are looking for a *martyr*." She flicked her head back towards me as she wrapped her long fingers against the door handle. "Perhaps you'll be inconsequential by tomorrow morning." The first smile she had shown since she slithered into my room crept onto her face. Her eyes narrowed to make room for her teeth to show.

Her snake-like smile sent cascades of goosebumps down my spine. I forced myself to hold eye-contact with her as the door swung open, the pit in the bottom of my stomach widening with each passing second.

She snapped her head away at the last second. The door swung shut with a loud thud. I leaned forward, resting my entire weight against my knees, my breath coming in hard and fast. A sheen of sweat dripped down the back of my neck.

"I might be in trouble," I rasped. I tried to pull myself up, taking a few more shaky breaths. My hands clenched against my knees as I tried to steady myself.

I sunk down on the soft bed, my body sinking in too deep to be comfortable. My head folded into my hands, and I twisted side-ways to shimmy up into the semi-foetal position—my protruding stomach getting in the way.

With a sigh, I forced my eyes shut, my brain circling on repeat.

"I might be in trouble," I whispered with no one but myself to hear me.

CHAPTER THIRTY-FOUR

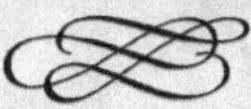

6 A.M

A BLARING ALARM STARTLED ME AWAKE. I TWISTED AND TURNED AND fumbled to move, enveloped in the bedsheets.

"What the—" I murmured, shaking my arms, my limbs lead-like.

A soft, robotic voice cooed, *this is your one hour alarm*. I groaned, tugging at my feet that were still trapped under the entangled sheets.

I waved the alarm off, realising after I did so that it had already stopped and the remaining noise was the ringing in my ears.

With a sigh, I rubbed my aching eyes. I stared at the floor, my mind foggy with lack of sleep. I had barely slept last night thinking about the interviews, Dr. Hidalgo, and the meteoric rise of Alice Avery.

Four loud raps on the door made me jump, my body still half-suspended in the art of getting out of bed at twenty-weeks pregnant.

Instead of moving, I watched the door, knowing it would swing open regardless of my personal invitation.

As always, I was right, and a few seconds later several Suits filed in, followed by the Executor and the Director, side-by-side.

I raised my eyebrows as the eight Suits lined themselves up, four on each side. Each pair of hands held a different item.

"To what do I owe the early morning pleasure?" I drawled, my voice cracking as I stifled a yawn. It was six in the morning. and there were ten people already crammed into my room. If this was any indication of my day, it was going to be long and challenging.

The Director's eyes narrowed as if she could hear my thoughts. Her irritation with me was obvious from the offset.

"Your transportation leaves at 7 A.M." The Executor's hands were clasped in front of her body. "You must be ready by then."

Her words must have been a secret signal because the first Suit in line darted forward, closing the gap between us.

With lightning fast movements, the Suit placed a silver scale on the floor. The numbers jumped around for a few seconds before returning to zero. Without a word, the Suit's hands were on mine, tugging me up out of bed and extricating me from the twisted sheets.

With another soft tug, I stepped forward, my feet landing in the centre of the scale. I decided early that I wouldn't fight here, not with the Suits. I'd save my fighting for later. Three soft beeps echoed, and the Suit pulled me down, returning me to solid ground and giving me a curt nod. She tucked the scale under one arm as she stepped back into line, her head bowed.

The Suits cycled through one-by-one, stepping forward to strip me off, measure me down to the smallest centimetre, dress me up, prime my face, pin my hair, and place beautiful, black, ankle-high boots on my swollen feet. They must have sized up, because my feet somehow felt comfortable.

When the final Suit stepped away, her eyes fluttered up-and-down, up-and-down, looking me over inch-by-inch. With a twist of her head, she bowed at the other women, each standing silently in the centre of the room, their eyes pinned to me.

"Miss Avery." The Executor shattered the long silence that had stretched out as the Suits worked.

"Enough pleasantries," the Director waved, her eyes narrowing to pinpricks as she looked me up-and-down. "We have five minutes to spare."

The two women exchanged glances, and with a long, overdone eye-roll, the Director twisted on her heel, clicking her fingers. She stalked away, shoes echoing, tailed by the eight Suits, their heads bowed. They gave slight nods towards us both as each of them passed by.

At the snap of the door, the Executor let out a loud sigh, pinching the bridge of her nose so tightly it turned a funny shade of red-purple.

"Miss Avery," she said again, dropping her hand and staring at me. "Many executives are very upset about the breach." She was choosing her words carefully, and I wondered what kind of chaos was happening within Epitome Labs and on the outside. "It has created quite a stir. International news, tabloids, splashed far and wide across social media." She said this seriously, but a slight sparkle in her eye and a small twitch of her lips almost gave away her amusement.

I nodded, biting my lip. I knew the Executives would be putting the blame squarely with me, but I had no regrets about what I said, and I wasn't the leak.

"And today, we are allowing the new poster child of the revolution to speak publicly, *again*." She was smirking. It seemed she thought this was funny, and I couldn't quite work out why.

"All I want is for all women to have the right to choose." I shrugged. "I wanted to choose to *not* have a baby. Thousands of women want to choose *to* have a baby, and it's unconscionable that the government can enforce their choice on an entire generation of women." My heart beat rose, the anger that had been dulled in my isolation roaring again. It beat through my bones and swept over me in waves. If the Executor had planned to sway me, to try and persuade me to be silent, it wouldn't work.

"You're passionate," she interjected. "It's written all over your body that you want to speak, to *fight*."

My already red cheeks flushed an even deeper shade. She had me figured out, and I wondered what that meant for both of us.

"You'll have the stage today," she said, returning to what must have been part of the script for this morning. "What you say. The words you choose. The choices you make today…it will be broadcast *live*." She emphasised that last word.

"Live?" I gaped.

"Live." Her voice was firmer this time.

I tried to swallow past the large rock that had lodged in my throat. I wanted to speak, wanted to do something big, but I had to hope the broadcast team would cut out my stutters.

"Understood," I murmured. My eyes dropped towards the ground, my head pounding. Sometimes you had to speak even if your voice wavered. "I assumed they would want to *alter* parts of what I said." I forced my eyes up to meet hers. None of this made sense, and my brain was trying to process the absurdity.

She shook her head. "The Director wanted that type of broadcast, but someone above her made the final decision. No edits, no altering." Three loud raps echoed through the room. "Miss Avery," she said, her eyes darting from the door to me as the door swung open.

The Director stood in the doorway, her arms crossed against her chest.

"Our transportation is here," she snapped, turning on her heel, her long hair waving behind her as she spun and stalked away.

The Executor gave me a firm look, her eyes boring into mine, a solid nod completing the conversation between us. I wished she had finished that last sentence. Instead, the unknown hung in the air.

She hurried out of the room. Her quick footsteps disappeared behind the door in a matter of seconds.

I took a deep breath, my chest rattling.

I followed a few steps behind, my shaky legs carrying me towards where the Director and Executor had stopped a few feet away.

"Now," the Director said with a loud bark and a sharp snap of her fingers. Her harsh demeanour lowered a dark cloud over the room. But her lack of control explained her level of rage—it was just directed at the wrong person.

Two Suits stepped out from behind the Director, flanking me. Their hands wrapped handcuffs around my wrists.

I didn't manage to even stutter a complaint before my eyes were covered, a thick, black piece of cotton obscuring my vision. I winced, trying to stay calm as my breathing hitched.

I tried to lift my right hand up to tug at the fabric, but the heavy cuffs pulled at my wrists, shooting a sharp, stabbing pain through my arm.

"As we are going to an undisclosed location," the Director's voice echoed in my ears—she was close to me, and I could have sworn I could hear her smiling, "you will be cuffed and blindfolded until we deem appropriate."

"Blindfolded, I understand." My voice sounded muffled through the cotton wrapped around my head. "But cuffs?" I said it as a question, but no one answered.

I stood there awkwardly as the silence seeped out, spreading between us with each passing second. I wasn't sure what to do. I couldn't see and I couldn't fidget, so I stood still, focusing all my effort on listening to the sounds around me.

A loud click echoed, making me jump. A soft chuckle to my right made my lips purse. The Director thought this was fun; her own personal game of taunting me.

"Come," her voice commanded.

Both my arms were yanked forward, rough hands grasping me under the armpit. The sudden forward momentum made me trip over my own feet.

Without another word, they tugged me forward. My feet managed to walk as we twisted and turned throughout the labyrinth. They led me left then right, up two flights of stairs, and then stopped before jolting upwards, the floor beneath me shaking.

"Are we in an elevator?" I asked the surrounding crowd with only a loud tongue click as a response. I wasn't going to get any information while the Director was around.

The door creaked open, and I fumbled on my feet. The wind howled and filled my ears, whipping my hair around my face.

With a push in the middle of my back, my feet hit the edge of a set of stairs. Both of my arms were gripped tightly as we ascended; each rung was too small or too big for my awkward footsteps.

At the top, I shuffled forward, knocking my head into something hard.

"Ouch," I mumbled, trying and failing to rub my head with my hand-cuffed hands.

I looked right and left, glaring through my black blindfold. I glimpsed patches of bright sunshine, but no details.

"This way," came the Executor's voice, calmly tugging my arm to the left and leading me forwards. "Sit," she said after only a few steps.

"Right back?" I said, not wanting to sit down only to find no chair there to catch me.

"Yes, Miss Avery, right back."

I lowered myself down, squatting until I finally felt the cool fabric underneath me. The chair bounced high, holding me in a straight upright position as I wriggled myself back-and-forth and side-to-side to get comfortable.

With a sigh, I twisted my body to the left, banging my knees into something.

"Miss Avery," the Director's sharp voice snapped from beside me. "Do you not even know basic seat etiquette?"

I raised my eyebrows underneath my blindfold.

"Madam Director." I planted a fake smile on my face. "I cannot see a single thing, so forgive my never-ending rudeness." I rolled my eyes under my thick mask. This whole charade seemed silly. I was going to say what I wanted to say *regardless* of the new, secret location.

A loud sigh was her only reply. It felt strangely good to be scolded by the Director, like I was doing something right.

I tried to sit still, but my legs kept bouncing and fidgeting. With a loud sigh and the click of fingers, someone pulled my blindfold off. The sunlight streamed onto my face, blinding me.

Blinking, my eyes watered and itchy tears spilled over. I held my head back and looked up at the ceiling. Above me was a small, circular light and a seat-belt sign, illuminated in a soft shade of green.

"Are we—" My head snapped down and flittered from left to right.

"Yes, Miss Avery." The Executor nodded.

"We are flying to the next location," The Director said, cutting her off again with a sharp, side-ways glance. She may not have been in charge of everything, but she certainly pulled rank here.

Silence fell between the three of us as I fidgeted with the seat belt, lengthening it to fit it over my belly. There were so many little things pregnancy affected, and it felt strange thinking about all the changes.

As I heard my belt *click* in and gave it another few tugs to be sure, the sound of footsteps rang in my ears.

"Eyes front and centre," the Executor whispered, casting a sharp glance my way before positioning herself to look straight ahead, her eyes twitching.

With a frown, I complied as the footsteps got louder, overlapping with each other. My eyes darted to the very side of my periphery, my head tilting to glimpse the source of the noise.

Even with the strain, I caught only a shadowy glance of black suits as a set of curtains was ripped open and then closed.

I felt the Executor breathe a sigh of relief. Her shoulders slumped.

"Who were *they*?" I whispered, turning my head towards the curtains, the fabric still swaying. The thudding noise of men settling in was still audible.

"Silence," the Director snapped, her voice quiet but harsh.

A loud ding made me jump, The seat belt sign above my head illuminated, casting a faint glow across my face.

My hands reached for my seat belt again, giving it another firm tug before I settled back and squeezed my eyes shut.

"Are you scared of flying, Miss Avery?" the Director asked, amused and quizzical. She had made it clear she was the kind of woman who delighted in others' discomfort, and I hated that she was about to see one of mine.

"No," I said, keeping my eyes shut as the plane shuddered, lurching forward. "I'm afraid of take-off." I finished my sentence with a loud sigh, gripping the sides of my seat, my fingernails digging into the fabric as the plane shuddered. I wished I could have laughed off the snide remarks, but here I was, obviously terrified.

The loud *click* of two additional seat belts unnerved me as the plane crept forward, twisting right before lurching to a stop. It was the stop-start of take-off that unnerved me, the uncertainty of it all.

"Welcome to private flight 247," a chirpy voice interrupted my internal monologue. "In T-Minus 13 seconds, we are cleared for take-off. Buckle up," the voice sang before cutting off abruptly.

The sound of engines roared, and I sucked in a deep breath. The plane jerked and sped forward. My head sucked back into the chair. The plane thundered forward. My eyes clamped shut and my body tilted skyward as we took off.

I counted to ten over-and-over again in my head, forcing myself to breathe in and out at each interval. It was all I could do to keep myself grounded; numbers were always comforting in their simplicity and consistency.

"Miss Avery," I heard the Executor speak my name, but I didn't move, still focusing on my breathing.

"Miss Avery," the Director snapped, louder and firmer this time.

I cracked open one eye, her sharp glare darting from me to the side.

"Miss Avery," a third voice rang out—deep, rich, and unknown.

This strange voice was enough for my other eye to pop open, my head twisting towards the unfamiliar voice.

"Hello, Miss Avery," he said with a warm, straight-toothed smile, extending his hand out to me.

With shaking, sweaty palms, I clasped his hand, shaking it once before dropping my hand again into my lap.

"Would you care to join us?" he said. The seat belt sign flickered off.

I looked at the Director. Her face was red-hot and glowering, and she directed a barely perceptible shake of her head at me.

"I would," I said, finally finding my voice again. I was thankful that the plane seemed to have reached cruising altitude and was sailing smoothly through the air.

With a quick movement, I unclipped myself and stood, wobbling as I stepped into the aisle.

"After you," the man said, his tie so tight it pressed into his fat neck.

I wobbled forward, the plane steady but my legs shaky.

Pulling the curtain back, three additional men turned to look at me, their eyes scanning me up-and-down.

"Gentleman," came the voice from behind me. "You all know Miss Alice Avery."

With a nod, I shuffled forward, finding myself seated in the centre of the four men, each of their eyes glued to me. It was a strangely invasive set of stares. Each man expected something.

"Good Morning," I said, more confidently than I felt.

A chorus of greetings poured out from the small group, each voice intermingling with the one before. I stayed silent.

"Allow us to introduce ourselves," the man who had escorted me in said. He took a seat opposite me and to my right. "We are the four Vice Presidents of Epitome Lab. I am Vice President Alpha," he said with a grin. "This is VP Bravo." He gestured to the man to his right. His bald head shone under the bright plane lights. "VP Charlie." His hand extended towards the man seated to my right, his high-arched eyebrows and wide-set eyes almost scary. "VP Delta," he finished, as his hand moved across to my left. The final Vice President gave me a small head bow. His black suit was more faded than the rest of the pack.

I nodded and smiled with each introduction, unsure whether they expected me to speak or stay silent.

"The flight is short," VP Alpha said, his moustache wiggling.

"So we won't keep you long," VP Charlie said. His head twisted towards me, making him look almost like a mannequin.

I nodded again, the pit in my stomach dropping and sinking further. These men were at the helm of *the lottery*, and they clearly had an interest in me. I wasn't sure whether that was flattering or dangerous.

"As directed, I assume you are now aware the finals are now going to be televised live," VP Alpha said, the corners of his mouth twitching as he took back the conversation. He clearly wanted to lead this little chat.

I gave him a quick nod. My eyes flitted across the two rows of seated men. There was an uncomfortable hierarchy at play here, and I felt like I was teetering in the middle.

"So you understand, Miss Avery," VP Alpha continued, his voice sharpening, "what you say will be *unfiltered. Unedited.*"

I wondered if he spoke that way for dramatic effect, and I forced myself not to roll my eyes.

"Yes, I understand how live television works." The words came out snarkier than I had expected, but garnered a small chuckle from each of the men except Vice President Alpha. His eyes narrowed as I smiled sweetly back at him.

"We have no intention of censoring your words. We will not pull the live feed."

I nodded and shrugged at the same time.

"It'll be nice to have a woman *uncensored*. Maybe share an entire thought before being cut-o—" I snapped, the heat bubbling up into my chest.

"Miss Avery," Vice President Alpha cut me off.

"As if to prove my point." I rolled my eyes and raised my eyebrows.

"This isn't a game," he said.

"Oh, but it is, Vice President. The game is called *the lottery*. It's just that no one wins." I planted a smile on my face. "If you'll excuse me." I pushed myself up, forcing myself not to groan out loud at the effort this now took. "I'll be returning to my assigned seat."

I stepped over the men, crossing the small first-class area of the cabin without stopping.

"Miss Avery," VP Alpha called as my hand hovered to pull back the curtain.

I turned my head back to look at the men, all still seated, their faces ranging from shock, to disgust, to anger.

"The country is interested in what you have to say. Choose your words carefully," he cautioned, a deep, indented frown creeping across his face. I would have thought this was a concern for my situation, but it was clear he was concerned about the continued implementation of the lottery, and probably what it meant for his reputation, job, and paycheck.

I rolled my eyes, this time not bothering to hide it.

"How original," I said. "A man cautioning a woman on sharing her thoughts."

I pulled the curtains back and closed them with too much force. I hovered behind the closed curtain for a few seconds, the blood rushing from my face.

I wanted to stamp my feet like a small child having a tantrum, to rip the curtain back open and say more to the men about how I felt. Instead, I swivelled on my heel and stomped back to my original seat.

I stood in the small aisle, hovering over the two women who sat there, their faces looking up at me expectantly.

"I need a few questions answered," I snapped, stepping over them and plopping myself down in the middle. I folded my arms across my chest, my eyes shooting between them. "Who is going to tell me the truth?"

CHAPTER THIRTY-FIVE

LIGHTS, CAMERA, ACTION, LIVE

I STOOD BEHIND A LARGE RED CURTAIN AT THE BASE OF THE STAGE. MY legs wobbled and my fingers picked at the skin-tight black tights wrapped around my thighs.

Sucking in short, shallow breaths, I squeezed my eyes shut, straining to listen to the muffled, microphone-echoed words that were bouncing around the stage.

All that came through was a garbled mess, followed by a curt round of applause and a muffled cheer here-and-there.

"I'll just..." The Executor huffed and tugged at my dress, pulling at my zipper, then poked and prodded my hair.

I waved her off. How my dress hung or hugged my body was the least of my worries.

"How many people are here?" My eyes were still stuck on the closed curtain.

"A few thousand," she said with a nonchalant shrug, fixing a final stray hair as my head snapped towards her.

"Thousand?" Our eyes met, and I knew shock was written all over my face. I had expected a small crowd—this was an army.

I hadn't managed to compose myself fully when the curtain ripped open and a ball-gown clad Mrs. Astley stepped through the open space.

She paused for a few seconds. Her deep brown eyes hyper fixated on mine, her unblinking gaze boring into me. I would have loved to say something witty and quippy, but she spoke before I got the chance.

"Best of luck." Her tone was condescending as she swept her hands over mine, giving me a little squeeze.

Without another word, she swivelled on her heel, gliding away, her gentle footsteps followed by two Suits. I cursed internally, but what was the point in besting her here? If I was to win, it would have to be on stage with the swarm.

"Miss Avery." Another voice broke through the silence that had fallen.

"Yes." Faking confidence, I turned to face the Director.

Now my mouth *really* hung open. She was dolled-up, clad in a figure-hugging, deep blue dress. Her eyelids sparkled in the same vivid blue as she stared down at me, the same burning dislike in her eyes as before.

"They're ready for you," she said curtly, with a brief nod towards both me and the Executor. "I won't give you any final warnings," she said, her eyes returning to mine. "We both know you'll ignore them anyway." This wasn't said *to* me so much as *at* me. I know she wished she could stop me from speaking—and from continuing the competition—but someone above her truly pulled the strings.

That alone made it easier to give her a fake, cheery smile. She would never know how I really felt as my stomach bubbled and twisted itself in knots.

She slunk away from me, pulling herself up the small flight of stairs behind the curtain. Reaching the top, she flung her shoulders back. Microphone in hand, she belted out a quick introduction. I must have missed Mrs. Astley's introduction in my nervous pacing, and I wondered what they had said about the pastor's wife.

"Please welcome to the stage..." It appeared I had also missed my own introduction.

I lost all sense of sound as I ascended the steps. The Executor's hand pressed into my back. My legs wobbled like jelly, shaking and stumbling. I hit the top step, and my name rang out at the same moment. I had never been more grateful I hadn't been forced into high heels.

Two bright lights flickered on above, shining golden streams onto me as I stumbled across the stage, the Director still talking.

In the centre of the stage were two oversized green velvet chairs, their backs shaped like large clam shells with thick pearl buttons.

"Here she sits, Alice Avery," the Director's voice cut through my mind fog. I sunk into the chair.

The noise filtered into my consciousness. The crowd was an eruption of clapping, screaming, and people chanting my name. I stared out at the sea of tiny heads and bodies, too far away for me to make out a single feature, but close enough to hear their words.

My face turned a bright shade of red, my mouth coated in a sticky paste as I tried to swallow. I wasn't sure how I was going to appease the crowd, whose chorus was both enamouring and terrifying. This felt different—this was a *speech* to a *crowd*. Until that moment, I had only been talking, not expecting anyone to listen.

"Well, well," came the smooth, new voice of the Moderator. "It seems a few fans of Alice Avery are in the audience tonight."

The crowd erupted again. Their cheers and shrieks rang in my ears.

"Well, don't you want to hear from her?" the Moderator boomed, raising his arms up high and standing up, forcing himself into my line of vision.

He was clad in an emerald green suit, an exact colour match for the chairs. His high quaffed, blonde hair was distracting, even from the back.

He swivelled back, shooting me a quick wink before throwing his hands out to quiet the crowd.

From my left, a Suit jutted into my vision, handing me a silver microphone before disappearing back into the shadows.

"Well now," his deep voice rang out. "Quite the warm welcome."

I shot him a weak smile, unsure if I was supposed to speak. My mouth was now coated in a thin layer of bile, and I forced the vomit back down. I wasn't one for public speaking, and this crowd was outside all of my wildest imaginings.

"A lot of people here have heard your words," the Moderator went on. I stared at the creases on his forehead. The lines became more pronounced the longer I stared. "But—" he said, pausing for a few seconds too long, as the crowd settled down into a dull roar. Only the rogue clap or scream pierced the hall.

I swallowed. The sudden lack of noise almost felt more deafening.

"—we don't really know *you*," he finished. "Who is *Alice Avery*?" His eyes widened and gave me the silent queue that I needed to start participating in the conversation.

I held the microphone up to my lips, a little squeak ringing in my ears.

"Who is Alice Avery?" I repeated. My voice sounded loud, odd, and distorted in my own ears, like it was both too loud and too soft. "Who is Alice Avery?" I repeated for a second time, trying to buy myself a few more seconds to think, my mind drawing an immediate blank. "First and foremost, I-I'm a scientist," I forced out. It was the only thing I could think of that might buy me enough time for my brain to return.

"A scientist?" the Moderator repeated.

"A biologist." I tried not to cut in over the top of him. My breath hit the microphone awkwardly as I hastily pulled it away from my face. I was sure all the crowd would see was a silly girl playing dress-ups.

"A biologist?" he repeated, giving me a little smile as he raised his eyebrows and looked out at the crowd. From the side, his nose protruded a little too far, and was a little too crooked. "Forgive our ignorance," he smiled as the crowd hollered behind him, "but what exactly does a biologist *do*?"

Now it was my turn to smile. I could answer *that* question with no trouble.

"We do a host of different things." I almost tripped over my own words in my eagerness. "We study plants, animals, and humans." I let my words linger on the last word. The crowd fell a little quieter. "We help humanity understand environmental issues. Understand the genetics of species." I sucked in another deep breath. The crowd was now silent.

"Fascinating, fascinating." The Moderator's words hurrying me along. This wasn't what he was looking for. It wasn't what I wanted to talk about either. "So all this knowledge...you must have a pretty good understanding of the human body?" He looked directly at me now, his eyes piercing into mine.

"Y-yes," I stuttered, forgetting to raise the microphone. "Yes," I repeated, and my words boomed across the room. I was glad I sounded more confident the second time.

"So you understand conception," he said, raising an eyebrow at me. "The concept of creation." His little smile turned up at the corners of his mouth. Here it was, the moment where the goading would begin. I was surprised I'd been given this much grace.

"Yes," I said, rolling my eyes. "Do you understand the concept of free will? Of choice?" I retorted, my own words ringing in my ears. I had no interest in discussing how babies were made or debating life at conception or at a certain gestation. I wanted to get straight to the point.

"The age-old concept of choice," the Moderator shot back. *This* was the conversation he wanted to have—and I was ready. I had *always* been ready.

I sucked in a deep breath. The corners of my mouth twitched as I waited for my turn to speak.

"Your choice, my choice, their choice," he rambled on, pointing between himself, me, and the crowd. "What about *their* choice?" He jabbed his slender finger at my stomach.

A few stagnated claps emanated from the audience.

"Are you..." I trailed off, my mouth still half open as the words stuck in my throat, "...arguing an embryo should have the same rights as a grown woman?" The twitch in the corner of my mouth migrated to my left eye. "We live in a country where there is *no* choice," I continued, cutting over the top of his next half-formed sentence. I didn't want him to answer that ridiculous question. "The Australian Government ripped that away. First, we're tested, trailed, drawn and quartered, because all we amount to is aptitudes and intelligences that might be passed on to the next generation." The crowd cheered, and the blood that shot through my veins felt like acid, electrocuting me from the inside; it rattled my organs, my nerves, my soul. "Some of us are deemed unworthy. Untrustworthy. Unusable. So we are sterilised. Discarded." I sucked in another breath. My heart thumped in my ears as I got to my feet, almost running towards the front of the stage. "Others, like me—" I paused for a few seconds to steady my knocking knees and wobbling ankles—long enough to look at the bright lights and scattering of unrecognisable faces. "Are denied even that *privilege*. I was deemed *too* intelligent for sterilisation, but not intelligent enough to make my own decisions." I gathered myself as I reached the front edge of the stage. From the edge, a horde of quiet faces stared back up at me. They blurred together, a sea of unblinking eyes, swollen with tears, mouths curved into smiles or sobs. "Our reproductive freedom has been stolen. Our ability to choose has long been taken." I swivelled around, facing the man who leaned back in his squishy, emerald green chair, a wide smirk painted on his face. "The Government mandate dictated that no children will be born outside of the lottery for twenty-five years—this has affected an entire generation," I said. "We're thirteen years into that term, and we've stopped fighting." I felt a strange pull in my throat. I now hovered over the still-seated man, who gestured at me to re-take my place next to him. I knew I had gone off-topic, but this conversation was too important to only answer the question posed.

"It's an interesting argument, Miss Avery," the Moderator said as I sunk back into the seat beside him. "That the want of the individual should be greater than the needs of a country."

I sat silent, letting his words wash over me.

"That the wants of young women outweigh the impacts of homelessness?"

I held myself still, my breath coming short and shallow. I waited silently, and my body slowly filled with a kind of seething anger that made me calm and calculating.

"That the ideals of young women are *that* important? The truth is messy, Miss Avery. And change and choice are complicated subjects." His words rang out to a near silent hall, bouncing off each wall.

I turned my head to look directly at the man sitting in the chair beside me. His wide, bright eyes lit up as he stared out at the crowd. He was pushing every button in my body, but I had my answer ready.

"Maybe," I said with a smile, "all men should be tested instead." Surprise rippled across his face. "All unintelligent men can be forced to have a vasectomy." I forced my eye roll down and spoke carefully. The last thing I wanted was the word "hysterical" or "emotional" printed beside my name in the news—even though I had every right to be both. "Why is it always women that are sacrificed for the greater good?"

The Moderator paused and looked at me, wrapping his fingers together, his head tilting to the side.

"*That* is a good question, Miss Avery," he said by way of a non-answer. His surprise had turned to amusement, as if the thought had never crossed his mind—and of course it hadn't. Women were born to suffer so men didn't have to.

"And?" I prompted. I wanted more than a TV host prepped to press my buttons could give me.

"Unfortunately, I do not have a good answer," he said, shrugging. "I don't pretend to understand the radical changes it takes to keep a country functioning. Life and death are complicated." His tone was almost morose. I'd said a lot in a short time, and I was no closer to any answers.

I looked out at the crowd. All I could see was a sea of clasped hands and shining eyes. They looked at the stage with such hope that my heart began to crack.

I ducked my head for a few seconds and stared at my feet.

For the first time in a long time, I was lost for words.

"Tell us more about *you*, Miss Avery," the Moderator pushed, placing a gentle hand on my knee and giving it a quick squeeze. It wasn't his fault, but the contact shot a shiver down my spine, forcing my mind back into the present moment—back to the fight.

"Is there a man in your life? Someone special?" he prompted, eyeing me.

I bit my lip, not sure how much I wanted to share with a host of spectators. "This was the product of a one-night-stand." My voice shook as images of Mason flashed through my mind. I hoped he would either forgive or appreciate what I said next. "For the record, he is a good man, and I c-care for him very much."

I sucked in another deep breath. I couldn't let myself get sucked into relationship chat, this chance was too important. "He's not what I want to discuss." My voice sounded stronger than I felt.

"Please," he said, waving his hand and giving me the stage. There was a kindness in his easy movements, and I wondered if he'd been directed to keep me talking.

I stood and walked forward a few paces, my mouth quivering as I reached the front half of the stage again. I stopped a few paces from the edge, the sea of faces all blurring together again.

"The single most important factor for women's advancement in our society," I said, my words coming out strong, "is our ability to control our own fertility." A round of short claps echoed from the crowd. "Without reproductive freedom, we are trapped. By pregnancy, childbirth, and child-rearing. By the lottery and its intense testing and scrutiny. By our inability to choose our lives."

My words rang out, and the short claps turned into a horde of noise. The noise filled me up, creeping up my limbs and sending tiny shockwaves through my body.

"Being female has become an unbearable burden." My voice echoed over the noise of stamping feet and beating hands. "Reproductive rights are as much to do with the freedom not to have an abortion as the freedom to have one. Before this, abortion would have been my choice as I was denied a sterilisation *three times*." The words stuck in my throat. Louder cheers coupled with a few harsh boos from the crowd rang out.

I knew sharing that part was risky, but for me to speak, I knew I had to share my own story and truth.

"This should be an individual choice for every woman faced with an unwanted pregnancy."

I swallowed. My mouth felt dry, as the hairs on the back of my neck prickled.

I lifted the microphone again, but the crowd had erupted, the noise deafening. I took a step back before a glass bottle soared past my cheek, smashing a few centimetres to my left.

My heart thumped in my ears. I stared at the pieces of broken glass shattered across the stage. Their translucent red reflected a distorted view of my face. I caught the shimmering movement of two Suits that had tentatively inched forward as the sound reverberated.

I couldn't look at them, I had to keep speaking. I took one last deep breath and turned back to the crowd. This felt like my last chance to say something important.

"Every single woman should have the right to decide what to do with her own body!" I yelled. My voice ached and my words barely cut through the chaos. "Government regulations shouldn't factor into our decision. We should have the right to choose our own path. Sterilisation, abortion, IVF, pregnancy. All of these things have the same ultimate argument!" I was barely able to hear myself over the raging noise as two more bottles soared over my head and smashed in a heap behind me. Splashes of red slashed across my calves, seeping into my shoes. The Suits rushed backwards instead of forward; clearly they were completely unprepared for what was unfolding.

I stumbled back a few paces, the microphone still gripped and pressed up against my lips. I was sticky, but I wouldn't be silenced.

"All of these things are fundamental to female empowerment and equality, and it's time we spoke up!" I shouted, my voice ringing out above the noise.

I dropped the microphone and stumbled back as more glass and plastic bottles hit the stage with loud blasts and shatters. They were aiming for the lottery banner, and most were falling short.

The front line of the crowd, held behind a high, black metal fence, looked wild as they shook the slats.

Stepping back again, I collided with another body.

"Come, Miss Avery," the Suit said, her voice shaking. The grip on my arm was too tight as she wound her other arm around my opposite shoulder and frantically pulled me away.

We ducked as the first fence paling broke. The body of a young woman clambered onto the stage, her top half bare, thick black writing scrawled across her stomach. I threw her the microphone as the Suit pulled at my body. Two more people climbed up onto the stage, their cheers and yells ringing in my ears. They felt like friends, but the Suits treated them like foes.

A few Suits were trying to push back the women, but they were being overrun by the horde. The Suits that flanked me forced me down the stairs with their bodies. The Moderator hurrying a few steps ahead of us, his head covered in a white towel held by the three Suits flanking him.

"Subjects secured," my Suit said into a black walkie-talkie. The door closed behind me. A large wheel lock turned and locked into place.

Three loud bangs echoed from behind the door, the metal scraping and shuddering under the weight.

"What's happening?" I already knew, but I wanted him to say it.

"You incited a riot," the interviewer said plainly.

"A riot?" I said, deadpan. I could have pretended, but speaking up meant I was finally having fun.

He stood there with his arms crossed, staring at me.

"Yes, Miss Avery, *a riot*." He sighed as he looked me up and down. He answered even though we both knew it wasn't a question. "You're a tiny little thing," he said with a shake of his head. "But you've got guts."

"Come." the Suit behind me said, with her hands up against the metal door. She ran her fingers down the locked door, a few small dents sunken into the metal. "Our next location has been secured."

CHAPTER THIRTY-SIX

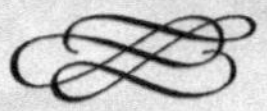

THE LAST DAYS

I SAT STILL ON THE UNCOMFORTABLE BED, MY EYE TWITCHING. I HAD been staring at the door for what felt like hours, willing it to finally open and reveal my fate.

Footsteps echoed down the hall, and I froze, waiting until they passed my door and continued in the opposite direction. I let out a sigh, dropping my head into my hands as my door suddenly swung open.

"D-Dr. Hidalgo?" I stuttered in surprise. Another figure stepped into the room beside her, I eyed her cautiously as another familiar face joined her. "Dr. Aslan?" I breathed, blinking and staring at her, a friendly face within the chaos. My mouth gaped and I almost questioned the figure that looped in beside Dr. Hidalgo to clear the doorway. They stood side-by-side and hand-in-hand, both clad in casual jeans and plain tees, no clipboards, charts, or tablets to be seen.

Peeling myself off the short bed, I stumbled to my feet. One more person entered through the doorway, her brightly coloured scrubs the first thing I saw out of the corner of my eye.

Another familiar face appeared and I recognised my sweet Nurse. "Amy?" I forced myself not to call her *Nurse Amy,* and to stay rooted on the spot and not lunge forward for the hug that I was craving.

I stared at the row of strong women, my eyes prickling. All three of them had held my hands through the most gruelling moments and months of my life. They were here because something was about to crack and shatter, I could *feel* it.

"What...?" I shoved out, my throat burning. I couldn't manage the full sentence, but as each woman looked at me with sympathy, they knew what I wanted to know.

"There's one more," said Dr. Hidalgo with a smile. I was grateful she sounded like her normal self again. My eyes shot back to the open doorway.

"Alice?" came Darcy's familiar voice, her question replaced by a running hug, our bodies smashing into each other, arms flying, tears pouring. She never used my first name, and my stomach dropped as I sobbed, pulling her back and looking her up and down. Her muscled arms pulled me back in, holding me. My chest heaved, racked with sobs. My tears fell onto her white t-shirt, leaving huge wet patches.

"K-Kit?" I squeaked out, still attached to Darcy's chest. I had never been a hugger, but in that moment, my whole body craved her arms around me.

"Only one support person allowed," Darcy whispered, "and I drew the longer straw between Kit...." She paused and grinned. "...and Mason." She whispered his name more softly. She seemed proud and happy; just his name alone sent a tingle down my spine.

I forced the tears down and cleared my throat, running my eyes across the line of women once more. Their physical differences were astounding, but the kindness they had shown me throughout still hung in the air.

"Can someone—" I got a few words out before Amy waved me off.

"Avery," she said, taking charge, her smile both sweet and sad, "as you know, twenty-four hours ago they broadcast the two finalists of this quarter's lottery to the public."

I nodded, biting my lip hard; the sound of shattering glass and heaving screams still rang in my ears.

"Your words," Darcy interjected, "caused a riot." She let out an honest and familiar chuckle.

"But not only in the live audience," Dr. Aslan said. "Simultaneous riots broke out across the states."

I blinked a few times. My mouth dropped open as the dry, acidic taste returned.

"Women left their homes, their jobs, their families," Dr. Hidalgo said, her smile widening. "And they marched. *Together*." A single tear ran down her cheek, and I was glad they were letting her talk freely today, even if the sense of foreboding that came with it sunk in deeper with each piece of information.

"They were all targeted. Every local senator, cabinet member, administrator, minister, court justice, and every single member of Parliament. The list goes on." Dr. Hidalgo swallowed, squeezing hands with Dr. Aslan.

"Women flooded the streets, Avery," Amy said. "Your words inspired a whole country." She winked at me now. Her face was the only one glowing with happiness with no intermingling of sadness or fear. I was grateful for her enthusiasm as my heart thumped in my ears. My chest rattled with every ragged breath. The hideous hospital gown I was wearing stuck to my back and chest with sweat.

"Riots? Like, back when they first changed the law?" I said, vaguely remembering a handful of protests as a seventeen-year-old. But all I remembered was a few picket lines and a few women warning us how this law was going to change *everything*—and no one listened.

"No," said Dr. Aslan. "This is nothing like what came before."

I was lost for words. "And the reason you are all here? In this room, together?" I forced myself to get to the point.

Darcy wrapped her arms around my shoulders again and I saw the raw indent in her lip as she hesitated. "The Director called each of us. The other contestant won the lottery." She squeezed me tight as I nodded again. It wasn't a shock, it wasn't even a surprise, but hearing Darcy tell me straight felt like a punch to the gut. Everything felt messy and jumbled and I struggled to keep myself together; I no longer needed a pregnancy to have a voice, and yet, my participation in *the lottery* being ripped away *just like that* still stung.

"Avery," Amy spoke up in Darcy's silence.

I could feel her squeezing my arm, her fingers trembling.

"The lottery only has one winner in each round; you are not the winner, and therefore, your pregnancy will be terminated here." My heart ached, not for the foetus, but for me— the woman at the centre. In all of this, *I* was the one who got hurt.

"Today," Darcy whispered. Her fingers indented into my skin and left tiny divots and large red marks. I knew she was telling me because I needed to know, needed to prepare, but it felt like another physical blow. No chance to catch my breath.

"Can I ask you a purely medical question?" I turned to the three medical women who stood in front of me. I couldn't let myself give in to the overwhelming guilt until I had all the answers.

Each of them nodded. Their sad smiles sent a strange itch up my spine and into my neck. I swallowed down the bile rising in my throat. "Today I am twenty-one weeks pregnant." It was a fact, but it still felt strange to say it aloud. "I never wished for this, but it is my reality." I struggled to keep my voice calm. "I wanted an abortion when it was a clump of cells." I swallowed hard and pushed myself to continue. "But now, due to *endless* testing and talking, the *foetus* is almost at the age of viability." I could feel my voice rising. The women all lowered their heads. I couldn't bring myself to call it a *baby,* not now, knowing what I knew now. "I am not a monster," I said quietly. "This is now more than a clump of cells," my lips trembled. "How ca —" My mouth now quivered too much for me to speak coherently. The tears burned my eyes, leaking out even as I tried to keep them in.

"Avery," Dr. Hidalgo stepped forward, placing both hands on my shoulders and looking me dead in the eye. "The situation you are in is not enviable. Many women have found themselves here, saying the same words, feeling the same gut-wrenching heartbreak." Without a doubt I knew this was true, and it turned my stomach. "*The Lottery* provides an alternative." It was barely more than a whisper.

"An alternative?" I asked, the frown on my forehead sinking deeper. The lines carved themselves in as Dr. Hidalgo nodded and handed over Dr. Aslan. This was why all three had been sent. The burden was too much for one doctor or friend to bear alone.

"The alternative is adoption," Dr. Aslan's words were quiet and tortured. "Rich couples who don't want to bribe government officials to carry their own pregnancy buy babies from runners up."

"No." I shook my head, my knees trembling so severely that I felt myself hit the hard mattress without a clear idea of how I had sat.

My eyes glazed over. Each of the women turned into a blur of colour as the tears flowed, and I thought through what Dr. Aslan had just said. I knew what each word meant, but it felt as though the sentence as a whole didn't make sense.

"Was that woman?" I said, grappling for meaning, trying to catch my breath, My chest rattled, my fingers turning into fists.

Dr. Hidalgo sat down on one side of me, and Darcy took her place on the other side.

"Women are housed in facilities," Dr. Hidalgo said, "even if they aren't competitors." Her voice was so soft and kind, but her words burned like acid, and what she didn't say was that pregnant bellies were hidden away here; the public none-the-wiser.

"She looked vacant," I said, my voice breaking.

Dr. Hidalgo sighed and closed her eyes, a grimace painted on her face. "A hire," she said, her eyes meeting mine and holding them. "This facility…" She trailed off, and for the first time I truly considered what atrocities she had seen—what atrocities she had committed.

"Suitable uteruses can be provided for a fee," Dr. Aslan said, finishing the sentence that stuck in Dr. Hidalgo's throat.

My hands shook and my feet bounced against the carpeted floor.

"Whichever option I choose, I lose." I lowered my face into my hands, my trembling fingers clawing at my skin, ripping at my seams. I felt like I might break apart, like I could split down the middle and never be whole again. It was too much for one soul to bear.

"There is a folder of options for adoption," Amy said, kneeling down gently in front of me. Her soft, warm hands pried my hands off my face.

I stared at her through tears, begging her to tell me none of this was true, but she didn't. She just sat quietly, waiting for the reality to sink in.

"Are any of t-them good p-people?" I stuttered, my words sticking against the roof of my mouth. I didn't know why I asked, but it seemed to be the right question in my muddled mind.

"Some." Amy nodded, her hand now gripping mine. "But first you have to decide if that is your choice. No one in this room would think less of you for choosing abortion." She squeezed my hand tighter. The word crawled across my skin. I had always been pro-choice, pro-women, but I was judging myself harshly for considering it now. In this moment, I wanted to be selfish; I wanted for once to make a choice purely for me. And yet I hesitated, wracked with guilt and sorrow that I was stuck in this position.

"I *never wanted this*," I pleaded, my heart shattering with the weight of this reality.

"None of us will *ever* judge you." Darcy knelt down on my other side and took my other hand. "We will all be here to support you." She squeezed it three times in quick succession, her tears spilling over. Darcy's tears made my own tears stream down my face.

"Why do people think this is a choice we make lightly?" I sobbed through tears. "Either choice I make, either decision..." Tears ran down my neck. I knew no matter what choice I made today, it wasn't really *my* choice. That had been snatched away a long time ago.

"We know," each of the women spoke in unison.

"Avery," Dr. Hidalgo leaned down, her voice soft. "I've had eight forced abortions." Her teary eyes flicked to the other women in the room as if she was encouraging them to share.

"Two," Amy said. "The first I would have chosen. The second I wouldn't." Her eyes lowered. The shame I felt radiating from her made me physically ill.

"I've had twelve forced abortions," Dr. Aslan's voice cut through the room, slicing into me. "Each wanted, but I was never enough." She sighed and shook her head. Of everyone here, Dr. Aslan knew heartbreak more than most.

"And I will never get to choose," Darcy whispered. "Because I didn't meet the basic intelligence criteria, and was sterilised at eighteen." Her voice wavered on her last word, but her tears had finished.

"One year after the lottery was introduced, I was stripped of my chance to *ever* choose."

Darcy's words hung in the air. The four women stayed silent for a few seconds as their tears overtook their words. As if in unison, each of us grabbed onto the other, our hands and fingers intertwining with the woman beside us. We held each other for a long while, our unified sobs echoing through the room.

"I know what I want to do," I said calmly, wiping away my tears and those of the other women one-by-one.

This time, the choice was mine, and I would make the one I thought was right; I would stand up and fight.

CHAPTER THIRTY-SEVEN

CHOICES

I LOUNGED BACK IN THE PLUSH WHITE CHAIR. IT SQUEAKED WHEN I moved around, my sweaty body sticking and un-sticking to the leather.

"Miss Avery," the Organiser said, sitting across from me in her own white leather chair. Her posture and poise was unshaken by my fidgeting.

"To what do we owe the *pleasure*?" the Director said, her eyes narrowing. Her disdain towards me was palpable.

The women sat side-by-side, each with a different look on their face. The Director silently fumed, her crumpled eyebrows and fierce, glaring eyes pinned on me from the moment I entered the room. The Organiser seemed to have taken a more curious approach as she slumped in her chair, her eyes switching between frowning at me and darting towards the Director. I had hoped the Executor would join us, but she must have been busy recording sound bites—as the face of *the Lottery,* she must be too important for this. It was strange, the Director, the Organiser and the Executor were different women; all distinct, all dedicated— and yet it felt like they were simply different faces with the same mentality. Still only titles and puppets of *the lottery*.

I let my silence hang for a few seconds past comfortable. My eyes floated between the two women.

"I want to discuss my options," I said, refusing to blink until I had stared both of them in the eye for a few seconds.

"Your options?" The Director's mouth ticked and squeezed into a tight circle, her voice incredulous. *"What options do you think you have?"* Her mouth opened and closed a few times. I enjoyed her squirming resentment.

"Oh, I'm sure I have a few." I felt the smile creep onto my face as she fished out her signature pack of cigarettes.

The Director shot a quick, furious glance at her, but she didn't stop. She lit her cigarette and took a deep breath in.

The Organiser blew a puff of smoke sideways out of her barely open mouth. The smoke circled behind her. "We're all ears," she said, the Director's glare still fixed on her.

"I hear I have two options," I said, trying to remember what I wanted to say. "Late term abortion…" I paused. "Or womb for hire." The sigh I had been holding in escaped, along with those last few words.

The Director's eye twitched. I could tell she wanted nothing more than to shove me out, but something kept her here—and If I had to guess, it was money.

"You are *hardly* a womb for hire," she snapped.

"A classic closed adoption situation." I shrugged. "I understand the criteria for an *actual* womb for hire is much stricter," I continued with a grimace. "Not women who have a one-night-stand and end up pregnant." I clasped my hands together in my lap, my sweaty fingers slipping. "But you understand what I mean." I smiled sweetly.

Her unblinking gaze bored into my face. She was trying to read me, to get a sense of my intentions.

"The Government is well awa—"

"Is the public?" I cut her off. "I wonder how those with a few notches under their forced-abortion-belt would feel?" My words hung in the air for a moment. "What is happening at this facility is reprehensible." My voice lashed out harsher than I intended. "And what's worse? There are a host of *women* at the top."

I lowered my eyes for a second. I sucked in a deep breath as I stared at my mottled hands, the next words dancing on the tip of my tongue. "I expect to get screwed by men in power," I seethed, venom seeping out. "I expect those who do not understand our bodies to legislate and regulate my choices. It's infuriating and unacceptable… but I expect it." I sucked in another deep breath. "What I didn't expect was how many *good* women this scandal has entangled." The lump in the back of my throat returned, and I swallowed hard. "This has gone *too far*," I pleaded. "It's deviated from the original intention." I could barely breathe, my chest heaved with the heaviness of the words I had finally spoken. The words I should have said years ago.

"It has," the Organiser cut over me. The cloud of smoke around her obscured her face. "This lab was always intended to be a research lab. A place for knowledge and learning." She sucked in another deep, rattling breath. "We have achieved that, but we lost our humanity somewhere along the way." She sighed, the cigarette now planted in her mouth, the puffs of smoke increasing by the second.

"Speak." The Director's narrow eyes ricocheted between the two of us. "What is it you want?" Her readiness to make a bargain unnerved me.

I chewed my lip, my teeth indenting hard into my flesh. "I-I…" The words stuck in my throat. It was harder than I expected to ask for everything I wanted.

"Don't hesitate now, Miss Avery," she snapped, her voice quivering at the end.

"We should hesitate sometimes," I said, "especially when we know we are about to cross a moral boundary." I frowned at my own words. When had I become so righteous?

"There are two things I want," I finally forced the words out.

"Name them," she shot back.

"The first is simple," I said. "The choice of adoptive parent should be mine alone, not from a predetermined list of rich, snobby couples."

I forced myself not to roll my eyes. Instead, I swallowed my anger, letting it swirl in the pit of my stomach.

The Director didn't hide her disdain. Her eye twitch was now accompanied by an eye roll and a little shake of her head.

"Ridiculous," she said, huffing and puffing. "What is the second condition?"

"No non-disclosure agreement," I said. "I've never had any interest in fame, but now that I've got a little—thanks…" I threw in a wink for extra annoyance. "I plan to use it for the greater good."

Without another word, the Director shot up. She stormed forward, her legs shaking, straight past me, before coming back and retaking her seat.

"The first condition *may* be a possibility," she snapped.

"We occasionally make exceptions," the Organiser chimed in, her body now slumped in her chair. The steady flow of cigarette ash dropped to the floor around her like a flower crown.

"However," the Director said, "we cannot agree to no NDA."

I looked at her closely. The large vein on her forehead protruded, her pale skin struggling to contain it.

"No negotiation?" I said with a fake pout. But I had expected push-back and was ready to try a new tactic.

"No, Miss Avery," she retorted. "I think…" Her eyes glittered in the harsh, bright light. "…this decision might have to be taken out of your hands."

She lunged forward, almost leaping past me in a swift, spinning motion. Blocking the door, she took a deep breath, her eyes locked onto mine.

"This is what happens—" She ran her hands through her hair, gripping and ripping at her scalp. She looked wild.

I jumped out of my chair, my footsteps echoing as my feet stepped out of her reach.

"—when silly girls *think* they have power." She spun on her heel and slammed her hand against a large red button.

My feet backed me into the Organiser, a soft tune humming from her lips.

I shot her a look, but she stayed in her chair, her eyes vacant. She was here, but not *really*.

"Thirty seconds," she barked from across the room, a gleeful smile painted on her face. She counted down for me with her fingers. With each passing second, her smile grew wider, until it had taken over her entire face. "I knew you were trouble from the start," she spat. "Women like you..." She shook her head, but her whole body vibrated. "Smart, educated...you *think* you understand how the world works?" The sound of loud marching footsteps thumped down the hallway, growing closer to the door. "But you know *nothing*."

The door swung open and eight Suits filed into the shrinking room. My body knocked up against the Organiser as the Suits squished in, creating a small semi-circle around the Director.

She muttered something to them before shouting, "Seize her!" with a harsh, angry bark.

I backed away, scooting around the Organiser, my stomach bumping against the back of her chair. I stopped in my tracks, staring down at my protruding stomach. I wasn't going to win this fight.

I raised my hands and walked forward. "Fine," I sighed. The first two Suits lunged forward, grappling with each of my arms.

"Gentle," I cooed sarcastically. They pulled both my arms behind my back, latching a thick, silver pair of cuffs around both my upper biceps and wrists.

"Take her to lab three," the Director ordered. The Suits pulled me forward, my feet now dragging across the ground. My black boots squeaked as I tried to walk, my steps out of sync with those holding me.

"I'll be taking care of this one myself," she whispered when the Suits dragged me past.

My body flailed as they carried me down the corridor. I tossed my shoulders from side-to-side, throwing, twisting, and turning my body. The grip against my shoulders and arms only tightened, their fingernails and the metal handcuffs cutting into my skin.

When we turned another corner, two Suits jogged ahead of the pack before turning left together and disappearing out of sight.

"Where are you taking me?" I asked, looking right and left at the two burly male Suits that held me. Their expressionless faces looked straight ahead, eyes unblinking.

Swallowing roughly, my eyes darted around. We turned another corner, and the corridor they pulled me down narrowed. The Suits jostled me as we shuffled along into a sea of bright, red doors.

"A-am I on the termination wing?" I asked, not expecting an answer. I wanted someone to tell me the truth, to confirm with me what was about to happen. My gut twisted. "A-am I on—" My words trailing off. I glimpsed the two Suits that had run ahead, their slender bodies pressed up against a red door that was separated from the rest.

The single door loomed, twice as big as any of the others.

I gave one last struggle, ripping my arms as fiercely as I could. My only reward was the nails of the Suits holding me ripping against my skin. Their grip tightened when the red door swung open.

With a last tug of my body, the Suits let go of my arms, unclicking the handcuffs in one swift move. The door snapped shut behind us with a loud *click.* I stumbled back, my feet wobbling uncontrollably. I wrapped my own hands around the deep indents left on each arm.

Four Suits stood over me; two male, two female. They loomed in a semi-circle around me, creeping forward as my back hit the wall.

"It is time to get on the table, Miss Avery," the Suit to my left said, his voice robotic.

I scooted my body against the wall, trying to haul my body further away. My arms shook violently.

I shook my head, unable to speak. The Suits took two steps forward for every inch I moved away. Their hands collided with my body, and they wrapped around my wrists and ankles and ripped me forward.

My body swayed in mid-air as the Suits trudged backward. My body writhed between them, twisting and shaking in every direction. They hauled me up onto the hard metal table.

I kicked my feet hard, connecting with a Suit who stumbled back. Two others pounced, pouring their body weight onto me while a third latched my wrists above my head at an awkward angle. The brown leather cord pinched my skin when I tugged, sending a shooting pain through my forearms and shoulders. I let out a guttural scream; my chest felt tight and my heart thumped hard before shattering as the Suit latched my second ankle to the table.

I lost my will to fight and my body crumpled, my eyes fluttering closed.

"You win," I whispered to the Suits that now stood at the four corners of my latched body. I squeezed my eyes shut, and the room started to fade; the last few kicks in my belly were enough to remind me that this journey was almost over.

"The subject has been secured," the Suit near my right ear said.

"They always win," I whispered to myself. The door swung open for a second time, the red handle bouncing against the wall before springing closed with a loud *click*.

"Leave us," she barked, clicking her fingers manically at the four Suits crowded around me.

They filed out, and the room filled with the sound of shuffling footsteps. The door clicked shut for a final time. This time, the silence was deafening.

I struggled to hold my head up as the Director turned her back to me. She flicked a thick silver deadbolt closed across the midsection of the door. Her fingers tapped across the metal rhythmically before she spun around.

"Do you believe in fate, Miss Avery?" A calm smile was painted on her face. The anger she had flared at me before was gone. She had me right where she had always wanted me.

I stared at her for a few seconds, struggling to hold my head up, before I sighed and laid back.

"Yes," I murmured, my eyes affixed to the roof. It was true—and at that moment, I still believed.

Her footsteps crept forward, the echo of her high-heeled shoes bouncing off the small enclosed walls.

"Do you think *this* is fate?" Her hot breath sent a shiver down my spine.

I closed my eyes and shrugged my shoulders.

"All I know," I said, as the goosebumps on the back of my neck prickled, "is that I was not meant to be a mother. Not in this life." I cringed. It was true and heartbreaking at the same time.

"It's a shame," the Director said coolly, stepping away and spinning on her heel. She sauntered over to her desk and grabbed a large, silver tray.

"If we could have trusted you, you could have been crowned the winner."

She slammed the tray down on the small portable table near my head. The instruments clanged and bumped together.

"It wasn't meant to be," I said, tears prickling at the corners of my eyes. I wasn't sure if she was being cruel or kind in my most vulnerable moment.

"It wasn't meant to be, Miss Avery," she said, her voice soft. "And now..." Her fingers tapped against the silver instruments. "This journey must come to an end."

I nodded, the tears spilling over and streaking down my cheeks. I wasn't sure why I was crying—the lack of control, the lack of choice, the termination—any of these would be acceptable. But it was my failure that made the tears come.

"In the end, the choice was out of my hands," I whispered through my tears. "But it's the right one." The words stung my throat. I was being oddly truthful with a woman I despised.

The Director patted my arm. Her demeanour was almost kind as she bustled about beside my head, tapping and shuffling things.

"It's time." Her hand reached for my shoulder, her fingertips stopping a few centimetres short.

I looked up at her, my vision blurry from the tears.

"H-how—" I stuttered, but the she held up her hand to silence me.

"Miss Avery," she said, fiddling with a clear plastic mask in her left hand, the thick plastic tube crinkling as she checked the suction. "It is better not to know." She tapped the back of my head, and I lifted it up. A thin, blue strap flicked against my skull, and the mask was fitted onto my face.

A loud rap at the door made me jump. My hands and feet pulled against the restraints.

With a loud scrape, the Director flicked a loud switch behind my head, the mask filling with a strange smelling gas.

"Lay back," she said, her hand now pressing against my shoulder.

The door rattled again, louder this time.

With a sigh, she stalked away, flinging open the door.

"I was sent to assist, ma'am," a sweet voice piped up.

I blinked a few times, trying to focus on the familiar sound.

My eyes fluttered open and closed, the mask's fabric changing to a swirl of patterns— whites, greens, and blues.

I blinked again, opening my eyes to see a blurred smile above my head.

"I'm here," the voice cooed in a distorted, disjointed way. Ice-cold hands pressed down on my forehead.

I tried to smile, but my cheeks were uncooperative. My tongue rubbed against the inside of the mask, leaving a tiny trace of fog and saliva behind.

With a giggle, my eyes fluttered open and closed for a few seconds before pulling shut. A sweet, familiar smile and a kind face imprinted on my mind as my vision faded to black.

CHAPTER THIRTY-EIGHT

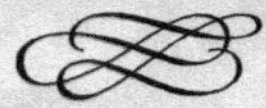

AWAKENED

I GROANED AND I ROLLED OVER, MY VOICE MUFFLED BY THE PILLOW pressed against my face.

"Ow, ow." I opened my eyes and a searing pain shot through my lower abdomen. I slowly wiggled my fingers and toes. I swallowed; my throat was itchy and sore.

"*She's awake,*" a kind voice broke through, soft but urgent.

I blinked a few times and slowly dragged myself to a seated position. My body ached with each movement.

"Stop, stop," came a more urgent voice, and ice-cold hands pressed against my shoulders. My eyes felt like they were fused shut; my whole body ached in different ways across different places.

Nurse Amy's face came into my vision, her sweet smile tormented, her eyes red-rimmed and watering.

"What—" I croaked. The last thing I remembered was the Director leaning over me. The vision sent a shiver down my spine, but I needed someone to tell me the truth.

"Avery," Nurse Amy said, her fingers now clicking in my face. I blinked, and her blurry figure finally came into focus.

"Where am I?" I blurted, looking around the room full of women.

"You are in the recovery wing," Nurse Amy said, her smile returning to normal.

"Recovery," I whispered, closing my eyes.

I placed my hand against my stomach. The bump was soft and pudgy, any hardness gone. A flash of pain seared the flesh where my fingers lingered. The pain shot through my stomach and then my heart as Dr. Aslan took over.

"Yes," said Dr. Aslan, shaking her head. The look in her eyes told me that my pregnancy was over.

"Why does it hurt?" I asked, looking between Nurse Amy, Dr. Aslan, and Dr. Hidalgo. The women looked at each other for a few seconds before Dr. Hidalgo spoke.

"At that stage of pregnancy, a C-section is the only appropriate method of termination." The grimace on her face grew bigger with each spoken word.

My fingers traced the puffy gauze that had replaced my bump. It felt surreal; they had removed the foetus—the baby—and yet my body still felt foreign.

"And now?" I looked at the women. I wanted someone to reassure me that physically I was okay, even if my mind spun and my stomach churned.

"Now, you recover," Nurse Amy said, her soft fingers running down the length of the sheets, tucking and primping them.

I leaned my head back against the propped up pillows, my fingers interlacing across my eyes.

Three hands placed themselves on different parts of my body as I shook, the sobs racking my chest violently. The tears flowed and hit the pristine white pillow-cases.

They let me sob. The tears ebbed and flowed, the anger coming and going, the grief rising and falling. The women didn't speak, each lost in their own memories of grief and loss, each gripping onto me as if my raw pain was the same as their buried pain.

"W-we cannot continue..." I whispered, my chest aching. I sucked in a deep, shaky breath. I kept my eyes shut, the last few tears flowing out of the corners. "T-this isn't life."

"Miss Avery." Dr. Hidalgo's voice pierced through my own. "This *is* life. This is the deck they have dealt us." She smiled at me, squeezing my calf where her hand was resting. She was being so kind and gentle with me, like I was breakable—and maybe right then I was. "It's not forever." I wasn't sure if that was comforting or terrifying.

I gritted my teeth and pulled myself up. The movement pulled at my stitched skin.

"No." My arms shook as I inched forward. "No," I whispered, quieter this time. "Do any of you have a phone?" I lifted my head, my lips tightening as I steeled myself. I was about to propose something insane.

Dr. Aslan and Dr. Hidalgo exchanged meaningful glances, each pulling out a phone. I was surprised they hadn't been confiscated, but if Dr. Hidalgo could be controlled by her chip, it didn't surprise me. They would think they always had control.

I looked up at Amy, who still hovered around my head. Her bottom lip was now stuck in her mouth, the large, red chew mark increasing with each passing moment.

I realised I looked nothing like a human woman, but a ghost, and that would have to be enough.

I turned to look between the two doctors, their deep frowns and pursed mouths almost identical. "Do either of you have a high enough clearance to connect to the internet here?" My eyes flitted between them wildly. Now that I had decided, I immediately wanted to get started.

Dr. Hidalgo nodded, her eyes boring into mine. I wondered if she was fighting internally or her own fear —I decided quickly *I didn't want to know..*

"And how would you feel about accessing it?" I pressed. I needed her to know what this meant.

A single, solid nod broke away from her neck. She flicked open her screen and tossed the phone to me. She might have been apprehensive, but she let her actions speak louder than her fear.

"Do you not have Instagram?" I asked, sniggering. It fit what I knew about her, but she shook her head with a smile.

"What's your plan?" she eyed me, her tone turning serious. They all turned their attention to me—no one breathed as I started talking. We shared a look, and I knew she already knew—we had talked about my voice, and about the power that held.

"I'm going to speak," I said with a shrug. "And I'm going to keep speaking. Until someone listens." I didn't say it, but I hadn't signed an NDA yet—and if they could slice into me without my consent, I could speak without theirs.

Dr. Aslan shook her head. "They'll silence you." Her eyes were full of worry and tears. It was the kindest type of worry, and what I imagined a mother's worry would feel like.

"Maybe," I swallowed the lump in my throat and hid behind another shrug. "Or maybe my voice will carry forward through a new generation of women. Maybe my voice will become theirs." I cleared my throat. "You three have done so much for me. But now, you should distance yourself." I swallowed hard. "Maybe I'm wrong. Maybe no-one will listen, but..." I looked between the three women who had bundled themselves together. "I have to speak now," I said. "So go, care for the next woman the way you cared for me. *Until this is over.*" A single tear spilled over, but my smile was unwavering. "And tell them I stole this." I held up the phone and waved it at Dr. Hidalgo.

The three of them leapt forward, eyes full of heartfelt tears as they wrapped their arms around my head and shoulders. It felt immensely powerful and personal to feel their bodies press against mine. Three women were risking everything on the whim and words of an almost-stranger.

"Good luck," they whispered in unison, backing out the open door. Dr. Hidalgo seemed to struggle to walk away, but Darcy's firm grip pulled her through the door.

"Last line of defence," Nurse Amy added. She flicked the door to a locked position, then pulled it closed. Her sweet smile was the last thing I saw before the red door clicked shut.

With a deep breath, I hit the download button. The tiny blue ring closed and flashed.

Clumsily tapping the keys, I logged in to my account. The backspace button was my best friend as I struggled to stop my hand from shaking. I knew once it was flagged, I would only have fleeting moments.

I looked down at my open profile, blinking.

2.5 million followers.

A nervous giggle escaped my lips. "Thank you, live games." I allowed myself ten seconds of pure panic and a handful of deep breaths to prepare for the most important moment of my life.

My eyes snapped open, and I tapped a few buttons, ending with the 'live' button.

I pulled at my matted hair and poked at my pale face and the bags under my eyes. The rawness of the last few days was etched into my skin. Every inch of my torso hurt, like the scalpel had punctured me in multiple places. The dull, slicing pain across my mid-section was only dulled by my rising adrenaline.

"Hello," I said. The live feed blinked from the phone, and I tried to find a more flattering angle.

The phone shook in my hands as the number of followers watching steadily grew, jumping by the hundreds with each passing second.

I closed my eyes and spoke. "I lost." The words flowed out of my mouth. "My journey as part of the elusive lottery has come to an end. Another pregnancy ending in late-term termination." I panned the camera down, showing a quick glance at my white and green striped hospital gown. My hand came to rest on my empty stomach, as if to prove my awful point. The thought of showing the incision crossed my mind, but scaring people away with blood and scars likely wasn't the best option.

I forced myself to look straight into the camera and speak.

"Women are not commodities," I said, my lips trembling. "We are not objects. We are not test scores. We are not categories."

My voice rose and cracked. I struggled to keep to a normal volume, the trembling inside my throat mounting.

"We are being robbed of our lives." I took a deep breath. "You've heard parts of my story, but the truth is, I never wanted to have children. What I wanted was control. A chance to make my own decision. I saw a ton of doctors as a young woman. I spoke with them about my wishes, and asked—with my mind made up and the decision carefully considered—for sterilisation. And yet, here I sit. Another failed contestant in the lottery. Another woman first denied a choice, then forced to continue a pregnancy." I swallowed hard. "And now I have been forced to have an abortion much later than necessary." The number of people now tuned into my rambling words was in the hundreds of thousands.

Underneath my strong voice and clear words, my hands shook.

"I never wanted to have an abortion," I said, forcing myself to keep talking. "Because I never wanted to be pregnant. If I had had the right to choose back then, the right to decide my own reproductive future, I wouldn't be sitting here today. Sporting a large, painful, C-Section sca—" My words were cut off by repeated banging on the other side of the red door. The door shook on its hinges.

"I'm in the *termination wing*—and we have company." I flipped the camera around to show the door shaking violently.

"Miss Avery!" the Director's voice flew through the tiny cracks of the door, piercing into the room with a loud vengeance. "Stop that stream at once!" Her muffled words came between the pounding from the other side.

I smiled at the camera, the little red flashing light giving me strength.

"How did we get here?" I said, as the banging ramped up. "How did women get here?" The cascade of fists on the other side of the wall hammered in quick succession, louder with each passing second.

"It's *way past time...*" I pressed my mouth against the speaker. "To fight!" The door burst open.

I fumbled to flick the camera around to face the horde of incoming people. The camera wobbled and jerked as the Suits poured in, four of them flanking each of my limbs.

With searing pain, I jumped up. The mattress shook beneath my feet, and my stomach pulled and split when I tried to stumble back.

The Director stalked into the room. The phone was still grasped in my hands, pointed at her.

"Women like her—" I screamed, my feet wobbling as I tried to jump backwards, the first two Suits grasping my ankles, "—have been led to believe they are working for the greater good!" My feet were yanked out from under me. My back bounced against the soft mattress, the phone landing less than five centimetres away from my face.

"Have compassion," I whispered. The Suit next to my head grappled with the phone, tapping the screen multiple times. "We all need more compassion!" I flinched as the Suit handed the phone to the Director. Her narrow, black eyes fixated on me.

She tapped the phone screen once and the live stream was cut-off. With more force than I imagined, she threw the phone against the wall.

The screen shattered, and tiny shards of glass and plastic exploded in every direction.

"You," she said, her voice steady. "*Get her out.*" She waved her hand at me.

The four Suits that surrounded me seized each of my limbs, yanking me to my feet. I tried to double over. Searing pain in my stomach ripped through my torso.

The Suits held me upright as I slumped between them, the beads of sweat on my forehead and neck prickling against my skin. The adrenaline ebbed, and I realised that I was split open at the seam, my stomach ripped apart. Everything blurred and blinding agony sliced through me. As the stitches pulled apart piece-by-piece, I could hear screaming and only realised a few seconds later it was coming from my own lips.

The Suits dragged me forward, my feet barely touching the ground. I couldn't stand any longer, my legs couldn't hold my weight.

The Director's lip was pursed in a snarl, her dark eyes fixed on me.

"We're not so different," I croaked when my face passed hers. "We were both doing what we thought was best." My mouth clamping shut as the pain in my stomach burned. My skin felt like a knife was raking across it, again-and-again, slicing me open again-and-again.

I dared to look down once—my white and green hospital gown was seeped with blood, and the line across my stomach grew each time the fabric brushed against my skin.

"Ow," I murmured. The Suits jostled me, hauling my body haphazardly through the winding corridors. I could barely manage to move my legs, but I could feel the blood dripping down my thighs

The Suits' unified footsteps rang out; the *click, click, click* against the wooden floor lulled my heavy eyes closed.

I swallowed, my mouth feeling hot and dry. My throat scratched as my eyes fluttered open and closed—the pain was beckoning me to drift away. The changing of coloured doors and concrete floors flooded my broken vision.

The glass made my head spin, each window depicting a fuzzy image of a ghostly pale woman in a hospital gown with a large red stain on her midsection growing in size by the second.

Is that me? I wondered with half-closed eyes. I listened first to the pounding thump between my ears, and then the rhythmic sound of stomping shoes. The two things bouncing off one another, overlapping and then separating.

A sudden gust of wind hit my face, forcing my eyes open.

The Suits dropped my body, and my knees collided hard with the pavement. The cobbled stones underneath my legs jutted out and poked my sides.

"Goodbye, Miss Avery," the Suit at the front said, her words soft. Her face was a blur of hair and rosy cheeks.

A smile tugged at my lips, and I let my body rest against the hot pavement. The Suits retreated, moving a few feet away with each slow blink of my eyes.

I rested my hand against my stomach. It was hot and wet.

"I'm bleeding," I whispered. My palm and fingers were soaked in red.

"What happened?" a hurried voice said.

"She's hurt," came another as I closed my eyes again, letting the hot concrete press into my face.

"Call an ambulance," came a long, drawn out voice. A smile danced across my lips.

"I'm still alive," I whispered before letting myself float away.

CHAPTER THIRTY-NINE

END

I FIDGETED WITH THE LAST TWO BUTTONS ON MY BLACK DRESS, MY fingers trembling..

"Here." Kit squeezed my shoulder before quickly doing them up.

I smiled down at her crouching figure as she fixed the rest that I had half-looped. She took a step back, her eyes running over me until she nodded.

"Very professional," Darcy chimed in, shovelling the entire bottom of a jam donut into her mouth. I could always count on Darcy to snap any lingering tension.

We laughed. We stood crowded in Darcy's small bathroom; the two women I loved more than anything were still standing beside me.

"Got your speech?" Kit whispered, tucking herself in behind me, her hands fidgeting with my hair.

I nodded and knelt down, wincing as the pain from my incision shot through my torso.

Kit ran her fingers through my knotted hair, then switched to a thick black comb.

"You sure about this?" Kit's voice crackled, and her eyes darted towards my stomach. "It's only been two weeks." Her eyes never left the spot under my dress where my stitches lay. I could feel the tightening of my skin as I steeled myself.

"I'm sure," I said, gritting my teeth and giving her a nod. I may have almost bled out on that hot pavement, but I had awoken with more fight than ever.

We stayed silent for a while while Kit tamed my curls and Darcy inhaled more food than one woman should be able to eat.

"Stress eating," she said, when I raised my eyebrows at her after her fifth jam donut. We all handled stress differently and my stomach gurgled in response—I was both impressed and nauseated.

"Can I really do this?" I whispered to them. Kit and Darcy each grabbed an arm and gently hoisted me to my feet.

"You were never one to stay quiet," Kit said. Her jaw was set. She was as serious as I had ever seen her.

"Or back down without a fight," Darcy said. She shoved the last bite of donut six into her mouth.

"Women have been working towards this *for years*," I said, looking between my two best friends. "And the Legislative Council meets today. It's our first and final shot." I clasped my hands together. My knuckles turned white.

Every fibre of my body felt tense and twitchy—like I was somehow wound up tight to fight, but would unravel at any moment.

"Will the opposition be there?" Kit asked, biting her lip before I answered.

I shrugged. "I'm sure they will."

Kit slid her hand into mine and squeezed. "Speak for all of us," she whispered, and I knew she meant it. All three of us had been affected by the lottery in different ways.

"I can't change the world with my voice alone." I tugged at the hem of my dress. "But I can tell my story." I held on tight, using the pressure to tether myself to the present.

A loud rap at the door made us all jump.

The three of us turned on our heels, exiting the small bathroom one-at-a-time. I flung open my apartment door. Amy stood there, her plain black pencil skirt and white button up making me pause until she smiled.

"You scrub up well," she said with a wink, stepping past me into the small living room.

Kit and Darcy stood hand-in-hand as Amy looked around the space.

"We've got five minutes," she said. "Are you ready?"

My hands sweated profusely, but I nodded at her. I tapped the small side pocket on my dress, the edges of my note cards sticking into my fingers. I could see the flurry of my messy handwriting scratched across the cards, and I willed myself to remember every word.

"I wish you could be there," I said, turning to face Kit and Darcy. They were now enveloped in a side-hug, their hands clinging to one-another's t-shirts.

I wiped my welling eyes and cleared my throat as two sets of arms flung around my shoulders, squeezing me.

"Tell them everything," Kit whispered into my ear.

"Speak loud," said Darcy. "Your words are your power."

They both squeezed me for a few seconds before stepping back and falling into each other instead.

I winked at them, swivelling on my heel and stalking out the door. I threw my arm in the air in a half-wave, half-fist as I crossed the threshold. I hoped they saw hope and strength in my back—even if my eyes swam with tears.

Amy caught up to me, her heeled shoes tapping against the concrete floor out of sync with my own heavy footsteps.

We walked in silence, descending the building's ancient stairs one-by-one. Our footsteps drowned the small space with noise.

As I pushed my way out of the small fire escape, Amy barrelled past me, turning right and jogging ahead.

A sleek, black car pulled around, and she waved at it. The dark tinted windows shimmered under the morning sun.

"Good luck!" came the high-pitched screams of Kit and Darcy from the outdoor balcony. Their faces were full of redness and tears.

I waved up at them, turning my body too fast and wincing in pain.

"We love you!" they yelled in unison.

I waved back, unable to speak. I sidled up to the car and opened the door. I was glad they had each other today.

As I folded my body in on itself, the stabbing pain in my stomach returned, and I gripped my knees to steady my spinning head.

"Still overdoing it, I see," came a familiar voice.

"I keep forgetting," I said, wincing with a smile at Dr. Aslan.

"They've already re-stitched you once." She shook her head at me, her scolding doctor's voice perfected after telling me off so many times. "You need to slow down."

"After today." I gave her a sharp grin.

The car snaked through the criss-cross of streets. I was grateful the others had organised transport, it was one thing I could leave to someone else.

As the silence in the car stretched, I wanted to ask about Dr. Hidalgo, about the other women of the Epitome Lab, but the words stuck in my throat. Mugshots had appeared all over the news and I knew the two women beside me had come close to the same publicised fate.

"We've only got a few minutes until we arrive," Amy broke the silence. "There is likely to be a large crowd."

We turned onto a side-street, and the car slowed to a stand-still.

I pressed my face up against the window, my breath creating small, broken wisps of steam.

"What…" My voice trailed off.

A wall of people stood in the street, their bodies pressed together, shoulder-to-shoulder. Some held large handwritten signs that they waved above their heads. Others stood talking to their neighbours with wide smiles on their faces.

"I don't think I can drive you any closer," came a quiet, familiar voice from the front seat.

My head snapped around.

"Mason?" My stomach knotted up, the feeling slinking upwards to my chest.

"I didn't want to intrude," he whispered. "But I did want to show my support." He looked weakly back at me, his smile tugging feebly at the corners of his mouth.

"Thank you." My face burned hot. I broke eye contact by looking down at my watch and realising we needed to move. Today wasn't a day to be late.

"Should we walk?" Amy said, biting her lip as she looked at her watch, too.

"I have an idea." I moved my body slower this time. "Give me three minutes. If it doesn't work, we'll have to run," I added with a shrug and a wink, not wanting to consider how much that would hurt.

Three voices called after me as I opened the car door, stepping out into the crowd. The noise was chaotic; snippets of conversations entered my ears.

I pulled myself onto the bonnet, swinging my legs up behind me and clambering to my feet. I held onto the roof of the car, steadying myself.

With a few careful steps, I stood on the roof of the glossy black car. My booted footprints spread across the bonnet, windscreen, and roof.

The crowd spanned for as far as my eye could see. All the streets were packed with women, and their faces blurred together.

The Administration Building was just in view in the distance. Its pale cream stone pillars shone in the sunshine.

I took a deep breath and closed my eyes. As I opened my mouth to scream, a piercing honk sounded from below me, making me jump.

Three more loud beeps rang out into the crowd. The car underneath me quivered and many sets of eyes turned towards me.

I cleared my throat.

"It's her," came the soft murmur from the crowd. The phrase was repeated as the women whispered to the person beside them.

Hundreds and then thousands of eyes turned towards me. Women as far back as I could see turned my way.

Thousands of hands came together, and their clapping and cheering flooded the streets. More and more women turned to face me.

With no words, the women parted, squishing their bodies together out of the driving line of the black car.

I sat down on the roof, tears falling down my cheeks. I rapped on the side of the car.

Mason's soft hand shot out of the window before he restarted the car, giving my limp fingers a tiny squeeze before inching forward.

I waved awkwardly on the roof as we crept towards the entrance of the Administration Building, the large, arched windows shining in the morning sun.

Women continued to clap, stamp their feet, and whistle at us. They weren't rioting yet, but I could *feel* the tension rippling through every jostling body. Like me, they wanted this to be the beginning of the end —*today*.

Mason gracefully parked the car at the side of the entrance. He inched as close to the large bricked barricade as possible, stopping a few metres from the open doors.

When the car came to a halt, I swung my legs back over the windscreen. Scooting myself down onto the bonnet, I ungracefully returned my feet to the floor while the other three exited the car.

"Big crowd," Mason said, nudging me with his shoulder. His smile had returned, although he looked somewhat nervous. He tried his best to smile and hide it from me.

I nodded at him, gripping the sharp edges of my notecards. They were still there, my polished words, and I was here; I had made it almost in one piece.

"Miss Avery," a curt voice interrupted my spiralling panic. I swivelled around, catching myself with a wince.

A gentleman stood before me with a large clipboard and a thick black ear piece. His face was familiar.

"As always, a seamless entrance," he said, his tone flat and dry. "Please accompany me inside." He returned to his business-like demeanour and scanned the enormous crowd of women pressing closer to the Administration building.

A muscle in his jaw ticked, and he swivelled on his heel and stalked away. A small, almost-hidden gate sprang open after he entered a punch code. I lingered for a second and looked back at Mason. He nodded his head at me, and the soft, goofy smile on his face pushed me forward.

I stepped away and forced myself not to look back at Mason as the other women crowded in beside me.

We walked under the small archway to the left; the thick red hued brick cracked in places.

I hurried forward, closing the gap once again between us.

"Your hearing is in conference room three," the man said, turning down another corridor.

The four of us took a few more turns, the wide hallways deserted except for our drumming footsteps. Each wall carried a straight line of Australian landscape photographs through history, their frames all gold but un-matching.

My eyes lingered on some of the bigger portraits. The acrylic colours of our old town fascinated me. I wondered if they had realised back then how far we would get off track.

I took one step too many in my daydreaming and ran into the man who was escorting us. His thick shoulders and wide back bounced me back a few steps.

I gritted my teeth and swallowed an apology, my face flushed. He swung open the wooden double doors in front of us—without turning to look at us at all.

He stepped inside and toward the left, pressing his thick frame up against the back wall, his hands resting intertwined in front of him. It was clear his escort duty was done and he wanted nothing more to do with us.

Heads from across the room snapped towards me. A flurry of flyers and papers flickered as all eyes turned towards me.

It wasn't exactly a warm welcome, but I pushed my shoulders back and walked between the long, curved desks.

A large, wood desk sat at the front of the vast room, its light panelling swallowed up by the six men that sat behind it. Their crossed arms and interlaced fingers were only bested by their harsh eyes.

I continued forward, my legs like jelly, my feet numb and tingly. Outwardly, I hoped I appeared steely-eyed and poised. I had no intention of letting any man here know I was nervous.

"Mrs. Avery," a booming, female voice addressed me from the side of the room.

I faced her as she spoke to me through a thick, black microphone.

Miss! I wanted to correct her, but pursed my lips shut. I would hold my words until I had the floor.

"Welcome to the Melbourne Council meeting and introduction of Bill 247," she said, smiling at me.

"Please take a seat with your—party," she finished after looking each of us up and down with a slight pinch of her mouth and flare of her nostrils. "You will have your chance to speak after the particulars have been run through."

She clicked off the microphone and sat back, her hand gesturing towards the empty desk to our left.

We found our seat in silence, and the rest of the desks filled up around us. The large room held twelve curved desks, each slowly filling with a different cohort of people.

Behind us, a group of six women scooted along, their vibrant red dresses catching my eye as they sat down, each looking nervous.

I tried not to stare and instead turned back to the front and fished out the small notes from my pocket.

"It's packed," I whispered to Amy and Dr. Aslan, who leaned towards me. Their wide, unblinking eyes unnerved me. I wished silently that Dr. Hidalgo had been released from her cell so she could be here. It felt strange knowing she was the one imprisoned for her part in the lottery, but it looked like she would be released soon, *as soon as she answered all their questions.*

"Psst," came a soft, interrupting voice.

Amy jerked her head towards the women who were seated behind us. Her eyes bounced between them and me as I turned around.

A woman clad in a thick, red dress with puffy sleeves beamed at me while the rest of the women looked away or bowed their heads.

"We're huge fans," she whispered, smiling. "We're here because of you," she added, quieter still. The women beside her looked up.

"Are you here to speak?" I whispered back, smiling at her.

She nodded, casting her eyes down. "We call ourselves the *sisters of blood*." Her voice was almost ominous as she said the last three words, but her smile never faltered. "Forced sterilisation," she mouthed, her eyes darting around the room as if she had said something taboo.

My smile drooped and my lip quivered. I felt myself nodding, wishing I could reach out and hold her hand. Darcy should get to be here too—to tell her story. They all suffered the same fate, and yet their stories would be so different.

"Thank you," she mouthed again, her voice inaudible above the noise.

As I turned back to the front, I swallowed hard. The giant lump in my throat refused to go down.

The men at the front desk laid out stacks of paper, touching the edges to line them up. They talked amongst each other, jovial and smiling.

My eye twitched. The six policy makers with their stacks of paper — men who would never carry children, here to determine the reproductive choices of women.

Amy nudged my arm, and I pulled my glaring eyes away from the men. The anger bubbling in my stomach didn't subside as I turned to face her.

She intertwined her fingers in mine, squeezing my hand without a word.

I dropped my head, focusing on the cool palm and fingers pressed up against mine, breathing in and out as a loud, squeaking microphone sputtered to life.

With a pop of my head, my eyes darted to the woman who had introduced me. She stood serenely on a high, wood-panelled pedestal. Her eyes were alert and wandering the room, and each group quieted down when she ran her eyes over them.

A shiver ran down my spine.

"It begins," I whispered and steeled myself for all that was to come.

CHAPTER FOURTY

GIRL, UNINTERRUPTED

I held my breath as the woman introduced Bill 247.

"This Bill will debate the lawfulness of introducing Bill 135," she said towards the end of her short spiel. "We will hear from *some...*" She paused dramatically, her eyes looking over to where we sat."...of the women who have lived through an experience relating to Bill 135." Her words were soft, but powerful. "Then we will hear from those that believe the Bill should remain in place." Her eyes narrowed at the last few words. The six men at the front of the room nodded in unison. The men were like clones of each other, each paunchy and red-faced.

"First," she continued, "opening arguments will be heard from both parties. Let the debate begin." Her last few words fell flat, as if she had lost interest in the conversation.

She nodded at two men standing behind her on the right and left, each clad in dark black suits, with thin black ties. They parted their hair on opposite sides, but otherwise, their looks were almost identical.

"Pick the politician," I whispered to the two women beside me without breaking eye contact. The men both shuffled a few papers.

I saw two smirks out of the corner of my eye as the first man stepped forward to the mounted microphone.

"Thank you, Madame Speaker," he said with a nod in her direction, his voice crackling as he spoke. "Welcome." He looked up at the crowd, then his eyes darted back to his notes. "To the introduction of Bill 247." He fell silent for a few seconds while he shuffled his papers.

My eyebrows pinched. He may have looked the part, but the fumbling hands and sweaty forehead made me think this was his first time. As I opened my mouth to make a snide comment to Dr. Aslan, another man stepped forward, and the two seamlessly traded places.

The smiling face of Mr. Dunn stared back at me. He wore his arm in a sling, and the tinge of yellow-purple bruising shimmered under his eyes in the bright lights.

"This Bill is an important correction to our legislation," Mr. Dunn spoke confidently. "Today we will hear from brave women who have endured the outcomes of Bill 135." He looked up, his words flowing. "I don't pretend to understand or comprehend what it is like to be a woman in Australia right now." He paused as if he wanted to look every woman listening in the eye. "By introducing Bill 247, those of us with a shred of power hope to make some amends for the wrongs our fellow man has allowed."

His straight, perfect teeth shined under the bright lights. He was here to represent us—he had kept his word. I appreciated his easy tone and straightforward script more than he would ever know.

"Thank you, Madame Speaker," Mr. Dunn said, grabbing his paperwork by the fist-full and backing away from the stage. He nodded to the other men huddled on his side of the room, and I wondered if he was a last minute addition or if he took over because he felt he should.

"A quick introduction," Madame Speaker said as she stepped forward, wiping down the lectern and microphone before gesturing for the opposition speaker to move forward.

"Thank you, Madame Speaker," the gentleman said with a soft smile. "Ladies and gentlemen." He leaned forward casually, as if this was easy, as if he wasn't nervous—and he likely wasn't. His body wouldn't be affected based on today's debate.

I shifted in my chair. His smooth voice made me uncomfortable.

"I will keep this as brief as my counterpart," he said with a not-so-subtle eye-roll. "Bill 135 was instituted for the greater good. Our population growth was out-of-control. Famine was rife. Homelessness was rising at an alarming rate." He rattled off the list of reasons the original Bill *had* to be implemented without really saying anything. "There is an end date," he said, clasping his hands together. "We are already seeing *striking changes* through the Bill's effects." His eyes roved and searched through the crowd. "Twenty-five years is a long time to ask the Women of Australia to sacrifice—but we are thirteen-years in."

I bit my lip hard, irritated that I understood his argument. That's why this experience had been so harrowing—because I was both a scientist and a woman. Both rational and irrational. Both torn and angry.

"Please," he said, shaking his head. "I understand the hurt this Bill causes the women of Australia." His eyes darted towards me and the two tables of women in the room. "I am sorry your life has been so deeply affected." His words sounded almost sincere. "But that doesn't change the fact that it is the *right thing to do*." His eyes looked almost pleading. "Thank you, Madame Speaker."

My head spun as I held myself in place. My fingers gripped the edge of my chair.

With my stomach swirling, I placed my hand on my scar and took a deep breath. His argument was smooth, it addressed the hot topics in politics—but it left out one crucial part: humanity.

I gritted my teeth, reminding myself that no woman should have to go through what I did within the Epitome Lab. The breath I held in my chest slowly seeped out as I watched the men; their jovial smiles and easy conversation was a stark reminder of our differing situations, of the different ways we paid the price.

"We will take a brief intermission," Madame Speaker said cheerfully into the microphone. "Please return to your seats in fifteen minutes." Her voice chirped and gnawed at my inner ear, sending a shiver down my spine. I pushed myself up, twisting on my heel and power-walking out of the room.

I had to get out; I could feel my sharp, shallow breaths coming. The cool air conditioner blew into my face as I turned left and half-ran down the hallway.

I twisted and turned, my blood pounding in my ears. I tried a few doors until one opened. With a quick look behind me, I slipped inside, clicking the door shut.

The room was small, with a pile of unused student desks piled into two corners, stacked haphazardly atop each other. A thick layer of dust had already settled on them.

I backed myself up against the nearest wall, fanning myself as I sunk down into a seated position. I pulled out my notecards, the thick black trim on the edges blurring. I forced myself to breathe. The words became unrecognisable.

"What if he's right?" I whispered, dropping the notecards beside me and staring up at the ceiling. Tears filled my eyes, blurring my vision and spilling down my cheeks. I blinked a few times, forcing out the last of my tears and shaking myself.

I slowly shook my head, forcing in the reminder with every movement. "Bill 135 is inhumane." I pulled myself to my feet, wiping my face over-and-over again while I paced back and forth, mumbling to myself. "The Bill started off with good intentions. Privatised. Allowing the rich..." My eyes only fluttered open when I felt I was getting close to the wall. I had to focus on the words, or I would unravel at the seams.

"Interesting commentary," a harsh, male voice cut through my babbling. I whirled around and snapped my eyes open. An older man in a black politician's suit stood in the doorway, his arms folded across his chest. His silver slicked back hair pulled his forehead as his eyes narrowed.

I stared at him, my curiosity turning into a frown.

"Can I help you?" My voice sounded stronger than I felt.

"The fifteen minute interval is up," he said with a smirk. "I thought the mumbling woman behind this door might want to know."

He shrugged and turned away. The sound of his footsteps echoed after the door closed behind him. He had looked at me as if I had lost my mind, and I knew he was partially right—this fight had rattled me.

Sucking in a deep breath, I yanked the door open, jogged down the hallway, and returned to my seat.

"Where did you…" Dr. Aslan whispered, her voice scolding until she laid eyes on me. She trailed off, smiling at me instead. The sympathy in her eyes unnerved me, and I wished she would stick to scolding.

"We will now hear from the women who wish to speak about Bills 135 and 247," Madame Speaker announced as the rest of the room filled up with people. "There are two sides to each story. Today, we finally hear both of them."

Madame Speaker stepped back, folding her hands in her lap. If I didn't know better, I would have sworn we had an ally in her.

The women behind me scraped their chairs against the floor. The clunking sound filled the entire room. I could hear the footsteps behind me as the three women made their way forward.

I took a deep breath when they passed, their brilliant red dresses shimmering under the bright lights. They ascended the stairs, holding hands in a tight grip.

The woman who spoke to me stepped forward, pressing herself into the small wooden lectern. The other two women crowded in beside her, their bodies less visible.

"Thank y-you, Madame S-Speaker," she said, her voice shaking.

I gulped in a deep breath, settling in to hold it.

"We met in the most u-unfortunate of circumstances," she said, her voice still quivering. "Our uteruses ripped from our bodies in our late teens due to one-to-many failed intelligence exams." My heart thumped in my ears. The breath I was holding still stuck in my throat as I thought of Darcy. "We failed at maths and science questions." Her lips tugged into a small smile.

My lips tingled when I smiled back at her, before closing my eyes as her words washed over me.

"We failed grammar and syntax and English. We failed tests of robustness and calm, of sadness and sorrow. We failed at the pillars of human society, *according to our examiners*." Her tiny breaths fluttered into the microphone. "We were not intelligent enough, afflicted with mental illness in the way that can be passed onto the next generation. According to those results, the offspring we would produce would not be valuable or desirable. Like me, they may suffer from depression and anxiety. Like Mona, they may struggle to do basic maths. Like Rach, they may struggle with the written word, when dyslexia jumbles the letters and regurgitates them in the wrong order." Her voice was rising, no longer wavering.

I stared at her pale face, the small creases around her frown line deepening.

"We failed," she repeated, "and yet, here we stand. A muralist with hundreds of commissions lined up." Mona stepped to the side and forward, waving. Her face flushed a brilliant shade of red. "A best-selling poet." Rach stepped to the other side and forward, her head bowed as she waved, her hand no higher than her chest. "She may not write quickly, easily, or without difficulty, but her passion and success outweigh her struggle."

I swallowed the lump in my throat, my eyes swimming with tears, turning the women in the red dresses into coloured blurs.

"And me," she said, raising her own hand in the air in a fist instead of a wave. "A human being who has grappled with depression and anxiety since I was a teenager. I struggled. I battled. *And I won*." She smiled and looked at the two women who stood beside her. She bit her lip as she forced her face back to the front.

"Bill 135 instituted a war on my body," she said. "And Bill 247 strikes to repeal this war on women." Her teeth clattered together as she clamped her lips shut, pressing them into a taut, thin line. "Our damage is done, but the next generation of women are coming of age. Born into a time when their bodies are deemed defective. Born into an age where men still believe they should have the right to make decisions about women's bodies and steal their reproductive choices. Born into an age where they will have to fight to not have a forced abortion for a wanted child, or to fight to have an abortion because they were deemed a *successful* woman of merit and the foetus might be incredible." Her words ran over me, and I swallowed; we were opposites in every way and yet we weren't. "These decisions are not opposing. They are linked. Intertwined in our lack of the right to choose the trajectories of our own lives. Entangled in our inability to decide for ourselves if we wish to bear the burden of children." She took a deep breath. "I have always said that I am pro-choice. *Pro-letting-women-choose*. And I have recently discovered that I am also pro-voice." She smiled down at me. Her white teeth shone under the fluorescent lights surrounding the stage.

I took a deep breath and dropped my stinging eyes as they threatened to spill over again. Everything she said was how I felt, and listening to another woman speak what could be my words made my heart ache and swell with pride.

"Women's voices are rarely heard in this debate outside of the lawmakers and policymakers. Women discuss their political agendas, but not their personal experiences. We hear about homelessness, population growth, resource management. Facts, figures, statistics, data, numbers. Thrown in our faces one after the other." My skin crawled and bubbled with each word she said.

"And whilst these things may be important, they aren't human. There are women in this room that have clearly been affected by Bill 135, and who could be healed by Bill 247. Will you speak?" She looked around the room.

My eyes followed hers, dancing around the room as multiple women cast their eyes down, tugging at their black suit jackets and tussling the papers on their desks.

"Will you share your experiences? Here and now?" she asked, her eyes falling on one woman who quivered in her seat. I watched them lock eyes, the energy between them bristling.

The first woman in the crowd stood. Her shaking legs wobbled her forward as her four male colleagues tried to grasp at her suit jacket.

Her hands clutched to her chest, she walked forward.

"Why don't we speak up?" the red-dressed girl called again, this time waving at me to join her as well. "This is the moment; the time in history—the minute, the second." I rose to my feet.

"This is it," I whispered to Dr. Aslan and Amy.

"Yes," Amy said, getting to her feet beside me.

"It is," Dr. Aslan said, pushing her hands on the wooden table and rising.

We strode purposefully towards the podium. The cards that I had written and rewritten jostled in my pocket, their edges scraping against my sides. I knew I didn't need them; what I needed was my own lived experience.

I ascended the stairs first, the room deadly silent. The woman in the red dress wore a more genuine smile than I had seen in years.

She winked at me when she stepped back, her posse enveloping her in tight, locking her in a hug.

I swallowed roughly, the bright light shimmering above me almost blinding, the faces of the men below blurred. I squished my body into the small podium.

With a deep breath, I opened my mouth, and the words came tumbling out.

"I had sex," I said, blinking a few times to clear my vision. I sighed, my words catching the microphone. "Whilst I appreciate how many women would want to be in my position—finding themselves a competitor in the lottery—for me, it was akin to torture. I don't, and have never, wanted children." My voice shook with each passing word. "I argued for years to be put on a permanent form of birth control—*Not an option.* To have my tubes tied—*You'll change your mind.*" I forced an eye-roll inward. "To be sterilised—*too permanent,* what would your *future-non-existent-husband think?*" I looked out at the crowd and saw only women looking up at me, listening to me. The men had somehow found somewhere, *anywhere,* else to look.

"Bill 247 comes to an end in a few years—a line I heard *so many times.*" I intertwined my fingers atop the podium, leaning my body forward. "I don't give a fuck," I said. "Women are not commodities.

We are not machines. We are capable of having our own thoughts and feelings. We are entitled to long for children, or decide we have no interest in bearing them. Our rights have already been stripped away. Day-by-day, hour-by-hour, minute-by-minute, women are forced to have abortions they don't want, or forced to carry pregnancies they don't long for." I closed my eyes, the silent room swimming around me. "I carry the weight of a late-term, forced abortion on my chest and across my stomach. A large, red, raw scar—my permanent reminder that I had less rights than a clump of cells." My hand held my stomach at these words. "I am not vain, but this scar is a permanent reminder of my inability to choose and the horrors I faced in the lottery. We should not have to choose abstinence or a forced pregnancy. We should not have to choose sex or an abortion. Bill 135 slowly crept into our lives." The doors began to rattle loudly, the wood shaking against the hinges. "It stripped us of our freedom through amendments, our privacy through mandates." The wooden door creaked again as my words echoed out into the silent room. My eyes darted to Dr. Aslan, whose eyes were now fixated on the wooden doors. More women stood, their arms ripping away from the hands of the men around them.

"Bill 135 tore away our fundamental right to choose; our right to control our own reproduction." Three loud bangs rang out from behind the wooden door, the hinges shaking violently as the final few women stood—as we stood on the edge of change.

I could feel the body weight of Dr. Aslan and Nurse Amy pressing in behind me as the room filled with the scratching, booming sounds.

"Every woman deserves the right to choose!" I yelled, my voice almost drowned out by the noise. Its hinges gave way with a loud *snap*.

"We deserve to make our own choice! The freedom to choose our own path. The freedom to choose birth control. The freedom to choose a child-free life through sterilisation. The freedom to access a safe, legal abortion!" The doors fell, crashing down against the tiled floor. "Access to kind, comforting prenatal care *when we decide*! The chance for women to hold their wanted babies, to share the joy with everyone around them!" I didn't know what that joy felt like, but I imagined most women would.

A thick cloud of smoke and debris hovered above the door, the sea of small faces pressing in barely visible.

"All women," I shouted above the buzz, "deserve a voice! Deserve a choice! Deserve freedom!" The noise in front of me quieted.

A steady flow of women walked into the parliament room, their movements in-sync and calm.

The men fell silent. The shuffling of papers stopped, their bodies crumpling back into a seated position.

"Bill 135 has affected half of the population." I watched more women file into the room. Their smiling faces beaming up at me, becoming an instant blur of white teeth and wide eyes. "The time has come to speak up," I called, my voice echoing through the now-crowded hall. "This is the moment. The time in history, the hour, the minute, the second. Right now." My eyes welled up at the sea of female faces looking adoringly up at me. "The revolution is here, and it's time for women to be in charge of their own bodies."

I took a few stumbling steps back as the room erupted in cheers and applause. The soft hands of Amy and Dr. Aslan wrapped around me, and I sobbed, my chest heaving. A red-dressed woman squeezed her way in, her arms wrapping around me.

"This is it," she whispered in my ear.

"This is the moment in history," I whispered back, clinging to her. "We created a revolution." I pulled away and staggered back.

"*You did*," said the woman in the red-dress. I turned back to the front and threw my arms up as two loud *cracks* rang out.

My ears rang, the static fuzz dropping me to my knees. Beside me, the woman-in-red fell too, clutching her shoulder.

A searing pain stabbed into my thigh as I scrambled forward towards her.

"What happened?" I whispered. She laid back, her face pale and pained.

Her blood-soaked fingers shook, a bleeding hole blown open below her shoulder blade.

"O-oh m—" I stuttered. Amy and Dr. Aslan crowded in on me, pulling my body backwards and pushing hard pressure on my leg. "NO! Let me help he—" I couldn't force the words out. My own body gave way to a wave of pain.

"You're okay," Amy said, her hand gripping mine. "It's a minor wound… Dr. Aslan w-will…" Her voice morphed into panic.

My eyes stung. I whimpered and looked down, an identical hole gaping in my thigh. I looked into the terror-filled eyes of Dr. Aslan and Amy.

The room erupted.

EPILOGUE

I SLID INTO OUR FAVOURITE, CRAMPED BOOTH, SQUISHING MY BARE FLESH in against Kit, with Darcy piling in after me, her soft, tanned skin rubbing against mine.

"Oi!" I mock yelled, slamming into Kit again.

"There's less room than there used to be," Darcy rolled her eyes, squishing in closer.

"Come on, quit bickering," Charlie said, wearing her signature red-dress, her shoulders shoved in between Mason and Harry.

"We're here to celebrate." Harry grabbed Kit's hand and squeezed it. Our eyes all flicked to the television above the bar.

The closed captions touted information about another hot summer day, the degrees rising steadily.

"Before the live stream starts," Mason said, clearing his throat. "Let's take a second to cheers to the strongest woman I know." He smiled at me.

"And the woman who rivalled her on stage," Darcy said, lifting her glass up to Charlie. "You two sparked a revolution," she added with a wink.

I smiled at them, staying silent as my finger found the scar on my thigh. The divot was a permanent reminder of the cost to speaking out. Everything that had come out about *the lottery* in the last year had been horrifyingly reassuring. The head runners were in jail, charged with profiteering and allowing women to buy babies for a hefty sum. Most sickeningly, it came out a few months later that their staff had all been implanted with special control chips—a host of women forced to do their bidding. The women were both lucky and unlucky to have escaped jail based on the coercive control they faced, but it didn't make their scars any less heartbreaking. Tears prickled in the edges of my eyes, but I swallowed my sadness, bolstered by our mismatched group. The chatter changed from cheers to chit-chat to immediate bickering between Darcy and Harry.

"It's-starting," I stuttered, my eyes glued to the television that I couldn't hear.

Everyone's voices dropped as they craned their necks to catch a glimpse.

"Today is a historic day," the caption read as a pretty, blonde reporter stood in front of Parliament House, the thick, white columns shining in the background.

The bar turned quiet, and a bartender turned the volume up.

"After ninety-seven days of waiting, Bill 247 has passed into law today."

The bar erupted in cheers and loud whoops. My eyes spilled over, blurring my view of the TV. "Today will be remembered for years to come as the day women had their rights returned," the reporter went on, a huge smile pulling at her cheeks. "Bill 247 brings with it a huge number of other legislative changes. Women will now be able to access a safe, legal abortion until twelve weeks gestation. Funding for women's healthcare has skyrocketed."

Tears spilled down my cheeks as I smiled up at the TV. Darcy took my hand and squeezed it. I watched the screen, unable to pull my eyes away.

"And women will now be able to *opt* to access permanent methods of birth control or undergo sterilisation if they choose." The reporter beamed, and just for a moment it felt like she was talking directly to me.

I looked across the bar and raised my glass to the three women who helped me at my darkest. Dr. Aslan, Dr. Hidalgo, and Nurse Amy all already had their beers raised, their radiant smiles drowned out by the skyrocketing noise in the bar. It bounced off the walls and roof, but I barely heard it. I was thankful to all of them; they had allowed me to survive and fought for what was right in the end.

"We did it," I whispered to myself, biting my lip hard.

"A toast," Darcy called, squeezing my hand three times in quick succession, "to the strongest women I know," she said as I looked across at her. "Thank you…for fighting for us all."

My tears spilled over again, and Darcy reached out and hugged me.

"W-who would have t-thought?" I stuttered, laughing through my tears. "I'm crying in public." I wiped my face and stared around the table. "I guess all it takes to start a revolution is an unplanned pregnancy." The reality slowly sank in.

The table erupted in laughter, and Mason looked at me with a wide, sweet, goofy smile. I smiled back at him, forcing myself not to break eye-contact.

"To Alice," Mason said, pulling up his glass. "The toughest fighter I have ever met."

We all sipped our drinks, and my cheeks flushed hot. The pretty blonde reporter continued talking about a new health marketing gimmick.

"Our ten minutes of fame is over," Kit said, nudging my eyes towards the screen.

"It doesn't matter," I said. "Ten minutes was all we needed to change the world."

CHECK OUT MY WEBSITE
WWW.AMJOYAUTHOR.COM

FOLLOW ALONG FOR MORE
WORDS AND WORLDS

WANT TO FOLLOW ME ON INSTAGRAM AT:

AMJOY_WRITER

OR

SCAN ME

FOLLOW ALONG FOR MORE WORDS AND WORLDS

www.ingramcontent.com/pod-product-compliance
Lightning Source LLC
Chambersburg PA
CBHW032142050726
47591CB00001B/56

* 9 7 8 1 7 6 3 6 7 3 6 0 1 *